ARBITRATING THE CONDUCT
OF INTERNATIONAL INVESTORS

Investment arbitration has emerged from modest beginnings and matured into an established presence in international law. However, in recent years it has drifted from the reciprocal vision of its founders. This volume arises to serve as a comprehensive guide for those who might wish to reform international investment law from within, seeking a return to the mutuality of access that is in arbitration's essence. A detailed toolset is provided for enhancing the access of host States and their nationals to formal resolution mechanisms in foreign investment disputes. It concludes by offering model texts to achieve greater reciprocity and access to justice. This book will appeal to all those interested in the future of international investment law, including an international audience of scholars, government officials, private sector actors, and private citizens alike, and including diverse constituencies, communities, and collectives of host State nationals.

JOSE DANIEL AMADO is a founding partner of the firm Miranda & Amado in Lima, Peru and teaches international arbitration at the Pontificia Universidad Catolica del Peru. He earned his law degree at that institution and also holds an LLM from Harvard Law School. Professor Amado is a past scholar-in-residence at Wilmer Cutler Pickering Hale and Dorr LLP and a past visiting fellow of the Lauterpacht Centre for International Law and the Centre of Latin American Studies, University of Cambridge.

JACKSON SHAW KERN has acted as counsel across Africa, Asia, Europe, and the Americas, where he represents sovereign States, State entities, and State enterprises as well as private interests. He is a past visiting fellow of the Lauterpacht Centre for International Law, Cambridge, and frequent guest lecturer at institutions including the Peking University School of Transnational Law. He is a member of the Bars of New York, Washington, DC, and Montana, and is of counsel to the Addis Law Group LLP.

MARTIN DOE RODRIGUEZ is Senior Legal Counsel of the International Bureau of the Permanent Court of Arbitration (PCA) at The Hague, where he assists arbitral tribunals constituted under the auspices of the PCA to resolve investment treaty disputes, contract claims involving State entities and international organisations, and inter-State disputes arising under various international conventions and treaties. In addition, he advises and assists the PCA Secretary-General in regard to the roles given to the PCA under the UNCITRAL Arbitration Rules, and is also regularly called upon to assist in the diplomatic work of the PCA with its Member States and other intergovernmental organisations.

ARBITRATING THE CONDUCT OF INTERNATIONAL INVESTORS

JOSE DANIEL AMADO
Miranda & Amado

JACKSON SHAW KERN
Addis Law Group LLP

MARTIN DOE RODRIGUEZ
Permanent Court of Arbitration

CAMBRIDGE
UNIVERSITY PRESS

CAMBRIDGE
UNIVERSITY PRESS

University Printing House, Cambridge CB2 8BS, United Kingdom

One Liberty Plaza, 20th Floor, New York, NY 10006, USA

477 Williamstown Road, Port Melbourne, VIC 3207, Australia

314–321, 3rd Floor, Plot 3, Splendor Forum, Jasola District Centre,
New Delhi – 110025, India

79 Anson Road, #06–04/06, Singapore 079906

Cambridge University Press is part of the University of Cambridge.

It furthers the University's mission by disseminating knowledge in the pursuit of
education, learning, and research at the highest international levels of excellence.

www.cambridge.org
Information on this title: www.cambridge.org/9781108415729
DOI: 10.1017/9781108235051

First published 2018

Printed in the United Kingdom by Clays, St Ives plc

A catalogue record for this publication is available from the British Library.

Library of Congress Cataloging-in-Publication Data
Names: Amado, Jose Daniel, 1965– | Kern, Jackson Shaw, 1987– |
Doe Rodriguez, Martin, 1980–
Title: Arbitrating the conduct of international investors / Jose Daniel Amado,
Jackson Shaw Kern, Martin Doe Rodriguez.
Description: Cambridge [UK] ; New York : Cambridge University Press, 2018.
Identifiers: LCCN 2017043586 | ISBN 9781108415729 (hardback)
Subjects: LCSH: International commercial arbitration. | Investments,
Foreign – Law and legislation. | Capitalists and financiers – Legal status, laws, etc. |
BISAC: LAW / Arbitration, Negotiation, Mediation.
Classification: LCC K2400 .A963 2018 | DDC 346/.092–dc23
LC record available at https://lccn.loc.gov/2017043586

ISBN 978-1-108-41572-9 Hardback

CONTENTS

FIGURES AND TABLE

Figures

Table

FOREWORD

Private monies for centuries have been invested abroad. Over those centuries there have been numerous claims by the foreign investors that they were wrongfully treated by the host state, and there have been a correspondingly significant number of claims by host states alleging wrongful acts by the investors. In the last half of the twentieth century, a system was developed for the protection of foreign investment, known as investor-State dispute settlement (ISDS). But even as ISDS became increasingly relied upon, fundamental critiques of ISDS have gained momentum since approximately 1990. Even though ISDS continues to be employed somewhat more each year, it is clear that there is a substantial loss of confidence in ISDS by host states, investors and communities. The last fifteen years of ISDS have seen substantial reform both procedurally and substantively. But the critique, if anything, is more substantial. In the eyes of those critical of ISDS, reforms in the main have served only to tweak ISDS and do not address the concerns raised.

Simultaneously, from at least the 1950s, it has been clear that private funds for investment in developing states can exceed, or at least are a very important complement to, governmental or development bank funds. Amid the sustained critique of ISDS and the need for private investment funds, this slender volume makes an important contribution. It is important because it moves beyond either critique or reform within the ISDS model to asking how we might approach in other ways what is a crucial and complex challenge. This volume contributes to reconstructing our sense of how we as peoples and nations may cooperate – organise our affairs – so that entities may invest abroad and so that all nations may develop towards their objectives sustainably. 'Reform is not forged in rage and frustration,' our authors remind us. Most important for the authors is the recognition that peoples and nations around the world seek, indeed need, a way forward. The commitment of the authors to a fundamental rethinking and to the construction of mutually beneficial arrangements illuminates the possible directions to go. It does not exhaust the mapping of the way forward, but it has opened a crucial line of inquiry that others may now join.

It is the authors' intent that this volume assist those who seek to address 'concerns of diverse constituencies within the design of a new generation of instruments'. Critical to this intent, the authors eschew 'rage and frustration' and welcome all of these diverse constituencies as a part of this project. The challenge the authors pose for themselves is a generation of instruments that address the valid concerns of the many diverse constituencies present in foreign investment. It is the embrace of this complexity of the diverse valid interests in foreign investment that is the essence of their commitment to reconstructing our sense of a way forward.

The calculus that will govern the way forward depends greatly on the particular circumstances. The authors thus look to the territory of dispute resolution. A large part of that territory is the various national courts; those of the host state, the home state, or yet some other state. As the authors observe, however, the particular court matters, and national courts can be 'often poorly suited to ensure international enforceability of their judgments'. To the national courts is thus added the territory of international courts, and international arbitration. With an eye on both the historical use and future promise of these courts and tribunals, the authors sketch the models that will underlay a new generation of instruments pointing to the strengths and weaknesses of each.

It is said that as Lewis and Clark were returning downriver in 1806 from their expedition to map the Northwest Territories of the United States, they were passed by the next generation of explorers going upriver, both guided and inspired by the expedition's work. I wish such success for the present authors: that they may see scholars, diplomats and practitioners revisit and refine the frontier they have here pioneered.

David D. Caron

ACKNOWLEDGEMENTS

Arbitrating the Conduct of International Investors is born from a collaborative effort spanning over the course of the past three years. Each of us brings to this book different perspectives. We share the goal of offering tools for broadening the scope of international investment arbitration in order to surmount its inherent limitations and more widely avail the advantages of this progressive innovation.

We have benefited enormously from the guidance, advice, and support of many who have contributed in various ways, from providing inspiration in engaging discussions to offering extensive commentaries, and even lending research and editing talents. Without them, this book quite simply would not have seen the light of day. We owe thanks to numerous such friends and colleagues whose advice and support have been instrumental in the stages of inception, evolution, and publication.

Members of the Pontificia Universidad Catolica del Peru, including Marcial Rubio, César Guzmán-Barron, César Azabache, Manuel Monteagudo, Rigoberto Zuñiga, and Bruno Amiel, were critical for their encouragement at the origins of this project.

Special gratitude is owed to the Scholar-in-Residence programme of Wilmer Cutler Pickering Hale & Dorr, which provided the perfect environment for many of this book's core ideas to consolidate. We are especially thankful to Gary Born, Steven Finizio, Maxi Scherer, Danielle Morris, Victoria Narancio, Daniel Costelloe, and Manuel Casas.

We are similarly indebted to many in Cambridge, including numerous fellows and visitors of the Lauterpacht Centre for International Law, perhaps the world's leading institution in promoting the study and development of international law. Advice and encouragement from the late Sir Elihu Lauterpacht, Judge James Crawford, Marc Weller, Roberto MacLean Ugarteche, Michael Waibel, John Barker, Rumiana Yotova, Federica Paddeu, Lesley Dingle, Ridhi Khabra, and Yurica Ramos Montes is deeply recognised. We offer profound thanks to Kim Hughes and the Cambridge University Press.

xi

Thanks are also due to friends and colleagues at the International Bureau of the Permanent Court of Arbitration for their assistance and encouragement over the later phases of the project, including Hugo Siblesz, Brooks Daly, Julia Solana, Nicola Peart, Diego Mejía-Lemos, and João Pereira Gil Antunes, among many others who helped mould ideas into real-life application.

Finally, other friends recurrently illuminated our thinking on critical matters, including David Caron, Lucy Reed, Roberto Dañino, Michael Kuczynski, Won Kidane, Juan Luis Avendaño, Luis Miranda, Wendy Miles, Suzanne Spears, Zewdineh Beyene Haile, Elizabeth Bartholet, Nathalie Cely, Julie Maupin, Clara Brillembourg, Martins Paparinskis, Daniel Bethlehem, Tom Snider, Valeriya Kirsey, and Daniel Chua.

Our memories have likely betrayed our thankfulness to others whose contributions to this book also merit acknowledgement. Our apologies to them, and also to those mentioned, but whose expectations this book does not meet. Whatever flaws may be found are attributable to us alone.

TABLE OF CASES

TABLE OF INTERNATIONAL ARBITRATION CASES

Permanent Court of Arbitration (PCA)

Investment Cases

Inter-State Cases

Others

International Centre For Settlement of Investment Disputes (ICSID)

Stockholm Chamber of Commerce (SCC)

International Chamber of Commerce (ICC)

Ad Hoc International Arbitration

TABLE OF CASES AND OPINIONS OF INTERNATIONAL COURTS

International Court of Justice (ICJ)

Permanent Court of International Justice (PCIJ)

Inter-American Court of Human Rights

TABLE OF CASES OF MUNICIPAL COURTS

Canada

Allen Qui Tam v. *Jarvis* (1871) 32 UCR 56
Bank of Montreal v. *Royal Bank of Canada* [1933] SCR 311

England and Wales

Boyce v. *Paddington Borough Council* [1903] 1 Ch 109
Dallal v. *Bank Mellat*, Queen's Bench Division (Commercial Court), [1986] 1 All
    ER 239
Gouriet v. *Union of Post Office Workers* [1978] AC 435
Tranton v. *Astor* (1917) 33 TLR 383

Germany

BVerfG, Order of the First Senate of 07 December 2004 – 1 BvR 1804/03

India

S.P. Gupta v. *Union of India* (1982) 2 S.C.R. 365
Suo Motu v. *Registrar, High Court of Gujarat* AIR 2002 Guj. 388

Malaysia

Government of Malaysia v. *Lim Kit Siang* [1988] 2 MLJ 12
Kuala Lympur v. *Wan Kam Fong* [1967] 2 MLJ 72
South Johore Omnibus Sdn. Bhd. v. *Damai Ekspres* [1983] 1 MLJ 101
United Engineers (M) Bhd v. *Lim Kit Siang* [1988] 1 MLJ 50

Singapore

Jeyaretnam Kenneth Andrew v. *Attorney-General* [2014] 1 SLR 345
Tan Eng Hong v. *Attorney-General* [2012] 4 SLR 476

South Africa

Kaunda and Others v. *President of the Republic of South Africa*, South African Law
    Reports, vol. XLIV, 4, 235 (CC) (2005)

Sweden

Titan Corporation v. *Alcatel CIT S.A.*, Case No. T 1038–05, Svea Court of Appeal,
    Stockholm (2005)

Switzerland

United States of America

SELECTED ABBREVIATIONS

CARIFORUM	The Caribbean Forum
COMESA	Common Market for Eastern and Southern Africa
ICCPR	International Covenant on Civil and Political Rights
ICESCR	International Covenant on Economic, Social and Cultural Rights
ICJ	International Court of Justice
ICSID	International Centre for Settlement of Investment Disputes
ILC	International Law Commission
ILM	International Legal Materials
ILO	International Labour Organization
ILR	International Law Reports
NAALC	North American Agreement on Labor Cooperation
NAFTA	North American Free Trade Agreement
OECD	Organisation for Economic Co-operation and Development
PCA	Permanent Court of Arbitration
SADC	Southern African Development Community
UDHR	Universal Declaration of Human Rights
UNCAC	United Nations Convention against Corruption
UNCITRAL	United Nations Commission on International Trade Law
UNCTAD	United Nations Conference on Trade and Development
UNDRIP	United Nations Declaration on the Rights of Indigenous Peoples
UNGA	United Nations General Assembly
UNGP	United Nations Guiding Principles on Business and Human Rights
UNHRC	United Nations Human Rights Council
UNTS	United Nations Treaty Series

Note: This volume references a large number of instruments that fall within the two categories of bilateral investment treaties (BITs) and free trade agreements (FTAs). These instruments are often referenced in the format 'Japan-Uruguay BIT (2015)', 'US Model BIT (2012)', or 'Colombia-Costa Rica FTA (2013)'.

~

Introduction

Investment arbitration, once viewed by jurists as a curiosity, has emerged from modest beginnings and matured into an established presence in international law. Its present form might be unrecognisable to its creators. Consider this passage:

> The Convention [on the Settlement of Investment Disputes between States and Nationals of Other States of 1965, sometimes known as the Washington Convention or, more universally, the ICSID Convention] permits the institution of proceedings by host States as well as by investors and the Executive Directors have constantly had in mind that the provisions of the Convention should be equally adapted to the requirements of both cases.[1]

Fifty years later, we do not believe it controversial to observe that this aspiration often falls short of reality: there has been a departure from this reciprocal vision of the founders. Against this landscape, this volume arises with the intention to serve as a toolset for those who might wish to reform the régime from within, to foster reciprocity, and to restore the mutuality of access that is in arbitration's essence, by means of openly allowing for the adjudication of claims submitted by the host State and its nationals.

Scholars and practitioners alike have long observed the limited jurisdiction of the typical investment arbitration tribunal. They have struggled to propose reforms that might redress a perceived indifference to legitimate aspirations of the host State, and to those stakeholders who fall outside the

---

[1] *Report of the Executive Directors of the International Bank for Reconstruction and Development on the Convention on the Settlement of Investment Disputes between States and Nationals of Other States*, para. 13, available at: https://icsid.worldbank.org/ICSID/StaticFiles/basicdoc/CRR_English-final.pdf. Further consider the following comment of the former long-time general counsel to the World Bank, Mr. Ibrahim Shihata: 'The "balance" which pervades the provisions of the [ICSID Convention] is only natural; the system provides conciliation and arbitration facilities to host States and foreign investors alike, and the proceedings may be initiated by either party.' I. F. I. Shihata, *The World Bank in a Changing World: Selected Essays and Lectures* (1995) 426.

foreign investor-host State equation. This struggle stems from the tribunal's status as creature of consent and *juge d'exception*, and from the conventional belief that there is no means or mechanism to gain the assent of foreign investors to the requisite jurisdictional expansion, or to garner political support of States which are traditional exporters of capital. In a world of growing dissatisfaction with investment law, as the historical distinction between capital-exporting and capital-importing domains declines, and as a number of nations turn inward, those assumptions are now due for challenge.[2]

Meanwhile, across the globe, there are told and untold investment initiatives presently stalled or obstructed by debilitating conflict, impacting investors, host States, and their nationals alike. It is not unusual to see large natural resource or infrastructure projects that become mired in a vicious cycle. Host State nationals may feel obliged to oppose entire projects, in order not to be left without effective redress in case of harm. Host States may be disinclined to overrule such opponents, even in the face of pressing domestic needs and despite positive potential for economic development. Investors, even though willing to offer redress, may be left unable to proceed.

The premise for the proffering of this volume's toolset is simple and time-tested. As in any transaction, the success of responsible investment initiatives requires access by parties concerned to a dispute settlement mechanism that is empowered to render a binding result. Success does not require that such mechanism be availed. Success does require that such mechanism exist.[3]

---

[2] For prominent commentary on dissatisfaction with the investment arbitration régime, see M. Waibel, A. Kaushal, L. K. Chung, and C. Balchin (eds.), *The Backlash against Investment Arbitration: Perceptions and Reality* (2010). More recently, it has been opined as follows: 'Legitimately entrenched by deferential frameworks, ideologically encouraged by advanced economies, politically tolerated by developing countries, empirically justified by academics, commercially promoted by arbitral institutions, and economically rewarded by private interests, international arbitration has developed its own culture: a culture of legal flamboyance.' W. Kidane, *The Culture of International Arbitration* (2017) 285.

[3] Thus is the broad objective of encouraging the flow of private international investment, embodied in nearly all international investment agreements, best served. See *Report of the Executive Directors of the International Bank for Reconstruction and Development on the Convention on the Settlement of Investment Disputes between States and Nationals of Other States*, para. 9 ('[i]n submitting the attached Convention to governments, the Executive Directors are prompted by the desire to strengthen the partnership between countries in the cause of economic development. The creation of an institution designed to facilitate the settlement of disputes between States and foreign investors can be a major step toward promoting an atmosphere of mutual confidence and thus stimulating a larger flow of private international capital into those countries which wish to attract it').

National courts are often poorly situated to ensure international enforceability of their judgments. The virtues sought in the crafting of international arbitration's foundational instruments are the establishment of a forum for the expert, neutral, and independent adjudication of rights and obligations, the results of which are enforceable beyond the boundaries of national jurisdictions. If the mechanism is said to have achieved some degree of success for investors, it is equally capable to do so on behalf of host States and their peoples.

Thus, without considering the comparative quality of diverse national judiciaries (a matter into which this volume does not inquire), these actors might reasonably elect, in the exercise of their autonomy, to submit their claims to adjudication in an international arbitral forum. This choice heralds a demand for more than *amicus curiae* submissions, more than an opening of the hearing room doors, and more than the publication of awards, for a leap beyond mere transparency to offer an avenue for the vindication of rights of investment stakeholders, from investors and their home States to host States and their nationals.[4]

Owing to the novelty of embracing these latter claimants in investment arbitration, we offer guidance to vest content in those rights and obligations that may be considered as candidates for inclusion in future investment treaties, laws, and contracts. By assisting interested parties to negotiate and draft their definitions of eligible initiators or intervenors and to designate justiciable rights, the investment arbitration forum shall open to newly defined classes of claims and claimants in order to promote responsible investments by finally resolving existing and prospective investment conflicts. This volume, including its model texts, will aid all users in determining those who hold claims that may now become actionable upon the international plane.

It is our hope that this volume will, at its broadest, be of interest to all scholars and practitioners of international law in addressing concerns of diverse constituencies within the design of a new generation of instruments. It is our expectation that this volume will furnish tools to overcome a deficit of properly tailored mechanisms, and thereby to maintain the viability of investors' initiatives which are presently stalled or blocked precisely by the

---

[4] Drawing the distinction, one observer has noted that 'the push for transparency has aimed at opening a process controlled by the parties to the dispute to view (and in some cases to influence or review) by persons and entities who arguably have an interest in the outcome of the dispute, *but who are not formally parties.*' D. D. Caron, 'Regulating Opacity: Shaping How Tribunals Think', in D. D. Caron, S. W. Schill, A. Cohen Smutny, and E. E. Triantafilou (eds.), *Practising Virtue: Inside International Arbitration* (2016) 380 (emphasis added).

absence of effective organs for adjudication, equipped to ensure broad international enforceability.

We thus intend that this volume will be of use to government officials, private sector economic actors, and private citizens alike in discourse over the future of international investment law. It will be useful to sovereigns in negotiations of both investment treaties (including trade or other economic agreements featuring an investment chapter) and contractual instruments underpinning a particular investment initiative. In perhaps its deepest exigency, the model texts and accompanying commentary offer a timely toolset in negotiations seeking to unblock existing investment initiatives that are impacted or obstructed by conflict. Lastly, this volume will aid in the drafting and reforming of national investment laws, for the host State's use in acting as gatekeeper of investments.

It is our hope that this volume shall shed light for the world to see that reasonable responses to the backlash against investment arbitration are unlikely to emerge from political or ideological posture. Reform is not forged in rage and frustration. Rather, one must first inquire within an imperfect model in search of answers to the most uncomfortable questions that have arisen from the enshrinement of only the investor's bundle of rights. This volume is therefore intended as an act of provocation to all experts in international investment law. It is an instigation to explore. If merit is to be found in its conceptual elements, such shall be a consequence of solicitude for all key stakeholders in international investment. It is our conviction that the soundest solutions to legitimate questions raised in recent years will result from introspection into rebalancing the régime by a return to its origins, yielding a natural evolution of the mechanism conceived by the founders.

For thoroughness and rigour, one must first consider the structure of existing mechanisms for the settlement of international investment disputes as well as the doctrinal constraints and historical trajectory that have brought us here. This section is not intended to serve as an exhaustive investigation into these dimensions, for each of them could be (and indeed often is) the subject of discrete volumes in its own right. Rather, the purpose is to portray the architecture within which these new tools will operate.

Second, this volume presents various models designed to allow for broader jurisdictional access to the existing investment arbitration apparatus, including the structure born from the ICSID Convention. Four models by which the mechanism may be embodied are revealed.

Third, various means of achieving jurisdiction over the foreign investor are offered, including those which emerge from an enlightened perspective of the consent requirement. Fourth, further mechanisms that may prove useful in the case of mass-scale events are explored. Fifth, consideration is given to bodies of rights and obligations that may be brought within a tribunal's competence. Sixth, prospects for enforcement of resulting arbitral awards are presented.

The toolset itself is introduced in an annex to the volume. Model language is set forth for use by interested investors and home States as well as host States and their nationals, within both contractual and treaty instruments, and in national investment laws. All model texts are accompanied by commentary drawing upon the considerations of the volume, and developed in part from the writings and counsel of some of the finest minds in international law, in order to best inform decisions of draughtsmen.

In this manner, may we better afford access to justice, in order that all entrants to the régime not hold a right without remedy.

1

The Legal Landscape

One must begin by considering the objects and expectations of both investors and host States in international investment. A foreign investor aspires to effect an investment in order to realise (and, often, to repatriate) a profit under rule of law. The host State hopes to enjoy various benefits of capital inflows while free from harm. These come in the form of general economic activity and development and all that these may entail, including employment and enrichment of local human capital, technology transfer, and export revenues realised in the sale of extracted resources or value-added goods and services. Other benefits might directly satisfy local demands as in the case of, for example, power generation from a hydroelectric mega-project.

There is presently a patchwork of existing judicial and other machineries for the safeguarding of these expectations under the law. In drawing the legal landscape, this volume focuses only upon those which are (in theory) competent and capable to render a binding result. In other words, this volume foregoes discussion of grievance procedures or of such methods as negotiation, mediation, and conciliation.[1] These topics are excluded not because they are not useful (indeed, they are essential) but rather because the very premise of this book ultimately requires the existence (but not necessarily the use) of a binding mechanism. Such a mechanism's mere existence is essential separate and apart from the question of whether it is ultimately resorted to by any party.

---

[1] Further, the advent of regional and international human rights courts (such as the European Court of Human Rights, the Inter-American Court of Human Rights, and the African Court on Human and Peoples' Rights) is largely omitted, as these fora enable the bringing of claims by individuals as against sovereign States. The ability to bring such claims undoubtedly marks a commendable advance in the individual right of access to justice, particularly where States may be held accountable for their acts or omissions with regard to non-State actors. The focus of this volume is upon the relationship of host States and their nationals vis-à-vis the foreign investor.

Host State National Courts

The first port of call is in the national courts of the State to host the investment. While the precise governing principles will vary with the constitutional laws of the State in question, any given host State presumably possesses courts of general jurisdiction which are empowered to adjudicate the contractual and extra-contractual rights and obligations of parties to an investment relationship as to events falling within its territorial sovereignty.[2]

Host State courts offer certain considerable advantages. Relevant contractual instruments will often be designated as governed by the host State's body of law. Where a claim seeks to impose liability of an extra-contractual nature for harms that have transpired within the host State's territorial jurisdiction, the host State's laws are commonly preferred.[3] In these matters, the State's own judges are presumably unrivalled in their expertise.

National courts suffer a deficiency not of their own doing. The limited reach of treaties for the recognition and enforcement of foreign court judgments is a known phenomenon in international law.[4] Concerns of extraterritorial enforceability may not arise where the foreign investor in

---

[2] This jurisdiction vests by virtue of the territorial principle. The proposition presumes that the parties have not concluded a valid and exclusive arbitration agreement or choice of court agreement specifying otherwise. Even in such a case, such agreement might cause only the inadmissibility of the claims in the courts of the host State and not truly derogate from such courts' jurisdiction, depending upon how these concepts are defined in the relevant laws.

[3] In addition to outliers to this general principle, there also exist various international and uniform law instruments which regulate extra-contractual liability according to international rather than national norms, particularly in industries (for example, transport) whose activities are highly international by nature and dependent upon a high degree of certainty. These exceptions nevertheless capture a very small fraction of cases of extra-contractual liability in general, and even less so in respect of activities related to foreign direct investment as opposed to international trade in goods and services.

[4] The United States, for example, is not party to a single treaty in force for the recognition and enforcement of foreign court judgments. In 1976 the United States and the United Kingdom initialled a Convention on the Reciprocal Recognition and Enforcement of Judgments in Civil Matters, 16 ILM 71 (1977), but negotiations over the final text ended in 1981 without agreement. As such, enforcement of foreign judgments remains largely governed by the laws of the fifty federated states and the District of Columbia. For a view into this phenomenon, see, e.g., L. J. Silberman and A. F. Lowenfeld, 'A Different Challenge for the ALI: Herein of Foreign Country Judgments, an International Treaty, and an American Statute', 75 *Indiana Law Journal* 2 (2000). A large number of the states have enacted into law the Uniform Foreign-Country Money Judgments Recognition Act, either as is or with variations. This model law was first drafted in 1962 and most recently revised by the National Conference of Commissioners on Uniform State Laws in 2005.

question holds assets sufficient for the satisfaction of an adverse judgment within the host State's jurisdiction, and may reliably be prevented from withdrawing those assets during the pendency of a non-frivolous claim.[5] But where an investor does not hold assets sufficient to satisfy an adverse judgment for injury caused, or where the assets are of such a nature that they may be expeditiously expatriated, a judgment of the host State's courts as against the foreign investor is at risk never to be executed in full.[6]

Home State National Courts

Unlike the host State national courts, which will presumably be vested of jurisdiction to adjudicate disputes arising out of the investment on the basis of the territorial principle, the national courts of the investor's home State may or may not enjoy sufficiently broad reach. If either party wishes

Whether under this law or any other, enforcement of foreign court judgments remains considerably more burdensome than enforcement of foreign arbitral awards.

[5] There is an element of anticipation in this calculation. In other words, the appropriate question is whether the investor holds assets sufficient for the satisfaction of an adverse judgment, whether actual or anticipated, foreseen or foreseeable. However, the impact of large-scale and widespread injury within the host State is often not fully foreseeable at the time of the investor's entry, or is assessed at a low level of probability.

[6] One recent development must be noted in this regard. On 1 October 2015, the 2005 Hague Convention on Choice of Court Agreements entered into force, three months after its ratification by the European Union. See Convention on Choice of Court Agreements, 44 ILM 1294 (2005). The Convention provides for recognition of express choice of court agreements as between disputant parties (often known in the United States as forum selection clauses) and for the recognition and enforcement of resulting final judgments by the courts of contracting States without review on the merits, subject only to limited exceptions. See Arts. 5, 6, 8, and 9 of the Convention on Choice of Court Agreements. Significantly, the United States has signed (but not ratified) the Convention, as has Ukraine. Beyond the member States of the European Union (all except for Denmark), the Convention presently binds only Mexico and Singapore. Its future thus remains uncertain, particularly where the super-jurisdiction of the European Union already possesses its own freestanding mechanism for the enforcement of national court judgments as amongst its member States. See Regulation (EC) No 44/2001 of 22 December 2000 on Jurisdiction and the Recognition and Enforcement of Judgments in Civil and Commercial Matters, 2001 O.J. Eur. Comm. (L 12) 1, available at: http://eur-lex.europa.eu/legal-content/EN/TXT/?uri=URISERV:l33054 (replaced by Regulation (EC) No 1215/2012, commonly known as the 'Brussels I bis Regulation'). However, it is observed that under a first-to-file or first-seized rule such as that of the Brussels I bis Regulation (as opposed to an express choice of court, or an exclusive arbitration agreement), other difficulties may arise. On the dangers of the 'Italian torpedo', see, e.g., R. Brand and S. Jablonski, *Forum Non Conveniens: History, Global Practice, and Future under the Hague Convention on Choice of Court Agreements* (2007) 127.

to bring a claim in the home State's courts, that party is at the mercy of the governing principles that establish the outer bounds of those courts' jurisdiction.

Many States require a close factual connection to their territory in order for such jurisdiction to vest, imposing a minimum threshold for the opening of their courts, even where the parties might expressly select them by a choice of court agreement.[7] As to extra-contractual liability, once again, the home State's jurisdictional principles would have to permit the reach of its courts into matters where harmful events, although perhaps perpetrated or caused by its own national, have occurred outside its territory. Such is far from guaranteed.[8]

One further obstacle is observed in the common law doctrine of *forum non conveniens*.[9] Even where jurisdiction is established, this doctrine permits a court of the home State to stay or dismiss a claim where it determines that the claim is best heard elsewhere. Under the jurisprudence of this doctrine, cases wherein the injurious events have occurred inside the territory of another State are often dismissed in favour of that State's courts owing, amongst other things, to proximity of evidence.[10]

---

[7] See, e.g., *Titan Corporation v. Alcatel CIT S.A.*, Case No. T 1038–05, Svea Court of Appeal, Stockholm (2005).

[8] See, e.g., *The Globe & Mail*, 'Defeat of responsible mining bill is missed opportunity', 3 November 2010. The proposed bill 'would have required [as a matter of Canadian law] extractive companies operating in developing countries to comply with certain international human rights and environmental standards widely accepted by the industry as best practice'. Ibid. The measure thus would have exercised a sort of limited extraterritorial jurisdiction over Canadian firms operating abroad. Even this failed bill would hardly have opened the doors of the Canadian courts. Rather, failure to comply 'would have resulted in, among other things, Export Development Canada withdrawing financial support and Canadian trade commissions and embassies ceasing to support and promote those companies' activities'. Ibid.

[9] See generally R. Brand and S. Jablonski, *Forum Non Conveniens: History, Global Practice, and Future under the Hague Convention on Choice of Court Agreements* (2007). See also Z. Douglas, *The International Law of Investment Claims* (2009) 395–396 (noting that '[a]lthough the doctrine of *forum non conveniens* is a creature of the common law, some commentators have observed that the flexibility built into jurisdictional rules in civilian systems is such that the gulf between the two legal traditions in the respect is more apparent than real'), citing A. Bell, *Forum Shopping and Venue in Transnational Litigation* (2003) 72 (further citations omitted).

[10] This obstacle is readily observed in the case of *Aguinda v. Texaco, Inc.*, 142 F. Supp. 2d 534, S.D.N.Y. (2001). Once a case is dismissed in favour of the host State's jurisdiction on grounds of *forum non conveniens*, the question of enforceability of any resulting judgment of the host State courts arises anew. This is so even where the foreign investor does not challenge the quality of such sovereign courts by seizing an international tribunal to invoke a denial of justice. For the authoritative modern monograph on this doctrine, see J. Paulsson, *Denial of Justice in International Law* (2005). Furthermore, certain treaty

Lastly, the enforcement risk described in regard to judgments of host State national courts holds true in mirror image with regard to home State national courts. While the investor may be more likely to hold assets sufficient for the satisfaction of an adverse judgment in his home State, the same may not hold true as to assets of the host State or its nationals in the event of, for example, a counterclaim (or costs claim) by the investor over which the court accepts jurisdiction and renders judgment in the investor's favour.

These truths are symptomatic of a larger structural deficiency in the architecture for settlement of international investment disputes, namely the presently persisting potential for a multiplicity of parallel proceedings oftentimes yielding conflicting results only some or none of which can be effectively enforced.[11]

It is a landscape that is ripe for abuse.

International Arbitration

Where desired, gains may be made in legal certainty, efficiency, and finality by the establishment of a forum vested of exclusive jurisdiction for the final and binding resolution of investment disputes, accompanied by robust avenues of enforcement. To seek such a mechanism portends a shift from the present proliferation towards a unified forum for the settlement of all disputes arising from an investment. Where properly consented, constituted, and availed, such a forum may lie at international arbitration.

Arbitration holds a long history as the preferred mechanism for the pacific settlement of international disputes.[12] The modern era of international arbitration is often traced to Jay's Treaty of 1794, as between the

provisions are interpreted as imposing upon host States a substantive obligation as to quality of justice that rises above and beyond the mere threshold of denial of justice at general international law. See, e.g., *Chevron Corporation and Texaco Petroleum Company v. Republic of Ecuador*, PCA Case No. 2007-2, Partial Award on the Merits, 30 March 2010, paras. 241–248.

[11] In the parallel world of international commercial arbitration, Mr. Gary Born has opined that 'parties face the threats of parallel or multiplicitous litigation in different national court systems, often located on one another's home territory, often facing local courts that may have parochial predispositions against one party or the other, and often producing judgments that cannot be effectively enforced'. G. Born, *BITs, BATs, and Buts: Reflections on International Dispute Resolution* (2014) 10, available at: www.wilmerhale.com/uploadedFiles/Shared_Content/Editorial/News/Documents/BITs-BATs-and-Buts.pdf.

[12] See, e.g., Introduction by S. M. Schwebel, in U. Franke, A. Magnusson, and J. Dahlquist (eds.), *Arbitrating for Peace: How Arbitration Made a Difference* (2016).

United States and Great Britain.[13] By the creation of the Permanent Court of Arbitration, which is born from the Hague Conventions for the Pacific Settlement of International Disputes of 1899 and 1907, which remain in force amongst more than one hundred States, international arbitration is recognised as the 'most effective, and, at the same time, the most equitable means of settling disputes which diplomacy has failed to settle'.[14]

In 1934, when accepting the administration of its first arbitration involving a non-State party, the then-Secretary-General of the Permanent Court of Arbitration 'noted ... that Article 26 of the 1899 Hague Convention (which became Article 47 of the 1907 Hague Convention) permits the [Permanent Court of Arbitration] to "place its premises and its staff at the disposal of the Signatory Powers for the operations of any special Board of Arbitration", a flexible formulation that was interpreted as encompassing disputes between a State and a non-State actor'.[15] Twenty-five years later, what is recognised as the first bilateral investment treaty was signed by West

---

[13] Jay's Treaty, Arts. V, VI, and VII (1794), reprinted in H. Miller, *II Treaties and Other International Acts of the United States of America 1776–1863* (1931) 245. See J. Ralston, *International Arbitration from Athens to Locarno* (1929) 191 ('the modern era of arbitral or judicial settlement of international disputes, by common accord among all writers upon the subject, dates from the signing on 19 November 1794 of Jay's Treaty'); see also G. A. Raymond, 'Demosthenes and Democracies: Regime-Types and Arbitration Outcomes', 22 *International Interactions* 1 (1996) 3 ('interstate arbitration prior to the Jay Treaty of 1794 remained more of an episodic occurrence in world affairs than a patterned regularity').

[14] Art. 38 of the Convention for the Pacific Settlement of International Disputes of 1907. As to inter-State disputes, the Treaty of Versailles and the emergence of the League of Nations would later see the inter-war reign of the Permanent Court of International Justice (PCIJ). The succeeding International Court of Justice (ICJ) came into being with the Charter of the United Nations following the end of the Second World War. Like the PCIJ before it, the ICJ is a court whose jurisdiction generally vests from the consent of the States. See Art. 34 of the Statute of the ICJ.

[15] C. Giorgetti, *The Rules, Practice, and Jurisprudence of International Courts and Tribunals* (2012) 40. The arbitration referred to is that of *Radio Corporation of America v. The National Government of the Republic of China*, PCA Case No. 1934-01, Award, 13 April 1935, 3 UNRIAA 1621, 8 ILR 26, (1936) 30 AJIL 535. More recently, in a 1997 report to its Administrative Council, a steering committee found that disputes involving non-State parties could be accepted on two grounds: '(i) article 49 of the 1907 Convention [for the Pacific Settlement of International Disputes] could be interpreted as giving the Administrative Council the power to authorize the establishment by the International Bureau of optional rules, even those that expand the mandate of the PCA, or (ii) pursuant to Article 47, State-non-State arbitration could continue to take place on an *ad hoc* basis, outside the express scope of the Conventions.' Permanent Court of Arbitration, 1999 Steering Committee, *Final Report and Recommendations to the Administrative Council* (June 1997), para 48. The report was accepted by the Administrative Council at its 156th

Germany and Pakistan.[16] It is often overlooked that this treaty served only, in a sense, to codify the content of the substantive protections to be reciprocally afforded by each State to investor-nationals of the other. The treaty did not establish a direct investor-State arbitration mechanism.

Such would come nearly ten years later, following the establishment of a procedural architecture in the ICSID Convention of 1965 (itself inspired by the Permanent Court of Arbitration's early experience with mixed arbitration)[17] and within, for example, the Netherlands-Indonesia Agreement on Economic Cooperation of 1968.[18] In that instrument, it was provided that '[t]he Contracting Party in the territory of which a national of the other Contracting Party makes or intends to make an investment, shall assent to any demand on the part of such national' to submit given disputes to arbitration.[19] This is the familiar language of the so-called standing offer to arbitrate that is reciprocally extended by the States party to thousands of international investment agreements.[20]

meeting in October 1997. Two sets of such optional rules are the 1996 Optional Rules for Arbitration between International Organizations and Private Parties and the 2001 Optional Rules for Arbitration of Disputes Relating to Natural Resources and/or the Environment (the PCA Environmental Rules), the latter of which is available even in disputes between private parties. Further, under Art. 1(1) of the PCA Environmental Rules, '[t]he characterization of the dispute as relating to natural resources and/or the environment is not necessary for jurisdiction where all the parties have agreed to settle a specific dispute under these Rules.'

[16] Treaty between the Federal Republic of Germany and Pakistan for the Promotion and Protection of Investments, signed on 25 November 1959 (entered into force on 28 April 1962), 457 UNTS 23.

[17] The institutional structure of ICSID and its first set of arbitration rules were modelled upon those of the Permanent Court of Arbitration, including the latter's 1962 rules for arbitration of mixed disputes. A. R. Parra, *The History of ICSID* (2012) 16–17, 51–52.

[18] Netherlands-Indonesia Agreement on Economic Cooperation (with Protocol and Exchanges of Letters dated 17 June 1968), signed on 7 July 1968 (entered into force on 17 July 1971), 799 UNTS 13.

[19] Ibid. Art. 11.

[20] The theory of the standing offer is meticulously articulated in the case of *Lanco International Inc.* v. *The Republic of Argentina*, ICSID Case No. ARB/97/6, Decision on Jurisdiction, 8 December 1998, para. 40 ('[i]n our case, the Parties have given their consent to ICSID arbitration, consent that is valid, there thus being a presumption in favor of ICSID arbitration, without having first to exhaust domestic remedies. In effect, once valid consent to ICSID arbitration is established, any other forum called on to decide the issue should decline jurisdiction. The investor's consent, which comes from its written consent by letter of September 17, 1997, and its request for arbitration of OCTOBER 1, 1997, *and the consent of the State which comes directly from the ARGENTINA U.S. Treaty*, which gives the investor the choice of forum for settling its disputes, indicate that there is no stipulation contrary to the consent of the parties. It should be recalled that Article 25(1) *in fine* establishes: "When the parties have given their consent, no party may withdraw its

In text that appears to be now forgotten, it was further provided that '*any such national shall comply with any request of the former Contracting Party*, to submit, for conciliation or arbitration, to [ICSID] *any dispute that may arise in connection with the investment.*'[21]

The driving factor in the acceleration of the international arbitration régime over the past half-century, since the entrance into force of the United Nations Convention on the Recognition and Enforcement of Foreign Arbitral Awards of 1958 (the New York Convention) and the ICSID Convention of 1965, lies in the superior enforceability of arbitral awards beyond the boundaries of national jurisdictions.[22] While enjoying this auspicious advantage, arbitration also knows an austere limitation: the closely confined jurisdiction of the tribunal.

In the case of an arbitration agreement within an investment contract offered or awarded by the host State, the scope of jurisdiction of any ultimately constituted tribunal naturally derives from the *clause compromissoire* itself.[23] As such, these tribunals are very often vested of jurisdiction for the adjudication of those rights and obligations arising under the

---

consent unilaterally," in our case by the Republic of Argentina after the investor has accepted ICSID arbitration') (emphasis added).

[21] Art. 11 of the Netherlands-Indonesia Agreement on Economic Cooperation (with Protocol and Exchanges of Letters dated 17 June 1968), signed on 7 July 1968 (entered into force on 17 July 1971), 799 UNTS 13 (emphasis added). The agreement was ultimately terminated and replaced by a bilateral investment treaty bearing a more standard provision regarding investor-State dispute settlement. See Art. 9 of the Agreement between the Government of the Kingdom of the Netherlands and the Government of the Republic of Indonesia on Promotion and Protection of Investment, signed on 6 April 1994 (entered into force on 1 July 1995), 2240 UNTS 323. This latter treaty has itself now been terminated by Indonesia.

[22] While international commercial arbitration has a longer history, the advent of treaty-born investor-State arbitration would take time, with numbers of cases achieving a rapid increase by the late 1990s on the backs of the myriad investment instruments concluded over the preceding decades.

[23] Perhaps the most significant examples of such contracts include concession agreements granting rights of exploration and development over hydrocarbon or mineral resources, contracts for the provision of public services, or contracts for the construction of State infrastructure. See, e.g., Art. 1 of the US Model BIT (2012) ('"Investment agreement" means a written agreement between a national authority of a Party and a covered investment or an investor of the other Party . . . that grants rights to the covered investment or investor: (a) with respect to natural resources that a national authority controls, such as for their exploration, extraction, refining, transportation, distribution, or sale; (b) to supply services to the public on behalf of the Party, such as power generation or distribution, water treatment or distribution, or telecommunications; or (c) to undertake infrastructure projects, such as the construction of roads, bridges, canals, dams, or pipelines, that are not for the exclusive or predominant use and benefit of the government').

contract alone. Such limitation may operate to the derogation of rights or obligations arising from extra-contractual sources,[24] and to the exclusion of claims by all save for the parties to the contract.[25] In other words, such a clause affords, by agreement of the parties, a privileged juridical space for adjudication of the rights and obligations of the contract, ensuring for these alone a unique and exclusive forum empowered to render a result that is final, binding, and widely enforceable.

In the case of treaty-born investor-State arbitration, the scope of a tribunal's jurisdiction is more heavily circumscribed still.[26] As with contractual rights and obligations falling within the scope of a contractual arbitration agreement, the scope of a treaty-born tribunal's jurisdiction is often limited to the adjudication of those rights and obligations enumerated within the treaty instrument itself.[27] Further, in sharp contrast to a typical bilateral or synallagmatic contract, there is a failure of mutuality or reciprocity in the treaty model. Where the disputant parties in an arbitration are not the States party to the treaty, but rather one of those States and an investor-national of

---

[24] Where the parties so agree, nothing bars a contractual arbitration agreement from vesting arbitral jurisdiction over the adjudication of rights or obligations arising at their origin from an extra-contractual source. See, e.g., *Perenco Ecuador Ltd.* v. *The Republic of Ecuador et al.*, ICSID Case No. ARB/08/6, Interim Decision on the Environmental Counterclaim, 11 August 2015 and *Burlington Resources Inc.* v. *Republic of Ecuador*, ICSID Case No. ARB/08/5, Decision on Counterclaims, 7 February 2017, paras. 60–62. Indeed, the broad language used in most model arbitration clauses often encompasses extra-contractual claims insofar as they bear a sufficient nexus to the contractual relationship in question, especially under pro-arbitration interpretative presumptions regarding the scope of an arbitration agreement. See G. Born, *International Commercial Arbitration* (2014) 1348–1366. See also Annex, Model 2 (Contractual Arbitration Agreement).

[25] Within international commercial arbitration, to which a contractual dispute as between an investor and a host State is perhaps more akin than treaty-born investor-State arbitration, there have developed a limited number of grounds for jurisdiction over non-signatory parties, sometimes known as extension of the arbitration agreement. See G. Born, *International Commercial Arbitration* (2014) 1418–1484.

[26] This is illustrated by the 'disappearance' of certain text of the 1968 Netherlands-Indonesia Agreement on Economic Cooperation, 799 UNTS 13. It has been written that '[t]he language referring to the national's compliance with a host state demand for arbitration quickly disappeared from the provision.' K. Vandevelde, *Bilateral Investment Treaties: History, Policy and Interpretation* (2010) 458.

[27] A treaty may of course incorporate by reference rights or obligations arising from a domestic source, thus elevating those claims to the international plane. Perhaps the most common example comes in the form of the so-called umbrella clause, whereby a State's contractual undertakings may be, in a sense, transformed into treaty commitments. Indeed, the very first investment treaty contained such a clause (but not an investor-State dispute settlement mechanism). See Art. 7 of the Federal Republic of Germany-Pakistan BIT (1959) ('[e]ither Party shall observe any other obligation it may have entered into with regard to investments by nationals or companies of the other party'). Such a clause merely effects a reversion to the contractual constraint.

another, the substantive rights typically flow in a singular direction.[28] The treaty gives rise to obligations in the host State alone, with corresponding rights arising in the foreign investor.[29] Insofar as any 'obligations' might fall upon the investor, these are typically addressed via rules of admissibility or jurisdiction. In other words, an investor may face the need to satisfy certain conditions in order to avail his right to enforce the treaty's substantive guarantees, to gain access to the arbitration mechanism,[30] but there is no justiciable obligation imposed upon the investor.[31] The forum often operates as a one-way street.

There is thus little prospect under the text of present investment treaties for host State claims, or indeed even a host State counterclaim once an investor has elected to launch his own.[32] In the case of a host State counterclaim lodged in response to an investor's claim which is founded upon the

[28] The reciprocity rather takes the form that each State party reciprocally extends the same substantive guarantees to investor-nationals of the other State party (or parties). Historically, efforts to forge a multilateral treaty instrument have failed, and of the web of some 3,300 international investment agreements presently in force, the overwhelming majority remain bilateral treaties. The investment chapter of the NAFTA (with its three States party) and the Energy Charter Treaty mark early multilateral successes. Most recently, a text of the proposed Trans-Pacific Partnership was agreed in October 2015 as amongst a dozen States, and includes an investment chapter featuring investor-State dispute settlement. At the time of writing, this text remains subject to national parliamentary ratification processes, and the withdrawal of the United States has plunged the initiative into uncertainty. The People's Republic of China is presently in pursuit of its own proposed sixteen-nation Regional Comprehensive Economic Partnership, which would extend across China, India, and other member States of the Association of Southeast Asian Nations. This proposal would not require its members to take steps to protect environmental standards or labour rights.

[29] The most common of these treaty protections feature, for example, guarantees of fair and equitable treatment, full protection and security, national treatment, most-favoured-nation treatment, and the guarantee of expropriation only for a public purpose upon payment of compensation. See generally C. Maclachlan, L. Shore, and M. Weiniger, *International Investment Arbitration: Substantive Principles* (2008).

[30] See, e.g., *World Duty Free Company Limited* v. *Republic of Kenya*, ICSID Case No. ARB/00/7, Award, 4 October 2006; *Fraport AG Frankfurt Airport Services Worldwide* v. *Republic of the Philippines*, ICSID Case No. ARB/03/25, Award, 16 August 2007 and Dissenting Opinion of Mr Bernardo M. Cremades, 19 July 2007; *Hulley Enterprises Limited* v. *The Russian Federation*, PCA Case No. 2005-03, UNCITRAL, Final Award, 18 July 2014.

[31] This omission is sometimes justified by a sense that the host State enjoys a privileged position to directly enforce its interests via the machinery of the State, including, if necessary, its police powers. Yet such reasoning rests once again upon a flawed assumption of international enforceability that undermines the effectiveness of national courts.

[32] This latter statement is not made without a degree of hesitation. For example, Professor Michael Reisman strongly advocated an efficiency rationale in his separate declaration in the case of *Spyridon Roussalis* v. *Romania*. In that declaration, he wrote that arbitral jurisdiction over host State counterclaims

respondent State's treaty obligations alone, there often prevails a vacuum of justiciable obligations of the investor.[33] Prospects of any claim by a host State national are smaller still.[34]

> works to the benefit of both respondent state and investor. In rejecting ICSID jurisdiction over counterclaims, a neutral tribunal ... perforce directs the respondent State to pursue its claims in its own courts where the very investor who had sought a forum outside the state apparatus is now constrained to become the defendant. (And if an adverse judgment ensues, that erstwhile defendant might well transform to claimant again, bringing another [treaty] claim.) Aside from duplication and inefficiency, the sorts of transaction costs which counter-claim and set-off procedures work to avoid, it is an ironic, if not absurd, outcome, at odds, in my view, with the objectives of international investment law.

Spyridon Roussalis v. Romania, ICSID Case No. ARB/06/1, Declaration of Michael Reisman, 28 November 2011. In the later case of Antoine Goetz & Consorts et S.A. Affinage des Métaux v. République du Burundi, a unanimous tribunal appears to have adopted Professor Reisman's reasoning, finding that

> [t]o decide differently would be to go against not only the letter but the spirit of the [ICSID] Convention. Indeed, this would cause States to seize national courts of counterclaims which arbitral tribunals could not hear, even though those counterclaims relate directly to the subject matter of the dispute which had been submitted to arbitration. It would also force investors who were unhappy with the decisions of the national courts to challenge those decisions in new arbitrations. The very purpose and intention of Article 46 of the [ICSID] Convention is not to complicate the resolution of investment disputes, but to make it simpler, in the interests both of States and of investors.

Antoine Goetz & Consorts et S.A. Affinage des Métaux v. République du Burundi, ICSID Case No. ARB/01/2, Award, 21 June 2012, para. 280. On host State counterclaims generally, see Z. Douglas, The International Law of Investment Claims (2009) 255–263. For an early proposal regarding reactive claims by individuals within the host State, see T. Weiler, 'Balancing Human Rights and Investor Protection: A New Approach for a Different Legal Order', 27 Boston College International and Comparative Law Review 2 (2004).

[33] More recently, an arbitral tribunal has accepted jurisdiction over a treaty-born human rights counterclaim by the Argentine Republic, though the claim was ultimately dismissed on its merits. See Urbaser S.A. and Consorcio de Aguas Bilbao Bizkaia, Bilbao Biskaia Ur Partzuergoa v. The Argentine Republic, ICISD Case No. ARB/07/26, Award, 8 December 2016, paras. 1110–1221. In accepting jurisdiction, the tribunal notably drew a distinction between the language of the treaty that governed in Spyridon Roussalis v. Romania, ICSID Case No. ARB/06/1, Award, 7 December 2011 (referring to 'disputes between an investor of a Contracting Party and the other Contracting Party concerning an obligation of the latter under this Agreement, in relation to an investment of the former') (emphasis added) and the more open-textured Spain-Argentina BIT (1991). Ibid. n 424. It is posited that, where desired, the mechanisms proposed in this volume may be availed to establish greater legal certainty, to the advantage of all stakeholders.

[34] Numerous theories have emerged in the realm of international commercial arbitration whereby a non-signatory party might avail the advantages of (or be bound to) a private

It is recalled that the foreign investor aspires to effect an investment in order to repatriate a profit under rule of law, while the host State and its nationals seek to realise benefits of capital inflows while remaining free from harm. It is not controversial to observe that in terms of the attainment of these objects and expectations, in terms of the assurance of attendant rights and obligations, there is an existing imbalance caused by the asymmetry of the régime that is best suited to render an internationally enforceable resolution in the event that disputes should arise.

Across the globe, there are told and untold investment initiatives presently impacted or obstructed by debilitating conflict. Such conflicts often stem from fear on the part of host State nationals that they will be bereft of an effective remedy in the event that harm is incurred. It is posited that there are twin desirable ends of enabling initiation or inter-vention by host States and their nationals in investment arbitration. These are:

1. The potential for *positive influence upon the prospective conduct* of key actors in order to unblock conflicted investment initiatives, in parti-cular by assuaging the fears of vulnerable host States and host State nationals that they will be *sans* effective remedy in the event of injury incurred by investor infringement of their rights; and

2. Participation of host States and their nationals in the arbitral mechan-ism *as an end in itself* in the event that compensable harms are incurred in the course of the investment, in order to see the settlement

instrument, namely a contractual arbitration agreement. These include theories of implied consent, veil-piercing or alter ego, or 'group of companies'. See G. Born, *International Commercial Arbitration* (2014) 1418–1484. With the single exception of the named third party beneficiary, these theories do not obtain in the law of treaties. There is no ground for extension of an arbitration agreement that originates in treaty from sovereign to subject, from the host State to its national. Under the Vienna Convention on the Law of Treaties, '[a] right arises for a *third State* from a provision of a treaty *if the parties to the treaty intend* the provision to accord that right.' Art. 36(1) of the Vienna Convention on the Law of Treaties, 1155 UNTS 331, 8 ILM 679 (1969) (emphasis added). There is authority to indicate that such intent must be expressly recorded. See, e.g., M. Villiger, *Commentary on the 1969 Vienna Convention on the Law of Treaties* (2009) 485 ('[t]he intention is to be understood as a *written* invitation, or proposal, to *a third State* to participate in the operation of a provision of the treaty. Once the right *has been enun-ciated in the treaty*, the parties are estopped from individually refusing to accord the right') (emphasis added). *A fortiori*, one may justly conclude that any effect in favour of a host State national must be expressly articulated in the instrument, in the same manner as provisions giving rise to investor-State arbitration within contemporary investment treaties.

of a broader range of investment-related claims which presently lack a unitary forum in which to be finally resolved.[35]

Thus, the utility of the proposed mechanism lies in the emergence of greater legal certainty and finality from a presently fractured and fragmented landscape, with broader accompanying enforceability across the boundaries of national jurisdictions.

It bears emphasis that nothing in the oncoming models need derogate from the right of choice of investors and their home States, or host States and their nationals. Nothing need diminish the right to choose the State courts (or indeed any other that might accept jurisdiction) for the litigation of disputes where such is wished. Rather, the innovation lies in the premise that entrants to the régime might reasonably elect, in the exercise of their autonomy, to seize a forum whose rulings enjoy wider global enforceability, in order that they not hold a right without remedy.

---

[35] Where provided for, such may of course include pleading for provisional measures (also variously known as interim or conservatory measures) in order to forestall the realisation of potentially compensable harms during the pendency of proceedings. See, e.g., Art. 47 of the ICSID Convention ('[e]xcept as the parties otherwise agree, the [arbitral] Tribunal may, if it considers that the circumstances so require, recommend any provisional measures which should be taken to preserve the respective rights of either party') and Art. 26(1) of the UNCITRAL Arbitration Rules (as revised in 2010) ('[t]he arbitral tribunal may, at the request of a party, grant interim measures').

2

The Four Models

Four mechanisms to achieve initiation or intervention by host States or their nationals in investment arbitration are now presented. These are (i) the Direct Claims Model; (ii) the Espousal Model; (iii) the *Qui Tam* Model; and (iv) the Hybrid Model, the last earning its name by a merging of the prior two.

The Direct Claims Model

The Direct Claims Model includes three variations; see Figure 2.1. In the first two, it is the host State national that acts as claimant. In the third, it is the host State itself.

Direct Claims (I) Model

The Direct Claims (I) Model is conceived to escape 'the paternalistic model of governmental espousal of private claims', in order to 'advance the individual right of access to justice'.[1] Alongside the Direct Claims (II) Model, it is unique in offering an uninterrupted right of action in host State nationals.

As its name suggests, the Direct Claims (I) Model removes any role of the State (whether the home State of the investor or the host State of the investment) in arbitration, and establishes a mechanism for claims by the host State national that may lie immediately against a foreign investor.[2] Such a posture dispenses with issues of internal and international law that may arise where a State acts to prosecute a claim of its national,[3] where a

---

[1] F. Francioni, 'Access to Justice, Denial of Justice and International Investment Law', 20 *European Journal of International Law* 3 (2009).

[2] The State may have a role to play in the pre-arbitral phase, namely in the promulgation of a national investment law or in the negotiation and conclusion of an investment treaty or contract which grants third party rights to the host State national. See Chapter 3.

[3] See The Espousal Model, *infra*.

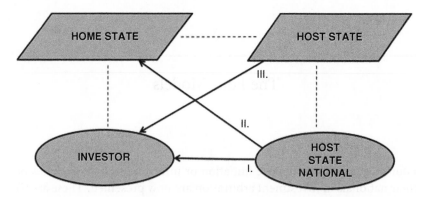

I.   Direct prosecution of claims held by the Host State National, and opposable to the Investor.
II. Direct prosecution of claims held by the Host State National, and opposable to the Home State of the Investor, where a Home State agency or other body acts as guarantor or insurer of the Investor's obligations.
III. Direct prosecution of claims held by the Host State, and opposable to the Investor.

Figure 2.1   Direct Claims Model

national acts to prosecute a claim of his State,[4] or both.[5] In essence, under the Direct Claims (I) Model, there is in the claimant host State national a unity throughout of party to the proceeding and holder of all relevant rights.

The Direct Claims (I) Model thus offers the least elaborate of the four, with accompanying gains by virtue of legal simplicity. In this manner, the host State national is not dependent upon the State to propound his grievances, but rather exercises unfettered control over the prosecution of his own claim, thereby gaining direct access to an international remedy.

Because the concerned host State national is not party to any agreement which confers arbitral jurisdiction over the investor (whether this jurisdiction arises at its origin from the host State's investment law, or rather from treaty or contract), there is an absence of privity. The right to arbitrate may be granted to the host State national as an interested third party.

In the case of a contractual agreement (for example, a concession agreement for exploitation of mineral or hydrocarbon resources, existing as between the host State and a foreign investor), such a third party right may be granted to the host State national by express language within the

---

[4] See The *Qui Tam* Model, *infra*.   [5] See The Hybrid Model, *infra*.

agreement itself.[6] Where a third party right in host State nationals arises in an investment law or a treaty instrument, such is in the image of the standing offer presently extended to foreign investors under the contemporary model.[7] In these latter cases, a further step may be required,

---

[6] See Annex, Model 2 (Contractual Arbitration Agreement). Where the investor's consent is conferred by a contractual instrument, such evokes the doctrine of third party beneficiaries of contract, which exists in both the common and civil law traditions. In crafting a contractual instrument to include an arbitration agreement that grants third party rights in host State nationals, the drafter must naturally be guided by the doctrine of third party beneficiaries appertaining to the body of law that governs the agreement. In particular, an express stipulation that the third party right is irrevocable may be advisable. In the United States, the doctrine gained widespread recognition from the middle nineteenth century following the decision of the New York Court of Appeals in the case of *Lawrence* v. *Fox*, 20 N.Y. 268 (1859), and the American law of this doctrine is heavily dedicated to discerning where a third party not expressly designated in the instrument itself may nonetheless act in exercise of contractual rights. Where, by contrast, a given third party is expressly empowered under the contract, little difficulty is likely to arise. In Britain, jurists long proved reluctant to recognise rights in third parties on grounds of doctrinal objection, where the third party had given no consideration. Parliament thus codified a law of beneficiaries within the Contracts (Rights of Third Parties) Act 1999. For an early view on the Act, see A. Burrows, 'The Contracts (Rights of Third Parties) Act 1999 and its Implications for Commercial Contracts', *Lloyd's Maritime and Commercial Law Quarterly* (2000) 541. In international soft law instruments, see chapter 5, sec. 2 of the UNIDROIT Principles of International Commercial Contracts, Art. 1.6(2) UNIDROIT Principles (2010) and Art. 6:110 of the Principles of European Contract Law, available at: www.cisg.law.pace.edu/cisg/text/textef.html#a6110. In arbitration, see G. Born, *International Commercial Arbitration* (2014) 1455–1459; see also A. Meier and A. L. Setz, 'Arbitration Clauses in Third Party Beneficiary Contracts – Who May and Who Must Arbitrate?', 34 *ASA Bulletin* 1 (2016) 62 (noting that '[t]hird party beneficiary contracts can be found in a wide variety of legal systems, including the systems of law built on the Roman and Anglo-Saxon legal traditions').

[7] See Annex, Models 3 (Host State Investment Law) and 6 (Contingent Consent Clause). For a thorough explication, see *ICS Inspection and Control Services Limited* v. *Argentine Republic*:

> The above analysis is bolstered by a brief consideration of the nature of arbitral jurisdiction for investor-State disputes arising under investment treaties. Whereas in public international law in the State-to-State context, the jurisdictional analysis usually focuses on the consent expressed in the instrument containing the arbitration provision, investor-State arbitration requires the additional and posterior consent by a non-signatory to that treaty: the investor. The formation of the agreement to arbitrate occurs through the acceptance by the investor of the standing offer to arbitrate found in the relevant investment treaty.
> The terms and conditions of the offer, however, were negotiated earlier and separately by the contracting parties to the treaty and are directed at investors of the other contracting State generally, rather than at any particular investor. According to the law of treaties, when exercising a right provided for it in a given treaty, a third party like the investor, shall comply with the conditions for the exercise of that right provided for in the treaty or established in conformity with the treaty.

for just as the concerned host State national is not privy to the legislative or treaty instrument, neither is the foreign investor.[8]

Once jurisdiction *ratione personae* is obtained, a dispute as lying directly between a host State national and a foreign investor gives rise to an arbitration that resembles any international proceeding as between two (or more) private parties.[9] The novelty then lies in expansion of the tribunal's jurisdiction *ratione materiae*, a tailoring of the bodies of rights and obligations of both investors and host State nationals that may be submitted to the tribunal's adjudication.[10]

An important caveat of the Direct Claims (I) Model is that, as these disputes by definition lie directly between the host State national and the foreign investor, ICSID jurisdiction cannot extend over them.[11] Thus, by electing the Direct Claims (I) Model, one forfeits access to the ICSID procedural framework. Such does not foreclose access to the Permanent Court of Arbitration. In a report to its Administrative Council, a steering committee found that 'article 49 of the 1907 Convention [for the Pacific Settlement of International Disputes] could be interpreted as giving the Administrative Council the power to authorize the establishment by the International Bureau of optional rules, even those that expand the mandate of the PCA.'[12] One set of such optional rules is the 2001 Optional Rules for Arbitration of Disputes Relating to Natural Resources and/or

---

ICS Inspection and Control Services Limited v. *Argentine Republic*, PCA Case No. 2010-9, Award on Jurisdiction, 10 February 2012, paras. 270–271. The tribunal noted 'the analogous context of treaties providing for rights for third States' as under the Vienna Convention on the Law of Treaties, Ibid. n 299, which states that '[a] State exercising a [third party right] shall comply with the conditions for its exercise provided for in the treaty or established in conformity with the treaty'. See Art. 36(2) of the Vienna Convention on the Law of Treaties, 1155 UNTS 331, 8 ILM 679 (1969).

[8] See Chapter 3.

[9] Where interests diverge as between the home State and its investor or the host State and its national, provision may be made in the relevant instrument for the State to file submissions, even arguing points in opposition. See, e.g., Art. 1128 of the NAFTA ('[o]n written notice to the disputing parties, a Party may make submissions to a Tribunal on a question of interpretation of this Agreement').

[10] See Chapter 5. Although the present focus is upon recourse to host State nationals, the laws or rules chosen by the parties may equally redress, by way of example, damage to an investor's property in the context of claims (or counterclaims) by the investor.

[11] It is recalled that the name of the foundational treaty is the Convention on the Settlement of Investment Disputes between States and Nationals of Other States, 575 UNTS 159, 4 ILM 532 (1965).

[12] Permanent Court of Arbitration, 1999 Steering Committee, *Final Report and Recommendations to the Administrative Council* (June 1997), para 48. The report was accepted by the Court's Administrative Council at its 156th meeting in October 1997.

the Environment (the PCA Environmental Rules), which is available in disputes between private parties. Under these rules, the Permanent Court of Arbitration has been authorised to provide and will provide full registry support even in cases where no State, State-controlled entity, or intergovernmental organisation is a party to the dispute.[13] Further, under the PCA Environmental Rules, '[t]he characterization of the dispute as relating to natural resources and/or the environment is not necessary for jurisdiction where all the parties have agreed to settle a specific dispute under these Rules.'[14]

As a further alternative within the Direct Claims (I) Model, the PCA Arbitration Rules may be used. Those rules provide that '[t]he involvement of at least one State, State-controlled entity, or intergovernmental organisation as a party to the dispute is not necessary for jurisdiction where all the parties have agreed to settle a dispute under these Rules.'[15]

Direct Claims (II) Model

The jurisdictional defect precluding access to ICSID under the Direct Claims (I) Model may be cured by rendering the investor's home State a

---

[13] To date, there have been five cases exclusively between private parties under the PCA Environmental Rules.

[14] Art. 1(1) of the PCA Environmental Rules.

[15] Art. 1(4) of the PCA Arbitration Rules 2012. The same provision states that 'where the Secretary-General of the Permanent Court of Arbitration determines that no State, State-controlled entity, or intergovernmental organization is a party to the dispute, the Secretary-General may decide to limit the Permanent Court of Arbitration's role in the proceedings to the function of the Secretary-General as appointing authority, with the role of the International Bureau under these Rules to be assumed by the arbitral tribunal.' Ibid. The authors are confident that the Secretary-General would exercise his or her discretion to provide full registry support to cases brought under the PCA Arbitration Rules 2012 in accordance with the model provisions given in the Annex, in particular in view of the public genesis and nature of the procedure envisaged, even where no public entity participates directly as a party to the proceedings. Where greater certainty as to the availability of the Permanent Court of Arbitration's services is desired, parties may instead opt to use the PCA Environmental Rules, which provide in their introduction that '[t]he Rules, and the services of the Secretary-General and the International Bureau of the PCA, are available to States, international organizations, and private parties.' Beyond the Permanent Court of Arbitration, there are other capable institutions that might equally administer disputes lying directly between the host State national and the foreign investor. Examples include the London Court of International Arbitration, the Arbitration Institute of the Stockholm Chamber of Commerce, the International Chamber of Commerce, the Hong Kong International Arbitration Centre, and the Singapore International Arbitration Centre.

guarantor of the investor's obligations.[16] Where the relevant instruments
are properly crafted, an arrangement that is akin to the common law of
joint and several liability might be achieved as between the investor and
his home State, with the claimant host State national to exercise a choice
of named respondent.[17] Where both the host State of the investment and
the home State of the investor are parties to the ICSID Convention, there
is, on the one hand, 'a national of a[] Contracting State', and, on the other
'a Contracting State', allowing jurisdiction to lie at the Centre.[18]

Direct Claims (III) Model

In contrast to the Direct Claims (I) and (II) Models, the Direct Claims
(III) Model serves in those instances wherein the rights allegedly
infringed by injurious conduct of the foreign investor are held not
uniquely by host State nationals, but rather by the host State itself. The
State thus holds an injured interest separate and apart from the summation of any individual claims arising from the unlawful conduct. Perhaps
the most useful example lies in the realm of environmental law, where
many obligations (whether arising in municipal law or another source)
are essentially public in nature, in the sense that it is often the State that is
entitled to enforce compliance.[19] Where the State is the right-holder, the
State may conduct the prosecution of its claim as directly opposable to
the foreign investor, before the Centre if it so wishes.

---

[16] For an extensive discussion on the passing of rights and obligations as between the State
and its national in the context of international investment law, see The Espousal Model,
infra. Such might be achieved in, for example, the form of a State-sponsored scheme of
international investment insurance. These schemes are established features of international investment, with the insurer commonly insuring against eventualities of political
risk, often including such classic investment law events as expropriation. In addition to
home State schemes and private insurers, there are examples of multilateral initiatives,
including a prominent one by the World Bank. See I. Shihata, *MIGA and Foreign
Investment: Origins, Operations, Policies and Basic Documents of the Multilateral
Investment Guarantee Agency* (1988). Under the Direct Claims (II) Model, the scope of
insurance is extended, encompassing liability of the investor to host State nationals, for
harms as may be inflicted in violation of their enumerated rights.

[17] See Annex, Model 14 (Home State Insurer or Guarantor). Under this mechanism's
operation, the home State is rendered a proper respondent in the form of its insurer,
with its maximum liability to be established under the terms of the insurance agreement, or perhaps with the insurer to be indemnified by the insured investor to the extent
that any ultimate recovery by the claimant host State national reaches beyond the scope of
insurance.

[18] Art. 25(1) of the ICSID Convention.

[19] See Areas of Law for Possible Incorporation, Chapter 5.

A Role for the Host State

The three forthcoming models are more elaborate than the Direct Claims Model, in order of escalation. In each of them, as in the Direct Claims (III) Model, the host State of the investment is party to the dispute vis-à-vis the foreign investor.

The assimilation of the State and its national within the forthcoming models is not motivated in any desire to deny legal personality to the individual at international law. Rather, a presently actionable path is chosen: the path of simple conformity to the *lex specialis* of international investment law, including, where desired, the ICSID Convention.[20]

The Long Shadow of Diplomatic Protection

To better apprehend the forthcoming three models, it is useful to examine a parallel to diplomatic protection, and to observe the inherent limitations of this analogue. Under the venerated practice, a State may espouse claims of its national as opposable to another State for violation of the latter's obligations in regard to the treatment of aliens. Such espousal is discretionary and may be manifest in any manner not prohibited by international law, including political or economic pressures (via consular actions or other diplomatic channels[21]), legal avenues (by inter-State arbitration[22] or by seizure of international judicial

---

[20] See, e.g., *Report of the Executive Directors of the International Bank for Reconstruction and Development on the Convention on the Settlement of Investment Disputes between States and Nationals of Other States*, para. 25 ('[w]hile consent of the parties is an essential prerequisite for the jurisdiction of the Centre, consent alone will not suffice to bring a dispute within its jurisdiction. In keeping with the purpose of the Convention, the jurisdiction of the Centre is further limited by reference to *the nature of the dispute* and *the parties thereto*') (emphasis added). Thus, the host State might be sought for purposes of gaining eligibility before the Centre in claims opposable to the foreign investor.

[21] Hersch Lauterpacht has eloquently described the phenomenon of diplomatic protection as follows: 'By a universally recognised customary rule of International Law every State holds a right of protection over its citizens abroad . . . every State is entitled to exercise this right when one of its subjects is wronged in his person or property, either by the State itself on whose territory such person or property is for the time being, or by the officials or the citizens of such State, if it does not interfere for the purpose of making good the wrongs done. This right can be exercised in several ways. Thus, a State whose subjects are wronged can insist, through diplomatic channels, upon the wrongdoers being punished according to the law of the land and upon damages, if necessary, being paid to its injured subjects.' H. Lauterpacht (ed.), *Oppenheim's International Law*, 8th edn., vol. I (1955) 638, 686–687.

[22] See, e.g., *Italian Republic* v. *Republic of Cuba*, Ad Hoc State-State Arbitration (UNCITRAL), IIC 507 (2008), Final Award, 15 January 2008.

organs such as the International Court of Justice[23]), or ultimately, in times past, by the use of force.[24]

Within the Commentary to the International Law Commission's Draft Articles on Diplomatic Protection of 2006, the origins of the practice are traced as follows:

> Diplomatic protection has traditionally been seen as an exclusive State right in the sense that a State exercises diplomatic protection in its own right because an injury to a national is deemed to be an injury to the State itself. This approach has its roots, first in a statement by the Swiss jurist Emmerich de Vattel in 1758 that 'whoever ill-treats a citizen indirectly injures the State, which must protect that citizen', and, secondly in a dictum ... in the *Mavrommatis Palestine Concessions* case.[25]

Indeed, one theory of espousal is concisely stated in the early *Mavrommatis Palestine Concessions* case, where the inter-war Permanent Court of International Justice wrote in 1924 that '[b]y taking up the case of one of its subjects and by resorting to diplomatic action or international judicial proceedings on his behalf, a State is in reality asserting its own rights – its right to ensure, in the person of its subjects, respect for the rules of international law.'[26]

---

[23] See note 90 *infra*.

[24] The legality of the use of armed force to protect economic rights fell into disfavour in the twentieth century. This modern trend is perhaps traceable to the 1899 and 1907 Hague Conventions for the Pacific Settlement of International Disputes, including the conclusion of the Drago-Porter Convention, Article 1 of which prohibits the use of force for the recovery of contract debts claimed from the government of one State by another, on behalf of its national. Convention on the Limitation of the Employment of Force for the Recovery of Contract Debts (Hague Convention II of 1907), signed 18 October 1907 (entered into force 26 January 1910), 36 Stat 2241, 1 Bevans 607. See also W. Benedek, 'Drago-Porter Convention', *Max Planck Encyclopedia of Public International Law* (2007). The Drago-Porter Convention came in response to the decision of an arbitral tribunal authorising the use of force in order to obtain compensation for pecuniary injury to investor-nationals in the case of *Preferential Treatment of Claims of Blockading Powers against Venezuela* (Germany, Great Britain and Italy v. Venezuela), Permanent Court of Arbitration, Award, 22 February 1904, IX UNRIAA 99. Also influential in this evolution were the Paris Peace Conference, the Kellogg-Briand Pact of 1928, and, of course, the Charter of the United Nations. For a contemporary view on the shift away from use of armed force in international investment law, see J. Paulsson, 'Confronting Global Challenges: From Gunboat Diplomacy to Investor-State Arbitration', Permanent Court of Arbitration Peace Palace Centenary Seminar (2013).

[25] Commentary to Articles 1 and 25, para. 3 of the *Draft Articles on Diplomatic Protection with commentaries*, ILC 2006, UN Doc. A/61/10, citing E. de Vattel, *The Law of Nations or the Principles of Natural Law Applied to the Conduct and to the Affairs of Nations and Sovereigns*, vol. III (1758) 136.

[26] *Mavrommatis Case* (Greece v. U.K.) (1924), PCIJ Series A, No. 2, 12. The Court further opined that '[i]n the case of the Mavrommatis concessions it is true that the dispute was at

In 1928, Brierly wrote favourably of this *Mavrommatis* principle:

> Such a view does not, as is sometimes suggested, introduce any fiction of law; nor does it rest ... on anything so intangible as the 'wounding of national honour'; rather it merely expresses the plain truth that the injurious results of a denial of justice are not, or at any rate are not necessarily, confined to the individual sufferer or his family, but include such consequences as the 'mistrust and lack of safety' felt by other foreigners similarly situated ... Such government frequently has a larger interest in maintaining the principles of international law than in recovering damage for one of its citizens in a particular case.[27]

In more recent times, within Article 1 of the Draft Articles on Diplomatic Protection, it is written that the practice

> consists of the invocation by a State, through diplomatic action or other means of peaceful settlement, of the responsibility of another State for an injury caused by an internationally wrongful act of that State to a natural or legal person that is a national of the former State with a view to the implementation of such responsibility.[28]

The following appears within the Commentary to this Article:

> Obviously it is a fiction – and an exaggeration – to say that an injury to a national is an injury to the State itself. Many of the rules of diplomatic protection contradict the correctness of this fiction, notably the rule of continuous nationality which requires a State to prove that the injured national remained its national after the injury itself and up to the date of the presentation of the claim. A State does not 'in reality' – to quote *Mavrommatis* – assert its own right only. 'In reality' it also asserts the right of its injured national.[29]

---

first between a private person and a State – i.e. between M. Mavrommatis and Great Britain', but '[s]ubsequently, the Greek Government took up the case', and '[t]he dispute then entered upon a new phase; it entered the domain of international law, and became a dispute between two States'. Ibid. The Court finally elaborated that '[o]nce a State has taken up a case on behalf of one of its subjects before an international tribunal, in the eyes of the latter the State is sole claimant.' Ibid.

[27] J. L. Brierly, 'The Theory of Implied State Complicity in International Claims', 9 *British Yearbook of International Law* (1928) 48. It has more recently been written that '[a]scriptions of nationality allow states to allocate control over a scarce and valuable resource: people.' M. Casas, 'Nationalities of Convenience, Personal Jurisdiction, and Access to Investor-State Dispute Settlement', 49 *New York University Journal of International Law and Politics* 1 (2016). Under such a view, a State might indeed act in the cause of its injured national, with a larger view towards preservation of principles of international law.

[28] Art. 1 of the *Draft Articles on Diplomatic Protection with Commentaries*, ILC 2006, UN Doc. A/61/10.

[29] Ibid. Commentary to Arts. 1 and 25, para. 3.

Fiction or not, investment arbitration as we presently know it is a child of espousal, with the foreign investor now holding a right of access to an international remedy, free from any need to seek the intervention of his home State.[30] Although debate remains as to whether the investor exercises a right directly or rather derivatively, as a proxy of his home State,[31]

[30] It is evident in the ICSID Convention that its drafters intended for an investor's right of action to supplant the practice of diplomatic protection. Article 27 provides in particular that '[n]o Contracting State shall give diplomatic protection, or bring an international claim, in respect of a dispute which one of its nationals and another Contracting State shall have consented to submit or shall have submitted to arbitration under this Convention.' There is a single exception for instances in which a contracting State fails to abide by an award. See also *Report of the Executive Directors of the International Bank for Reconstruction and Development on the Convention on the Settlement of Investment Disputes between States and Nationals of Other States*, para. 33 ('[w]hen a host State consents to the submission of a dispute with an investor to the Centre, thereby giving the investor direct access to an international jurisdiction, the investor should not be in a position to ask his State to espouse his case and that State should not be permitted to do so') and para. 45 (explaining that Article 64 of the ICSID Convention does not 'empower a State to institute proceedings before the [International Court of Justice] in respect of a dispute which one of its nationals and another Contracting State have consented to submit or have submitted to arbitration, since such proceedings would contravene the provisions of Article 27').

[31] Regarding the rights of the investor's home State, see, e.g., *North American Dredging Company of Texas (U.S.A.)* v. *United Mexican States*, 4 UNRIAA 26 (1926). In that case, the United States–Mexican General Claims Commission, commenting on the investor's waiver of diplomatic protection under a so-called Calvo Clause, asked whether '[u]nder the rules of international law may an alien lawfully make such a promise', and answered that he may, but at the same time held 'that he cannot deprive the government of his nation of its undoubted right of applying international remedies to violations of international law committed to his damage'. Ibid. 29. See also I. Brownlie, *Principles of Public International Law* (1979) 546; H. Lauterpacht (ed.), *Oppenheim's International Law*, 8th edn., vol. I (1955) 345; M. Sørensen, *Manual of Public International Law* (1968) 592; American Law Institute, *Restatement (Third) of Foreign Relations Law of the United States*, vol. II (1987), para. 713 cmt. g. As to rights of the investor, see Z. Douglas, 'The Hybrid Foundations of Investment Treaty Arbitration', 74 *British Yearbook of International Law* 1 (2003); *Republic of Ecuador* v. *United States of America*, PCA Case No. 2012-5, Award, 29 September 2012, para. 204 ('the question of to whom the obligations in [bilateral investment treaties] are owed revolves around the interpretation of the primary obligation'), citing J. Crawford, 'The ILC's Articles on Responsibility of States for Internationally Wrongful Acts: A Retrospect', 96 *American Journal of International Law* 4 (2002) 887–888; *Mondev International Ltd.* v. *United States*, ICSID Case No. ARB(AF)/ 99/2, Award, 11 October 2002, para. 116 (finding that 'both the substantive and procedural rights of the individual in international law have undergone considerable development', and thus indicating that certain rights under NAFTA are directly held by individuals); and *Société Générale de Surveillance (SGS)* v. *Republic of the Philippines*, ICSID Case No. ARB/02/6, Decision of the Tribunal on Objections to Jurisdiction, 29 January 2004, para. 154 (finding that 'under modern international law, treaties may confer rights, substantive and procedural, on individuals'). See also *Lagrand Case* (Germany v. United States), Judgment, 2001 ICJ Reports 466, para. 77; *Case Concerning*

it is established that investor-nationals of a State that contracts to a treaty comprising an investor-State arbitration mechanism may enjoy both (i) enumerated substantive guarantees of investment protection; and (ii) an effective means to demand their implementation.

It has been observed that '[w]hilst some aspects of the [investment treaty] system exhibit a symmetry and reciprocity evocative of mainstream commercial arbitration, many aspects exhibit a one-sidedness more reminiscent of its diplomatic protection past.'[32] Child of diplomatic protection though it may be, the investment treaty régime imposes no inherent limitation upon either (i) the nature of the substantive rights and obligations that may fall within its jurisdiction;[33] or (ii) the direction in which those rights and obligations may flow, as between a State and a national of another State.[34] A host State acting to prosecute a claim as opposable to a foreign investor is, in outward appearance, reversely akin to diplomatic protection.

As in diplomatic protection, two of the three forthcoming models require the State to take interest, via a sort of endorsement, in the grievances of its nationals, including classes or collectives thereof, and to offer an avenue for pursuing a claim to remedy allegedly injurious conduct. As a claim by a host State vis-à-vis a foreign investor does not (and could not) legalistically equate to a host State bringing a claim in diplomatic protection,[35] and because the claim arises under a self-contained régime of investment law, the traditional rules of diplomatic protection,

---

Avena and Other Mexican Nationals (Mexico v. United States), 2004 ICJ Reports 12, para. 40; and Commentary to Art. 33(2) of the Articles on Responsibility of States for Internationally Wrongful Acts, with Commentaries, *Yearbook of the International Law Commission*, vol. II(2) (2001).

[32] G. Laborde, 'The Case for Host State Claims in Investment Arbitration', 1 *Journal of International Dispute Settlement* 1 (2010) 121.

[33] See Chapter 5.

[34] See, e.g., Introduction, note 1. See also Z. Douglas, *The International Law of Investment Claims* (2009) 256 ('[i]f a general principle can be discerned ... it is that the jurisdiction *ratione materiae* of an international tribunal extends to counterclaims unless expressly excluded by the constitutive instrument'), citing *Installations Maritimes de Bruges* v. *Hamburg Amerika Linie*, 1 RIAA 877 (1921) ('*Att. que les deux requêtes introductives sont basées sur un seul et même fait, qui est la collision survenue le 25 octobre 1911 entre le vapeur Parthia et Duc d'Albe et un mur du port de Zeebruge, et que la seconde requête eût pu prendre la forme d'une simple demande reconventionnelle si l'article 29 de Règlement de procédure ne l'interdisait absolument*').

[35] It is recalled that diplomatic protection 'consists of the invocation by a State, through diplomatic action or other means of peaceful settlement, of the responsibility *of another State* for an injury caused by an internationally wrongful act *of that State*'. Art. 1 of the *Draft Articles on Diplomatic Protection with commentaries*, ILC 2006, UN Doc. A/61/10 (emphasis added).

such as nationality of claims and exhaustion of local remedies, do not of their own force apply.[36]

The Boundaries of State Behaviour

Where the host State proceeds to prosecute a claim, the empowerment of given personalities to act on its behalf must be achieved. In discerning the boundaries of State behaviour, guidance may be sought in the law of attribution. In this domain, the International Law Commission's Draft Articles on Responsibility of States for Internationally Wrongful Acts of 2001[37] are generally regarded as codificatory of customary international law.[38] Thus, '[t]he structure of the State and the functions of its organs are not in general governed by international law', and it is rather 'a matter for each State to decide how its administration is to be structured and which functions are to be assumed by government'.[39] These decisions, a

---

[36] The ILC's Draft Articles on Diplomatic Protection offer an authoritative statement of both rules. See Art. 3 ('1. [t]he State entitled to exercise diplomatic protection is the State of nationality') and Art. 14 ('1. [a] State may not present an international claim in respect of an injury to a national . . . before the injured person has . . . exhausted all local remedies. 2. "Local remedies" means legal remedies which are open to the injured person before the judicial or administrative courts or bodies, whether ordinary or special, of the State alleged to be responsible for causing the injury') of the *Draft Articles on Diplomatic Protection with Commentaries*, ILC 2006, UN Doc. A/61/10. See also ibid. Art. 17 ('[t]he present draft articles do not apply to the extent that they are inconsistent with special rules of international law, such as treaty provisions for the protection of investments').

[37] Articles on Responsibility of States for Internationally Wrongful Acts, with Commentaries, *Yearbook of the International Law Commission*, vol. II(2) (2001). Within the Commentary to these Articles, it is stated that '[i]n theory, the conduct of all human beings, corporations or collectives linked to the State by nationality, habitual residence or incorporation might be attributable to the State, regardless of any connection to government', but that 'in international law, such an approach is avoided'. Ibid. Commentary to Chapter II. Rather, 'the only conduct attributed to the State at the international level is that of its organs of government, or of others who have acted under the direction, instigation or control of those organs, i.e. as agents of the State'. Ibid. For an exhaustive view into the law of state responsibility, see J. Crawford, *State Responsibility: The General Part* (2013).

[38] See *Application of the Convention on the Prevention and Punishment of the Crime of Genocide* (Bosnia and Herzegovina v. Serbia and Montenegro), Judgment, 26 February 2007, 2007 ICJ Reports 43, paras. 385 and 398. See also *Legal Consequences of the Construction of a Wall in the Occupied Palestinian Territory*, Advisory Opinion, 9 July 2004, 2004 ICJ Reports 136, para. 140; *Case Concerning Armed Activities on the Territory of the Congo* (Democratic Republic of Congo v. Uganda), Judgment, 19 December 2005, 2005 ICJ Reports 168, paras. 160, 293; *Case Concerning Pulp Mills on the River Uruguay* (Argentina v. Uruguay), Judgment, 20 April 2010, 2010 ICJ Reports 14, para. 273.

[39] Commentary to Chapter II of the Articles on Responsibility of States for Internationally Wrongful Acts, with Commentaries, *Yearbook of the International Law Commission*, vol. II(2) (2001).

sovereign prerogative, manifest themselves in the statutory character of a State's organs, entities, and agencies, as under that State's internal laws.

Article 4 articulates the general posture with respect to State organs, and reads in full as follows:

> 1. The conduct of any State organ shall be considered an act of that State under international law, whether the organ exercises legislative, executive, judicial or any other functions, whatever position it holds in the organization of the State, and whatever its character as an organ of the central Government or of a territorial unit of the State. 2. An organ includes any person or entity which has that status in accordance with the internal law of the State.[40]

The rule reflected in Article 4 is sufficiently broad to encompass the sort of host State action envisaged in the forthcoming models, which action indeed entails legislative, executive, or 'any other functions'.[41] Moreover, under Article 4(2), designation as an organ calls for first assessment by reference to a given State's internal laws. Further sealing the role, the commentary to Article 4 notes that this provision 'explains the relevance of internal law in determining the status of a State organ', for '[w]here the law of a State characterizes an entity as an organ, no difficulty will arise'.[42]

Article 5 provides for a rule of attribution on the basis of a person's or entity's 'exercise of elements of governmental authority'.[43] Consequently, even the acts of those entities or personalities which are not 'organs' of the State within the meaning of Article 4 may nonetheless be attributable to the State. The commentary to Article 5 clarifies that 'an entity is covered even if its exercise of authority involves an independent discretion or power to act; there is no need to show that the conduct was in fact carried out under the control of the State', but rather the internal law in question must only 'specifically authorize the conduct as involving the exercise of public authority'.[44]

Finally, Article 11, entitled '[c]onduct acknowledged and adopted by a State as its own', first reflects the familiar principle that purely private conduct is not, as such, attributable to the State. Article 11 then recognises 'nevertheless' that conduct is to be considered an act of a State 'if and to the extent that the State acknowledges and adopts the conduct in question as its

---

[40] Ibid. Art. 4. Under the Commentary, '[t]he term "person or entity" is used ... in a broad sense to include *any natural or legal person*.' Ibid. Commentary to Art. 4 (emphasis added). These articles thus affirm the broad powers of the State to determine who may act on its behalf with binding effect at international law.
[41] Ibid.   [42] Ibid. Commentary to Art. 4.   [43] Ibid. Art. 5.
[44] Ibid. Commentary to Art. 5.

own'.[45] Indeed, 'provided the State's intention to accept responsibility for otherwise non-attributable conduct is clearly indicated', Article 11 may even capture a State's acceptance of responsibility 'for conduct of which it did not approve, which it had sought to prevent and which it deeply regretted'.[46]

Attribution versus Jurisdiction

Where discerning emanations of the State, there is a sharp distinction between attribution and jurisdiction. For purposes of the forthcoming three models, the question that arises is not one of whether given conduct may be traced to the host State so as to hold it internationally responsible (a question that not infrequently arises on the merits of affirmative claims by foreign investors), but rather of *whether given entities or personalities are authentically empowered by the host State*, and thus whether the host State's consent to arbitration is validly obtained, rendering the State a party to the dispute at the jurisdictional threshold.[47]

---

[45] Ibid. Art. 11. By analogy to the law of agency, such adoption is equivalent to what is there often known as ratification.

[46] Commentary to Art. 11 of the Articles on Responsibility of States for Internationally Wrongful Acts, with Commentaries, *Yearbook of the International Law Commission*, vol. II(2) (2001).

[47] On this sharp distinction between attribution and jurisdiction, see J. Crawford, 'Treaty and Contract in Investment Arbitration', 24 *Arbitration International* 3 (2008) 362 ('[i]t is sometimes argued that the question is one of attribution . . . but attribution has nothing to do with it. The issue of attribution arises when it is sought to hold the State responsible for some breach of an international obligation – including one arising under a substantive provision of a [bilateral investment treaty]. The problem here concerns jurisdiction, not merits; the formation of a secondary agreement to arbitrate, not the breach of a primary obligation concerning the protection of investments. In short, the question is one of interpretation of the jurisdictional offer, not attribution of conduct to the State'). Thus, a tribunal noted in its decision on jurisdiction that attribution was not *prima facie* relevant for determining whether the host State had consented to arbitration with the claimant. *Niko Resources (Bangladesh) Ltd.* v. *Bangladesh Petroleum Exploration & Production Company Limited (Bapex) and Bangladesh Oil Gas and Mineral Corporation (Petrobangla)*, ICSID Case No. ARB/10/11 and ICSID Case No. ARB 10/18, Decision on Jurisdiction, 19 August 2013, paras. 242–248. Instead, the tribunal concluded that consent to jurisdiction did not follow from attribution but remained a discrete require- ment. Ibid. para. 248 ('[i]n the present case the Government has not signed any agreement with the investor and has not on its own behalf agreed to ICSID arbitration. The Tribunal finds no basis on which an attribution of actions of BAPEX and Petrobangla to Bangladesh could justify the conclusion that the State of Bangladesh has agreed to arbitrate the present contract disputes with [the claimant]'). Similarly, in another case, while the tribunal did note that '[a]t this jurisdictional stage, there is no indication that either the courts of Bangladesh or Petrobangla could manifestly not qualify as state organs at least *de facto*', the tribunal did not determine these questions of attribution at that

One might be forgiven for questioning why the Articles on the Responsibility of States for Internationally Wrongful Acts are referenced in view of this distinction between attribution and jurisdiction, only the latter of which here concerns us. Attribution and jurisdiction are not only discrete inquiries: they flow in reverse directions. Attribution operates to *discern authority retrospectively*, whereas consent operates to confer jurisdiction, and thus to *grant authority prospectively*.

Even under the more restrictive standard of attribution, concerned as it is with preventing States from evading international responsibility, and wherein international law must thus exert a force, each of the forthcoming models, relying as it does upon *a prospective grant of authority* under the *internal laws of the host State*, surpasses the threshold of State behaviour.

A fortiori, each of the forthcoming models surpasses the threshold of State behaviour for purposes of jurisdiction. This is so where even the international law of attribution imposes only *negative* restrictions upon a State's ability to *disown* given conduct,[48] but no *positive* restrictions upon a State's ability to *own* given conduct.[49] The State is thus at liberty to designate agencies and appoint representatives of its choosing, for international law imposes no restraint upon a State's ability to positively empower, in accordance with its own laws, whomever it wishes to act on its behalf with binding effect at international law.

In sum, international law does not impose any limitation upon the nature of the agents or representatives via the person of whom a State may conduct itself. In sharp contrast to the question of attribution for purposes of discerning State responsibility (wherein international law is not content to merely defer to the internal laws of the State), where a State declares that given actors do act in its name and on its behalf, international

phase, which questions concern only State responsibility on the merits. *Saipem S.p.A.* v. *People's Republic of Bangladesh*, ICSID Case No. ARB/05/07, Decision on Jurisdiction, 21 March 2007, paras. 143–149.

[48] Thus, 'the conduct of certain institutions performing public functions and exercising public powers is attributed to the State even if regarded in internal law as autonomous and independent of the executive', for '[t]he State as a subject of international law is held responsible for the conduct of all organs, instrumentalities, and officials which form part of its organization and act in that capacity, whether or not they have separate legal personality under internal law'. Commentary to Chapter II of the Articles on Responsibility of States for Internationally Wrongful Acts, with Commentaries, *Yearbook of the International Law Commission*, vol. II(2) (2001).

[49] As noted, a State may claim conduct as its own even after the conduct in question has occurred, and even as to 'conduct of which it did not approve, which it had sought to prevent and which it deeply regretted'. Ibid. Commentary to Art. 11.

law imposes no test of their stateliness.[50] In the world of jurisdiction, the State alone determines the question of who is the State.

The ICSID Convention

In a further demonstration of the distinction between attribution and jurisdiction, manifested at Article 25(3) of the ICSID Convention, States party exercise unfettered control over which of their 'constituent subdivision[s]' and 'agenc[ies]' may gain access to (or be subjected to) ICSID jurisdiction.[51] To the extent that a State may act as a claimant (or counterclaimant) in a claim that is opposable to a foreign investor, its duly designated 'constituent subdivision[s]' or 'agenc[ies]' may freely do so as well. This vehicle of representation is viable, depending upon the constitutional structure of the State in question. If, for instance, an injured national falls within a properly designated federated state or region, the government of that 'constituent subdivision' may take up his claim at arbitration as against an allegedly wrongdoing investor. It has been observed that 'not only would [the term] cover municipalities and local government bodies in unitary States, but it would cover semi-autonomous dependencies, provinces or federated States in non-unitary States and the local government bodies in such subdivisions.'[52] Indeed, Professor Schreuer finds that '[i]t may be concluded that "constituent subdivision" covers any territorial entity below the level of the State itself.'[53]

Alternatively, or additionally, an agency of the host State may be established for the purpose of prosecuting claims, or the necessary powers may be conferred upon an agency already existing. The term 'agency' is broadly interpreted. Professor Schreuer has observed of Article 25 that

---

[50] This divergence is served by logic. A State may not be permitted to evade responsibility for internationally wrongful acts by simply defining the offending actor to be acting *ultra vires* under its own laws. Thus, international law imposes objective tests of attribution. See, e.g., ibid. Commentary to Art. 4 ('[a] State cannot avoid responsibility for the conduct of a body which does in truth act as one of its organs merely by denying it that status under its own law').

[51] Art. 25(3) of the ICSID Convention ('[c]onsent by a constituent subdivision or agency of a Contracting State shall require the approval of that State unless that State notifies the Centre that no such approval is required').

[52] C. F. Amerasinghe, 'Jurisdiction *Ratione Personae* under the Convention on the Settlement of Investment Disputes between States and Nationals of Other States', 47 *British Yearbook of International Law* 1 (1976) 233.

[53] C. Schreuer, L. Malintoppi, A. Reinisch, and A. Sinclair, *The ICSID Convention: A Commentary*, 2nd edn. (2009) 153.

[t]he concept of 'agency' should be read not in structural terms but functionally. This means that whether the 'agency' is a corporation, whether and to what extent it is government-owned and whether it has separate legal personality are of secondary importance. What matters is that it performs public functions on behalf of the Contracting State or one of its constituent subdivisions.[54]

In further deference to the State, Professor Schreuer has observed that 'a precise definition of the term "constituent subdivision or agency" is of subordinate importance' in view of the designation requirement, for '[d]esignation would create a very strong presumption that the entity in question is indeed a "constituent subdivision or agency"' of the State in question.[55] As to validity of the designation, an early observer wrote

[i]t would seem that under the scheme of the Convention such an approval is a unilateral act performed by the Contracting State and does

---

[54] Ibid. citing C. F. Amerasinghe, 'Jurisdiction Ratione Personae under the Convention on the Settlement of Investment Disputes between States and Nationals of Other States', 47 British Yearbook of International Law 1 (1976) 233–234 ('[i]t is probably necessary that the entity be acting on behalf of the government of the State concerned or one of its constituent subdivisions, and this is perhaps the main criterion. It would not seem to matter that the agency belongs to a political subdivision or that it has a separate legal personality from the government. Indeed, the use of the term "agencies" as opposed to "instrumentalities" may well indicate that it was intended to include even certain government-owned companies or government-controlled corporations. On the other hand, mere ownership by the government of shares in a public company may be inadequate for the entity to qualify as an agency'). This functional test is evocative of that given for purposes of discerning attribution. See, e.g., Commentary to Art. 4 of the Articles on Responsibility of States for Internationally Wrongful Acts, with Commentaries, Yearbook of the International Law Commission, vol. II(2) (2001).

[55] C. Schreuer, L. Malintoppi, A. Reinisch, and A. Sinclair, The ICSID Convention: A Commentary, 2nd edn. (2009) 154. Such a presumption is observed in the case of Noble Energy, Inc. and Machalapower Cia. Ltda. v. The Republic of Ecuador and Consejo Nacional de Electricidad, ICSID Case No. ARB/05/12, Decision on Jurisdiction, 5 March 2008, para. 63 ('Ecuador designated [the Consejo Nacional de Electricidad] to the Centre on 21 August 2002 for purposes of Article 25 of the ICSID Convention and [it] is thus to be considered as an agency of the Republic of Ecuador'). See also C. F. Amerasinghe, 'Jurisdiction Ratione Personae under the Convention on the Settlement of Investment Disputes between States and Nationals of Other States', 47 British Yearbook of International Law 1 (1976) 234 ('[i]f a Contracting State designates a body to the Centre as being an agency or constituent subdivision of that State, a strong presumption is raised that such body is in fact a constituent subdivision or agency, and it is not likely that a tribunal or commission will reject such a designation as being inconsistent with the Convention. On the other hand, it is, of course, the case that the Convention does not leave the ultimate determination of the issue to the Contracting State concerned. In the last resort such determination must be made on an objective basis by the tribunal or commission'). There is no known instance of deviation by a tribunal from this 'strong presumption', as indeed international law imposes no test of stateliness for purposes of consent to jurisdiction.

not depend for its validity on communication to anyone. On the other hand, since an overt act would be required for an approval, it would become effective only when it could be clearly said that the Contracting State has given the approval, for example when a Cabinet decision has been taken, or the legislature has resolved to approve, or the Minister concerned (if he has the power) has decided to approve. There should be some externalization of the act of approval, and it would seem inadequate that the official or organ merely intended to approve.[56]

The case of *Government of the Province of East Kalimantan v. PT Kaltim Prima Coal and Others* illustrates this conferral of consent (and thus jurisdiction), where the tribunal wrote that 'the form and channel of communication do not matter, provided that the intention to designate is clearly established.'[57] The tribunal further found that

> [t]he designation requirement in Article 25(1) must be read in conjunction with ... Rule 2(1)(b) [of the Rules of Procedure for the Institution of Conciliation and Arbitration Proceedings], which provides that '[t]he request [for arbitration] shall state if one of the parties is a constituent subdivision or agency of a Contracting State, that it has been designated to the Centre by that State pursuant to Article 25(1) of the Convention.' Consequently, the designation requirement may in particular be deemed fulfilled when a document that emanates from the State is filed with the request for arbitration and shows the State's intent to name a specific entity as a constituent subdivision or agency for the purposes of Article 25(1).[58]

Thus, one may discern that, in order for a designation to be validly effected, there must be only (i) an intention to designate; and (ii) some externalisation of an overt act of approval. Tellingly, the same Rule 2 of the Rules of Procedure for the Institution of Conciliation and Arbitration Proceedings (ICSID Institution Rules) states that required information 'shall be supported by documentation' under only three of

---

[56] C. F. Amerasinghe, 'Jurisdiction *Ratione Personae* under the Convention on the Settlement of Investment Disputes between States and Nationals of Other States', 47 *British Yearbook of International Law* 1 (1976) 237.

[57] *Government of the Province of East Kalimantan v. PT Kaltim Prima Coal and Others*, ICSID Case No. ARB/07/3, Award on Jurisdiction, 28 December 2009, para. 192.

[58] Ibid. para. 193. Separately, the tribunal found that the relevant instrument 'grants the [Government of Indonesia] the power to represent the Republic of Indonesia before ICSID tribunals in cases of investment disputes with a national of another Contracting State', that '[i]n this event, the [Government of Indonesia] has the "right of substitution" which must be understood as the right to nominate or designate a third party to assume such representation', but that '[t]his is not the case here ... the [Government of Indonesia] expressly indicated that it had never authorized such representation in the present case'. Ibid. para. 183.

its subparagraphs.[59] First, documentation must indeed be furnished to demonstrate 'the date of consent [of the parties] and the instruments in which it is recorded, including, if one party is a constituent subdivision or agency of a Contracting State, similar data on the approval of such consent by that State unless it had notified the Centre that no such approval is required'.[60] Secondly, documentation must be furnished to demonstrate 'with respect to the party that is a national of a Contracting State: if the party is a juridical person which on the date of consent had the nationality of the Contracting State party to the dispute, the agreement of the parties that it should be treated as a national of another Contracting State for the purposes of the Convention'.[61] Lastly, documentation must be furnished to demonstrate, 'if the requesting party is a juridical person', that 'it has taken all necessary internal actions to authorize the request'.[62]

The third and final requirement notably falls outside the subparagraph which is dedicated 'to the party that is a national of a Contracting State' alone.[63] It must therefore be read to apply to 'juridical person[s]' in the case of both the party that is a national of a Contracting State *and* the party which is a Contracting State. As for the latter, these 'juridical person[s]' presumably include the 'constituent subdivision[s]' or 'agenc[ies]' contemplated at Article 25 of the ICSID Convention.[64] ICSID Institution Rule 2 would therefore seem to impose an equal evidentiary requirement as to sufficiency of internal actions of authorisation within a State agency[65] *and* sufficiency of the very designation of that State agency to the Centre *ab initio*.[66] This equivalence is a further marker of the deference accorded to

---

[59] Rule 2(2) of the Rules of Procedure for the Institution of Conciliation and Arbitration Proceedings (ICSID Institution Rules).

[60] Rule 2(2) of the ICSID Institution Rules, referencing Rule 2(1)(c) of the ICSID Institution Rules.

[61] Rule 2(2) of the ICSID Institution Rules, referencing Rule 2(1)(d)(iii) of the ICSID Institution Rules. This provision is included to accommodate those permissive agreements that may be reached with regard to juridical persons of the Contracting State party to a dispute, but which remain under 'foreign control'. See Art. 25(2)(b) of the ICSID Convention.

[62] Rule 2(2) of the ICSID Institution Rules, referencing Rule 2(1)(f) of the ICSID Institution Rules.

[63] Rule 2(1)(d) of the ICSID Institution Rules.

[64] See Art. 25(1), (3) of the ICSID Convention.

[65] See Z. Douglas, *The International Law of Investment Claims* (2009) 78 ('[t]he law applicable to the issue of whether a legal entity has the capacity to prosecute a claim before an investment treaty tribunal is the *lex societatis*').

[66] See C. F. Amerasinghe, 'Jurisdiction *Ratione Personae* under the Convention on the Settlement of Investment Disputes between States and Nationals of Other States', 47

the internal laws of the State for purposes of consent, and thus jurisdiction.[67]

Arbitration Rules

The State's prerogative with regard to appointment of representatives in proceedings is seen in all relevant rules. The UNCITRAL Arbitration Rules provide that '[e]ach party may be represented or assisted by persons chosen by it.'[68] The PCA Environmental Rules are nearly identical.[69]

For their part, the ICSID Rules of Procedure for Arbitration Proceedings (the ICSID Arbitration Rules) provide that '[e]ach party may be represented or assisted by agents, counsel or advocates whose names and authority shall be notified by that party to the Secretary-General.'[70] This language is evocative of the reference to State agencies within Article 25 of the ICSID

British Yearbook of International Law 1 (1976) 237. See also *Government of the Province of East Kalimantan* v. *PT Kaltim Prima Coal and Others*, ICSID Case No. ARB/07/3, Award on Jurisdiction, 28 December 2009, paras. 192–193.

[67] A similar deference is accorded to internal law in the question of nationality, as under Article 25(2) of the ICSID Convention. It has been observed that '[i]n customary international law the position generally is that the law of the State whose nationality is claimed determines whether the claimant is a national of that State'. C. F. Amerasinghe, 'Jurisdiction *Ratione Personae* under the Convention on the Settlement of Investment Disputes between States and Nationals of Other States', 47 *British Yearbook of International Law* 1 (1976) 246. It is, however, generally accepted that international law does impose some outer bound to a State's power to confer nationality. See, e.g., Art. 1 of the Hague Convention on Certain Questions Relating to the Conflict of Nationality Laws, 179 LNTS 89 (1930) ('it is for each State to determine under its own law who are its nationals' and 'this law shall be recognised by other States in so far as it is consistent with international conventions, international custom and the principles of law generally recognised with regard to nationality'). Thus, in the law of diplomatic protection, 'a State of nationality means a State whose nationality that person has acquired, in accordance with the law of that State, by birth, descent, naturalization, succession of States, or in any other manner, not inconsistent with international law.' Art. 4 of the *Draft Articles on Diplomatic Protection with Commentaries*, ILC 2006, UN Doc. A/61/10. There is no known principle in international law that would circumscribe a State's ability to confer the status of agency; even less is there any indication that such designation would be offensive in the form prescribed for facilitation of the coming three models. It is thus appropriate to fashion the matter as one of municipal law alone.

[68] Art. 5 of the UNCITRAL Arbitration Rules (as revised in 2010).

[69] Art. 4 of the PCA Environmental Rules.

[70] Rule 18(1) of the ICSID Rules of Procedure for Arbitration Proceedings (the ICSID Arbitration Rules). It is recalled that parties to ICSID proceedings may select alternative rules of procedure should they wish to do so. See Art. 44 of the ICSID Convention ('[a]ny arbitration proceeding shall be conducted in accordance with the provisions of this Section and, except as the parties otherwise agree, in accordance with the [ICSID] Arbitration Rules in effect on the date on which the parties consented to arbitration'). In practice, such alternative selections have proven rare in the ICSID setting.

Convention – which states that '[c]onsent by a constituent subdivision or agency of a Contracting State shall require the approval of that State'[71] – The 'agents' contemplated at Rule 18 are evidently not in unity with any 'agency' contemplated by Article 25(3); Rule 18 is concerned with natural and not juridical persons.[72]

It has been observed that '[t]he various titles have little practical significance and is [sic] based on the Statute of the International Court.'[73] Thus, 'States are typically represented by "agents" that manage the proceeding on behalf of their party', and '[a]gents typically are diplomatic representatives, their statements directly bind the State party'.[74] The custom of appointing

---

[71] Art. 25(3) of the ICSID Convention.

[72] See, e.g., 'ICSID Rules of Procedure for Arbitration Proceedings (Arbitration Rules)', 4 *International Tax and Business Lawyer* 2 (1986) 380, available at: http://scholarship.law .berkeley.edu/bjil/vol4/iss2/15, providing as follows:

> It is not mandatory that a party select a lawyer to act on its behalf, though self-interest should ensure that the parties will select representatives of acknowledged competence in the law. The terms 'agent', 'counsel' and 'advocate' do not imply any specific legal or other qualifications and cover attorneys, avocats, barristers, solicitors, teachers of law, and other persons with appropriate legal or administrative training and experience. Hence, no party can object to a lack of professional qualifications of the opponent's representative.

[73] R. A. Schütze (ed.), *Institutional Arbitration: Article-by-Article Commentary* (2013) 952. See also Art. 42 of the Statute of the ICJ ('1. The parties shall be represented by agents. 2. They may have the assistance of counsel or advocates before the Court'). The custom of appointing agents to represent States before international courts and tribunals is traced to the first Convention for the Pacific Settlement of International Disputes. See Art. 37 of the Convention for the Pacific Settlement of International Disputes of 1899 ('[t]he parties have the right to appoint delegates or special agents to attend the Tribunal, for the purpose of serving as intermediaries between them and the Tribunal. They are further authorized to retain, for the defence of their rights and interests before the Tribunal, counsel or advocates appointed by them for this purpose').

[74] R. A. Schütze (ed.), *Institutional Arbitration: Article-by-Article Commentary* (2013) 952. See, e.g., *CMS Gas Transmission Company* v. *Argentine Republic*, ICSID Case No. ARB/ 01/8, Decision on The Republic of Argentina's Request for a Continued Stay of Enforcement of the Award, 1 September 2006, paras. 49–50 ('[t]he Committee notes that Dr. Guglielmino, Procurador del Tesoro de la Nacion Argentina, is Agent of Argentina in the present case. In this capacity, he represents Argentina as provided for in Rule 18 of the ICSID Arbitration Rules. He has authority to commit Argentina, as decided in many comparable cases by international courts and arbitral tribunals'). See also 'ICSID Rules of Procedure for Arbitration Proceedings (Arbitration Rules)', 4 *International Tax and Business Lawyer* 2 (1986) 380, available at: http://scholarship.law .berkeley.edu/bjil/vol4/iss2/15, providing as follows:

> In disputes between States, the parties are represented before international tribunals by 'agents', usually 'assisted' by 'counsel'. The general management and control of the case is in the hands of the agent who acts as intermediary between the party and the Tribunal and is the official and

'agents' to act on behalf of States is reflected in the PCA Arbitration Rules 2012, which provide that '[i]n disputes involving only States and/or inter-governmental organizations, each party shall appoint an agent' and 'may also be assisted by persons of its choice', whereas '[i]n other disputes under these Rules, each party may be represented or assisted by persons chosen by it'.[75]

Although designated by custom as 'agents', '[a] relationship of inter-national agency does not exist between the state and its organs for international relations, such as diplomatic agents and consuls', for '[t]hese organs ... do not have an international personality distinct from the state which they represent'.[76] These writings indicate the truth that there is a unity of the State and its duly empowered repre-sentatives; such representatives are the State itself in the eyes of inter-national law.

> full representative of the government. In some standing intergovernmental tribunals open to individuals, the latter must be represented by 'counsel' and States by 'agents'. On the other hand, some international arbitral or administrative tribunals permit individuals and, in certain cases, even States or intergovernmental organizations to appear 'in person'. Accordingly, Rule 18 permits, but does not require, representation by 'agents' or 'counsel' or 'advocates'. This will probably result in States being represented by agents, though it is not unthinkable that an 'agency' of a Contracting State might appear 'in person' through one of its officers rather than through an outside 'agent' (e.g., a diplomatic or economic representative of the government).

[75] Art. 5 of the PCA Arbitration Rules 2012.

[76] A. P. Sereni, 'Agency in International Law', 34 *American Journal of International Law* 4 (1940) 638. With regard to diplomatic protection, it has been written that '[n]o interna-tional agency can be recognized where the alleged principal, agent or third party is not an international person', and '[a] state, extending diplomatic protection to its citizens or juristic persons, does not act as their international agent, since the protected persons (the alleged principals) are not recognized as members of the international community'. Ibid. The relationship of a State with its diplomatic agents or consuls may of course be conceived as a relationship of agency under that State's internal laws. However, the international law of agency is concerned not with a State's power to appoint its repre-sentatives in international intercourse, but rather with the concept of agency *inter nations*. A true instance of international agency exists where a State empowers another State to conduct its international relations, to assert rights or incur obligations on its behalf under international law. This principle is reflected within the ICSID Convention itself. See, e.g., Art. 70 ('[t]his Convention shall apply to all territories for whose interna-tional relations a Contracting State is responsible'). For an account of international agency, see C. Giglio and R. Caulk, 'Article 17 of the Treaty of Uccialli', 6 *The Journal of African History* 2 (1965). The legal question that arose across diverging Italian and Amharic texts of the relevant article pertained to the very existence (or not) of an international agency, whereby the Kingdom of Italy claimed the right to conduct the international relations of the Empire of Ethiopia. The dispute ultimately led to war and Italy's defeat at the Battle of Adwa in 1896.

Lastly, perhaps owing to the identity confusion of the mixed-claims model, it has been observed of Rule 18 that

> [i]t is not intended – as in disputes between States – to draw a distinction between the authority of an 'agent' on the one hand and that of a 'counsel' or 'advocate' on the other. The party concerned must render it clear by the terms of its designation whether it is 'represented' or solely 'assisted' by an agent, counsel or advocate and what the scope of the authority of each such person is.[77]

Thus, what is ultimately controlling is not the usage (or neglect) of any particular term but rather the operative language that effectuates the appointment or designation, the instrument that confers a grant of power and delineates its scope. This is so whether a State confers consent to arbitral jurisdiction by designating a 'constituent subdivision' or 'agency'; appoints its chosen 'agents', 'counsel', or 'advocates' to appear on its behalf before an international tribunal; or both.

The State's role must be conceived in a manner such that its pursuit of a claim falls within the jurisdictional bounds to arbitrate an investment dispute. Dependence upon the intentions of the host State is inevitable where arbitral proceedings are to be brought in this fashion for, as in diplomatic protection, the State's participation ultimately remains in its own discretion. All lies within the power of the State to decide in accordance with its own constitutional laws, whether by legislation, executive act, or both.[78] There is

---

[77] 'ICSID Rules of Procedure for Arbitration Proceedings (Arbitration Rules)', 4 *International Tax and Business Lawyer* 2 (1986) 380, available at: http://scholarship.law .berkeley.edu/bjil/vol4/iss2/15.

[78] Guidance may be drawn from the law of diplomatic protection, wherein '[a] State entitled to exercise diplomatic protection ... should ... [g]ive due consideration to the possibility of [its exercise], especially when a significant injury has occurred.' Art. 19(a) of the *Draft Articles on Diplomatic Protection with Commentaries*, ILC 2006, UN Doc. A/61/10. Francisco Orrego Vicuña has written of a nineteenth-century Chilean law under which the Ministry of Foreign Affairs was obliged to send any request for protection to the Advocate General of the Supreme Court, whose legal opinion would then be binding upon the Government. F. O. Vicuña, The Changing Law of Nationality of Claims, Final Report Submitted to the International Law Association Committee on Diplomatic Protection of Persons and Property. Unpublished Manuscript (2000) 8. See also 'Chile', in E. Lauterpacht and J. G. Collier (eds.), *Individual Rights and the State in Foreign Affairs: An International Compendium* (1977) 138–141. Further, '[t]he Constitutions of many States recognize the right of the individual to receive diplomatic protection for injuries suffered abroad, which must carry with it the corresponding duty of the State to exercise protection.' Commentary to Art. 19 of the *Draft Articles on Diplomatic Protection with Commentaries*, ILC 2006, UN Doc. A/61/10, citing First Report of the Special Rapporteur on Diplomatic Protection, UN Doc. A/CN.4/506, 30. For example, by constitutional tradition in Germany, diplomatic protection is granted where it 'does not run counter to truly overriding interests of the Federal Republic'. W. K. Geck, 'Diplomatic

no obstacle to State prosecution of claims as opposable to a foreign investor, as under the forthcoming three models, designed to achieve this end.

The Espousal Model

The purpose of the Espousal Model is to grant standing to the host State as party to the dispute in those cases wherein the rights sought to be enforced vis-à-vis the investor arise at their origin in host State nationals. While not necessary for purposes of other institutions or rules, conformity to the ICSID Convention is achieved only by a return to 'governmental espousal of private claims'.[79] Further, viewing not only the law but also the history of diplomatic protection, given host State nationals may find the political heft of their State to accrue advantages, as well as greater resources or expertise. Under the Espousal Model, the host State national assigns his claim to the host State, in order that the State may then prosecute the claim as opposable to the foreign investor; see Figure 2.2.

The Host State as Espouser

The Espousal Model thus entails the participation of a State organ or entity. Its essential characteristic is that it remains an emanation of the State. Its essential functions may include the following:

- to conduct an evaluation of actual or anticipated conflicts between host State nationals and foreign investors;
- to render a *prima facie* assessment of any contemplated claim in view of the evidence and applicable law;

Protection', in R. Bernhardt (ed.), *Encyclopedia of Public International Law*, vol. I (1992) 1052. As a last resort, the courts may be seized. See, e.g., *Kaunda and Others* v. *President of the Republic of South Africa, South African Law Reports*, vol. XLIV, 4, 235 (CC) (2005) 32, para. 69 ('[t]here may be a duty on government, consistent with its obligations under international law, to take action to protect one of its citizens against a gross abuse of international human rights norms. A request to government for assistance in such circumstances where the evidence is clear would be difficult, and in extreme cases possibly impossible to refuse. It is unlikely that such a request would ever be refused by government, but if it were, the decision would be justiciable and a court would order the government to take appropriate action').

[79] F. Francioni, 'Access to Justice, Denial of Justice and International Investment Law', 20 *European Journal of International Law* 3 (2009). Evidently without irony, it is this paternalistic model whose inadequacies inspired the very institution of investor-State arbitration, which has itself been instrumental in furthering the discourse upon personality of the individual at international law.

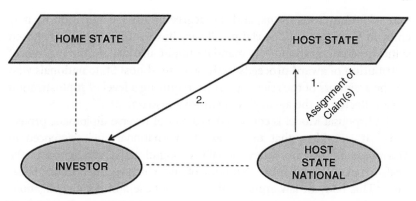

Figure 2.2 Espousal Model

- to accept assignment by host State nationals of favourably evaluated claims; and
- to advance these claims to arbitration, as opposable to the foreign investor.

The host State may establish an instrumentality mandated to perform these functions or may grant equivalent powers to one already existing. The body in question may most seamlessly take the form of a State agency.[80] The agency's statutory character and all aspects of its governance and operation, including the form and extent of any participation in arbitral proceedings by the assignor host State national, are matters to be decided in and governed under the host State's internal laws. Thus, participation by and representation of an injured host State national

---

[80] In one example of its possible functioning, a State may elect, upon the recommendation of an expert body or international organisation, to establish a specialised environmental agency dedicated to conflicts and claims arising out of investment activity of a nature that may produce environmental harm or degradation. This possibility is favourably mentioned in, for example, ChapterIII(A) of the United Nations Guiding Principles on Business and Human Rights, UN Doc. A/HRC/17/31. The implicated interests may hold great international significance, as in the equally notable case of indigenous rights. For an early view propounding international courts and tribunals as proper fora for the adjudication of indigenous rights, see M. Reisman, 'Protecting Indigenous Rights in International Adjudication', *Yale Law School Faculty Scholarship Series* (1995). The United Nations Declaration on the Rights of Indigenous Peoples, UNGA Res. 61/295 (Annex), 13 December 2007, which enjoys broad international acceptance, enumerates a series of rights that indigenous peoples enjoy, both collectively and individually. A host State may create a newly specialised agency tailored to represent indigenous peoples and to pursue their claims in international arbitration, or elect to empower an existing agency for this purpose.

may take numerous forms, and the degree of any participation he may enjoy in the pursuit of the claim will vary in view of the agency's chosen statutory configuration.[81] Its mandate might also dictate the manner of distribution of award proceeds to those injured host State nationals who are the assignors of the relevant claims, requiring a level of sophistication to be reflected in the agency's constitutive instruments.[82]

The Espousal Model is conceived as a sort of reverse diplomatic protection.[83] It is evident that the 'rules of international law' referenced in *Mavrommatis*[84] or the 'internationally wrongful act[s]' referenced in the Draft Articles[85] contemplate that body of law which regiments State behaviour. This body of law arguably does not impose affirmative obligations upon private persons such as foreign investors beyond a general prohibition as per *jus cogens* peremptory norms.[86] International law may, however, *grant rights* that flow *in favour* of private persons, causing diplomatic protection to be no longer as doctrinally constrained as it once was.[87] In the oft-observed

---

[81] By reference to the analogy of diplomatic protection, it is recommended practice that the host State should '[t]ake into account, wherever feasible, the views of injured persons with regard to resort to diplomatic protection and the reparation to be sought'. Art. 19(b) of the *Draft Articles on Diplomatic Protection with Commentaries*, ILC 2006, UN Doc. A/61/10. The State or its agency may empower an agent to act as representative of the State, in the interest of its nationals. Alternatively, a claim may be prosecuted in a form of joint representation, consisting of an agent of the State assisted by host State nationals (or their own representatives).

[82] By reference once more to the analogy of diplomatic protection, such purpose is evocative of the aspiration that the State should '[t]ransfer to the injured person any compensation obtained for the injury ... subject to any reasonable deductions'. Ibid. Art. 19(c). States might also elect to emulate language featuring within, for example, the NAFTA, requiring that an award 'shall provide that it is made without prejudice to any right that any person may have in the relief under applicable domestic law'. Art. 1135(2)(c) of the NAFTA. The instrument that governs the entity's duty of distribution, being a matter of municipal law, falls within the ambit of such 'applicable domestic law'.

[83] See, e.g., F. Francioni, 'Access to Justice, Denial of Justice and International Investment Law', 20 *European Journal of International Law* 3 (2009) 738 (advocating an opening of arbitration 'to private claims that the host state would endorse in a sort of reverse model of diplomatic protection: the territorial state would espouse the claim of its own citizens against the investor rather than vice versa').

[84] See note 26 *supra*.   [85] See note 28 *supra*.

[86] Examples are the prohibition of slavery, piracy, terrorism, and genocide, the prohibition to prepare or wage an aggressive war, or the use of force contrary to Article 2(4) of the United Nations Charter.

[87] It has been observed that

> [t]he essence of the evolution points towards the fact that in both the scenario of diplomatic protection and in that of direct standing of the individual, it is increasingly the right of the individual that is asserted in its own merits and no longer that of the state of nationality. The state may still act as a conduit, an

case of *Ahmadou Sadio Diallo*, the International Court of Justice observed that the role of diplomatic protection has 'somewhat faded, as in practice recourse is only made to it in rare cases where treaty regimes do not exist or have proved inoperative'.[88] In the *Diallo* case, although Mr. Diallo seems to have held individual rights vis-à-vis the respondent Democratic Republic of Congo, he held no avenue of recourse, and thus sought the intervention of his State of nationality, the Republic of Guinea, in order to prosecute his claims before the Court.[89] A State thus sought to enforce treaty rights held by its national, and successfully did so.[90]

> agent, or on behalf of the individual, but no longer substituting for his rights. This is not to say that the state may not consider that a wrong done to one of its nationals affects its own interest, but the latter will be the consequence of the rights of the individual and not of the state's own right. While the transition from a legal fiction to a different reality takes place, the interesting thought that a claim may actually have a 'dual nature' and represent the interest of both the individual and the state has been discussed.

International Law Association, *Final Report of the Committee on Diplomatic Protection of Persons and Property* (2006).

[88] See *Ahmadou Sadio Diallo* (Republic of Guinea v. Democratic Republic of the Congo), Judgment on Preliminary Objections, 24 May 2007, 2007 ICJ Reports 582, para. 88. Such seems an apt description in respect of international investment law and, perhaps, human rights law, where conventions have given rise to regional and international courts and tribunals before which the individual might enjoy a right of action.

[89] Ibid. para. 5 ('[t]he two contending States are both parties to the aforementioned treaties: Guinea is party to the Covenant on Civil and Political Rights since 24 January 1978, and to the African Charter since 16 February 1982, and the DRC is party to the Covenant since 1 November 1976, and to the African Charter since 20 July 1987. They are both, likewise, parties to the 1963 Vienna Convention: Guinea is party to it since 30 June 1988, and the DRC since 15 July 1976. The present case is, thus, significantly, an *inter-State contentious case before the International Court of Justice*, pertaining entirely to *the rights of the individual concerned* (Mr. A. S. Diallo), and the legal consequences of their alleged violation, under a UN human rights treaty, a regional human rights treaty, and a UN codification Convention. This is a significant feature of the present case, unique in the history of the ICJ') (emphasis added).

[90] On rights as may be held by the individual at international law, see, e.g., R. Portmann, *Legal Personality in International Law* (2010) 277–278 ('[a]s a matter of general international law, international treaties have direct effect upon individuals whenever the provision in question so indicates'). See also Commentary to Art. 33(2), para. 3 of the Articles on Responsibility of States for Internationally Wrongful Acts, with Commentaries, *Yearbook of the International Law Commission*, vol. II(2) (2001) ('a State's responsibility for the breach of an obligation under a treaty concerning the protection of human rights may exist towards all the other parties to the treaty, but the individuals concerned should be regarded as the ultimate beneficiaries and in that sense as *the holders of the relevant rights*') (emphasis added). Language has been adopted within the recent American Declaration on the Rights of Indigenous Peoples that might appear to ensure not only substantive rights but also legal personality, albeit perhaps only before municipal courts. See Art. IX of the American Declaration on the Rights of Indigenous Peoples, AG/

The unsettled state of the law of diplomatic protection is inconsequential. Under the Espousal Model, the host State national holds given rights not vis-à-vis a State, but rather vis-à-vis a private party, the foreign investor, who accepts to be so bound.[91] The Espousal Model is achieved not by entering the mould of diplomatic protection, but rather by resorting to the *lex specialis* of international investment law, including, where desired, the ICSID Convention.

The ICSID Convention requires that a 'Contracting State' be the 'part[y] to [a legal] dispute' vis-à-vis a 'national of another Contracting State'.[92] Existing authority does not allow one to conclude that a State which brings a claim against a foreign investor on behalf of its national – but is neither the right-holder nor the beneficial owner of the claim – may properly be considered such 'part[y] to the dispute'. All objective requirements of the Convention must be satisfied for ICSID jurisdiction to be established over such mode of prosecution.[93]

It is thus proposed that the host State national *assign his claim to the host State itself*, in the form of its designated agency, in order to achieve the host State's place as 'part[y] to the dispute'.[94] Further, it is proposed that in assigning his claim to the host State, the host State national *retain the financial interest* in award proceeds that may be procured. In this way,

---

RES.2888 (XLVI-O/16) 167, available at: http://cdn7.iitc.org/wp-content/uploads/AG07150E06_web.pdf ('[t]he states shall recognize fully the juridical personality of the indigenous peoples, respecting indigenous forms of organization and promoting the full exercise of the rights recognized in this Declaration').

[91] See Chapter 3.   [92] Art. 25(1) of the ICSID Convention.

[93] See, e.g., *Report of the Executive Directors of the International Bank for Reconstruction and Development on the Convention on the Settlement of Investment Disputes between States and Nationals of Other States*, para. 25 ('In keeping with the purpose of the Convention, the jurisdiction of the Centre is . . . limited by reference to the nature of the dispute and the parties thereto').

[94] The validity and effectiveness of such assignment are matters of municipal law, and thus must be provided for within the internal law of the host State. A special assignment of claims to the host State before the time that an injury is incurred becomes unnecessary where the investor consents to the assignment, or where the investor prospectively consents to jurisdiction over claims as may be assigned in future. See note 121 *infra*. Alternatively, it may be possible for the host State national to prospectively assign to the State, at or prior to the time an investment is effected, any and all claims that may in future arise vis-à-vis the foreign investor in respect of the investment. Furthermore, the requisite conveyance of claims to the host State may be prospectively effected by operation of host State law, with the host State then perhaps affording to its nationals an option of direct control over prosecution via the Hybrid Model. See The Hybrid Model, *infra*. Such mode of conveyance is naturally not immune from constitutional challenge in the host State.

legal title to the claim is detached from economic entitlement in its remedy.

Assignment or subrogation of claims as between a national and his State was the subject of extensive debate in the drafting of the ICSID Convention. At that time, certain delegations of capital-exporting nations proposed a provision that would have allowed, by exception, for an investor's home State to prosecute claims of the investor where the investor received indemnification from a State-sponsored scheme of investment insurance or guarantee.[95] However, following vigorous opposition from the representatives of 'Spain, the countries of Latin America, and certain African countries', the proposal was abandoned.[96] Thus, the investor's home State may not, even in the role of subrogee, act before the Centre in a claim opposable to the host State, as such is offensive to the exclusion of inter-State disputes.[97]

However, Professor Schreuer has observed that '[t]he denial of standing to the investor's home State and its agencies does not mean that ICSID is worthless in cases where the investor receives compensation under a national investment insurance scheme. It merely means that the

---

[95] See ICSID, *The History of the ICSID Convention* (1970), vol. II(1), Meeting of the Committee of the Whole, 28 May 1963 (not an approved record), 94; Fifth Session, 18 December 1963, 275; Sixth Session, 6 February 1964 348; Third Session, 18 February 1964, 397–399, 403–404, 406; Third Session, 29 April 1964, 503; Fourth Session, 29 April 1964, 503; Fourth Session, 30 April 1964, 528; Fifth Session, 1 May 1964, 543; and vol. II(2), Summary Proceedings of the Legal Committee Meeting, 2 December 1964, 759–762; Summary Proceedings of the Legal Committee Meeting, 4 December 1964, 794–795; Report of the Chairman of the Legal Committee on Settlement of Investment Disputes, 937; Meeting of the Committee, 16 February 1965 (not an approved record), 974–981; Meeting of the Committee, 11 March 1965 (not an approved record), 1017–1018; Meeting of the Committee, 17 March 1965 (not an approved record), 1025. Professor Broches has remarked on the broaching during the Convention's drafting of the question whether 'the exclusion of inter-State conflicts' from the 'competence of the Centre' extends to 'States (or international organisations) where they succeed to the rights of an investor after having indemnified him in performance of a contract of guarantee or insurance'. A. Broches, 'La Convention et L'Assurance-Investissement: Le Problème dit de la Subrogation', in *Investissements Etrangers et Arbitrage entre Etats et Personnes Privées* (1969) 161 (authors' own translation from the French).

[96] A. Broches, 'La Convention et L'Assurance-Investissement: Le Problème dit de la Subrogation', in *Investissements Etrangers et Arbitrage entre Etats et Personnes Privées* (1969) 166 (authors' own translation from the French).

[97] Professor Broches has opined that '[t]he history of the Convention removes any doubt in this regard. It indicates that the omission of the said subrogation clause was motivated by the desire to foreclose a sovereign State from acting before the Centre in an action introduced as against another State, whatever might be the capacity in which the first State appears. It seems thus to be an absolute prohibition.' Ibid. 166–167 (authors' own translation from the French).

claimant in ICSID proceedings would have to be the investor despite the insurance.'[98] Professor Aron Broches proposed precisely such a mechanism in remarks given in Paris in 1969, a mere three years following the Convention's entering into force. He proposed that, in order to achieve a sort of effective subrogation, an indemnified investor assign the financial interest in any award proceeds to his home State, while maintaining a claim before the Centre, with the consent of the host State.[99]

Professor Schreuer has further observed that such an arrangement

> may run into the problem that many legal systems will not allow the pursuit of claims by parties who are not the real parties in interest. Much would then depend on whether the question of . . . representation of the claim before ICSID is classified as a substantive question, to which the normal choice of law rules under [Article] 42 would apply, or whether it is classified as a jurisdictional question, to which the Convention and international law in general would apply.[100]

[98] C. Schreuer, L. Malintoppi, A. Reinisch, and A. Sinclair, *The ICSID Convention: A Commentary*, 2nd edn. (2009) 189–190.

[99] Professor Broches first suggested that 'the guarantor reserve a right of conditional payment to the insured, the condition being that the insured exhaust his remedies against the host State before the Centre', and that a payment 'would only become definitive where these remedies have not led to full compensation of the investor'. A. Broches, 'La Convention et L'Assurance-Investissement: Le Problème dit de la Subrogation', in *Investissements Etrangers et Arbitrage entre Etats et Personnes Privées* (1969) 164 (authors' own translation from the French). However, Broches then wrote that he 'would prefer a franker and more direct solution: the host State and the investor could accept, with the agreement of the guarantor, that the fact of indemnification by a third party would not affect the right of the investor to bring an action against the host State [before the Centre]'. Ibid. 168. His mechanism is embedded in present investment instruments. See, e.g., Art. 9 of the France Model BIT (2006) ('3. [s]i l'une des Parties contractantes, en vertu d'une garantie donnée pour un investissement réalisé sur le territoire ou dans la zone maritime de l'autre Partie, effectue des versements a l'un de ses nationaux ou a l'une de ses sociétés, elle est, de ce fait, subrogée dans les droits et actions de ce national ou de cette société. 4. Lesdits versements n'affectent pas les droits du bénéficiaire de la garantie à recourir au C.I.R.D.I. ou à poursuivre les actions introduites devant lui jusqu'à l'aboutissement de la procédure'). See also ICSID Model Clauses, Clause 8 ('Preservation of Rights of Investor after Compensation') ('[i]t is hereby agreed that the right of the Investor to refer a dispute to the Centre pursuant to this agreement shall not be affected by the fact that the Investor has received full or partial compensation from any third party with respect to any loss or injury that is the subject of the dispute [; provided that the Host State may require evidence that such third party agrees to the exercise of that right by the Investor').

[100] C. Schreuer, L. Malintoppi, A. Reinisch, and A. Sinclair, *The ICSID Convention: A Commentary*, 2nd edn. (2009) 188. Professor Broches voiced similar sentiment in his remarks of 1969, prior to proposing the solution of an express agreement by the host State that the fact of compensation by a third party would not affect the investor's right to bring an action before the Centre. See A. Broches, 'La Convention et L'Assurance-Investissement: Le Problème dit de la Subrogation', in *Investissements Etrangers et Arbitrage entre Etats et Personnes Privées* (1969) 168 (authors' own translation from the French) ('[o]ne risks that the

Within his commentary to the mentioned Article 42, Professor Schreuer has intimated the answer to this question. He has written that 'the problem of *jus standi* ... to submit claims to ICSID ... is not governed by [Article] 42. Rather, it is determined according to the applicable international investment agreements and [Article] 25' of the Convention.[101]

Within the context of debate over investment insurance schemes within the home State, Professor Broches further sought to articulate a jurisdictional test, writing that '[w]here the guarantor or insurer is juridically independent and distinct from the [home] State, and in particular if it is organized under the juridical form of a private institution, an action brought by such a guarantor or insurer as against the host State is in my view within the competence of the Centre.'[102] Depending upon the manner in which an insurance scheme is conceived and performed, the insurer may assume a position of beneficial ownership in the investor's claim, or become a sort of successor-in-interest to the remedy that attaches.

---

host State will defend against an action brought by the investor in advancing the argument, "no interest, no action". I will not hazard to pre-judge how this argument would be received by an arbitral tribunal, but I foresee problems of applicable law and qualification. The principle "no interest, no action" or, in the terminology of Anglo-Saxon law, the principle according to which the action must be brought by the "real party in interest", is it a principle of merits or of procedure? If it is a principle of procedure, does the rule of Article 42 [of the ICSID Convention], according to which, except in the case of contrary agreement, the law of the host State is applicable, does this law extend to the rules of procedure? It suffices to pose these questions in order to conclude that it is better to avoid them if possible').

[101] C. Schreuer, L. Malintoppi, A. Reinisch, and A. Sinclair, *The ICSID Convention: A Commentary*, 2nd edn. (2009) 553. Thus, in one case, a tribunal 'did not consider [a] legal distinction of [host State] law "determinant" because it found that "the applicable jurisdictional provisions are only those of the Convention and the [applicable bilateral investment treaty], not those which might arise from national legislation"'. Ibid. citing *CMS Gas Transmission Company v. The Republic of Argentina*, ICSID Case No. ARB/01/08, Decision on Jurisdiction, 17 July 2003, para. 42. This finding was explicitly endorsed by a subsequently formed ad hoc annulment committee. See *CMS Gas Transmission Company v. The Republic of Argentina*, ICSID Case No. ARB/01/8, Decision on Annulment, 25 September 2007, para. 68. See also, e.g., *Pan American Energy LLC and BP Argentina Exploration Company v. The Republic of Argentina*, ICSID Case No. ARB/03/13, Decision on Preliminary Objections, 27 July 2006, para. 217 ('[t]he instant case is not situated at the level of general international law but at that of treaty law – the [applicable bilateral investment treaty] and the ICSID Convention').

[102] A. Broches, 'La Convention et L'Assurance-Investissement: Le Problème dit de la Subrogation', in *Investissements Etrangers et Arbitrage entre Etats et Personnes Privées* (1969) 167 (authors' own translation from the French).

Two ICSID Cases

Some thirty years later, in a prominent case, the respondent State indeed submitted at the preliminary phase that the claim of a majority State-owned bank was excluded from the jurisdiction of the Centre. The respondent further submitted that the claimant's transfer of certain economic risks to its Ministry of Finance following the institution of proceedings had wholly rendered the matter into an inter-State dispute.

In rejecting this submission, the tribunal did not seek to evaluate whether the claimant entity was 'juridically independent and distinct from the [home] State'.[103] Further, the tribunal wrote that 'the question whether a company qualifies as a "national of another Contracting State" within the meaning of Article 25(1) does not depend upon whether or not the company is partially or wholly owned by the government.'[104] The tribunal found that

> [i]nstead, the accepted test for making this determination has been for-mulated as follows: ' . . . for purposes of the Convention a mixed economy company or government-owned corporation should not be disqualified as a "national of another Contracting State" unless it is "acting as an agent for the government or is discharging an essentially governmental function."'[105]

The tribunal then applied this test as follows:

> [I]n determining whether [the claimant], in discharging [its] functions, exercised governmental functions, the focus must be on the *nature of these activities* and not their purpose. While it cannot be doubted that in performing the above-mentioned activities, [the claimant] was promoting the governmental policies or purposes of the state, *the activities themselves* were essentially commercial rather than governmental in nature.[106]

Thus, where the claimant entity was 'juridically independent and distinct from the [home] State' but was majority State-owned, the tribunal chose to neglect both these facts and engaged instead in an inquiry into the nature or character of the entity's activities. The tribunal found these activities to be essentially commercial rather than governmental, found the entity therefore to be a 'national of a Contracting State', and thus found itself and the Centre to be competent. The authority cited by the tribunal in support of this 'accepted test' is none other than Professor

---

[103] Ibid.
[104] *Československa obchodní banka, a.s.* v. *Slovak Republic*, ICSID Case No. ARB/97/4, Decision of the Tribunal on Objections to Jurisdiction, 24 May 1999, para. 17.
[105] Ibid. (further citation omitted).   [106] Ibid. para. 20 (emphasis added).

Broches himself, the test being articulated a few short years after his early remarks in Paris.[107]

Further, with regard to the claimant's subsequent transfer of attendant economic risks, the tribunal found it to be 'generally recognized that the determination whether a party has standing in an international judicial forum for purposes of jurisdiction to institute proceedings is made by reference to the date on which such proceedings are deemed to have been instituted'.[108] Moreover, as Professor Schreuer observed, the tribunal found that 'even if it were to accept the contention that the [claimant's home State] had become the real party in interest it would not follow that there was no jurisdiction.'[109] The tribunal wrote that

> [t]his conclusion is compelled by the consideration that absence of beneficial ownership by a claimant in a claim or the transfer of the economic risk in the outcome of a dispute should not and has not been deemed to affect the standing of a claimant in an ICSID proceeding, regardless whether or not the beneficial owner is a State Party or a private party.[110]

For purposes of ICSID jurisdiction, the controlling terms are found at Article 25 of the Convention, whereby the 'parties to the dispute' must be a 'Contracting State' and a 'national of another contracting State'.[111] In the borderland that exists between a State and its national, one must determine whether a putative party, holding legal title to a claim, is one or the other.

---

[107] Ibid. para. 17, quoting A. Broches, 'The Convention on the Settlement of Investment Disputes between States and Nationals of Other States', 135 *Hague Recueil des Cours* 331 (1972) 354–355.

[108] Ibid. para. 31. A similar result, reflective of this principle, has been reached in recent cases involving third party funders, wherein a financing agreement that grants an interest in award proceeds is effected after the time of institution of proceedings. See, e.g., *Teinver S.A., Transportes de Cercanías S.A. and Autobuses Urbanos del Sur S.A. v. The Republic of Argentina*, ICSID Case No. ARB/09/1, Decision on Jurisdiction, 21 December 2012, paras. 255–259. See also Z. Douglas, *The International Law of Investment Claims* (2009) 466–467.

[109] C. Schreuer, L. Malintoppi, A. Reinisch, and A. Sinclair, *The ICSID Convention: A Commentary*, 2nd edn. (2009) 189–190.

[110] *Československa obchodní banka, a.s. v. Slovak Republic*, ICSID Case No. ARB/97/4, Decision of the Tribunal on Objections to Jurisdiction, 24 May 1999, para. 32. In beneficial ownership, specific property rights ('use and title') in equity belong to one person, even though legal title of the property belongs to another. *Black's Law Dictionary*, 2nd Pocket edn. (2001) 508. Applied by analogy to the Espousal Model, the property referred to is the claim itself, in which the host State national retains 'use and title' in equity, while legal title is assigned to his State.

[111] Art. 25 of the ICSID Convention. In a given case, the tribunal's jurisdiction may be narrowed (but not expanded) by the terms of, for example, an applicable investment treaty.

Where both relevant States are party to the Convention, upon sufficient assignment of a claim to the host State, the host State (a 'Contracting State') is party to the dispute vis-à-vis the foreign investor (a 'national of another Contracting State') under any test. A State agency is not 'juridically independent and distinct from the [home] State', nor is it 'organized under the juridical form of a private institution'.[112] As such, there is no question of ownership. The agency is not owned by, but is rather a direct emanation of, the State. Second, a State agency is, by its very nature and constitution, 'acting as an agent for the government', and is 'discharging an essentially governmental function' where it acts to enable for its nationals access to an international remedy, an end to which States may legitimately aspire.[113]

Thus, in Professor Broches' model for effective subrogation, the foreign investor conveys a financial interest in his remedy to his State, but retains legal title to his claim. He does so in order to preserve ICSID jurisdiction. In the Espousal Model, the host State national retains the financial interest in his remedy, but conveys legal title over his claim to his State. He does so in order to attain ICSID jurisdiction. In both cases, the relevant 'part[y] to the dispute' holds legal title to the claim, but not the accompanying economic entitlement in its remedy.

A recent decision suggests a divergence of authority on the implications of beneficial ownership for jurisdiction and *locus standi*. In partially annulling the final award in the case of *Occidental Petroleum Corporation and Occidental Exploration and Production Company* v. *Republic of Ecuador*, an ad hoc committee has found that '[i]n cases where legal title is split between a nominee and a beneficial owner international law is uncontroversial . . . the dominant position in international law grants standing and relief to the owner of the beneficial interest – not to the nominee.'[114]

The committee then reproduced the following quotation in full:

---

[112]   A. Broches, 'La Convention et L'Assurance-Investissement: Le Problème dit de la Subrogation', in *Investissements Etrangers et Arbitrage entre Etats et Personnes Privées* (1969) 167 (authors' own translation from the French).

[113]   *Československa obchodní banka, a.s.* v. *Slovak Republic*, ICSID Case No. ARB/97/4, Decision of the Tribunal on Objections to Jurisdiction, 24 May 1999, para. 17, quoting A. Broches, 'The Convention on the Settlement of Investment Disputes between States and Nationals of Other States', 135 *Hague Recueil des Cours* 331 (1972) 354–355. This proposition holds true irrespective of whether a tribunal inquires into the nature or purpose of the agency's activities, and cannot be questioned in the light of both the law and history of diplomatic protection, from which investment arbitration is born.

[114]   *Occidental Petroleum Corporation and Occidental Exploration and Production Company* v. *Republic of Ecuador*, ICSID Case No. ARB/06/11, Decision on Annulment of the Award, 2 November 2015, para. 259.

International law authorities have agreed that the real and equitable owner of an international claim is the proper party before an international adjudication, and not the nominal or record owner. This principle was espoused as early as 1876, and was a consistent element in early claims practice. Moreover, claims tribunals following the First World War explicitly enquired into the beneficial ownership of property at issue before them. The fact that the nominal owner did not have a real interest in the subject property, or that the beneficial owner was not of a proper nationality, was occasionally the decisive ground for dismissing a claim. Claims settlement commissions after the Second World War likewise continued this practice, and it has been observed recently in the jurisprudence of the Iran-United States Claims Tribunal. The notion that the beneficial (and not the nominal) owner of property is the real party-in-interest before an international court may be justly considered a general principle of international law.[115]

The committee then found that

[t]he position as regards beneficial ownership is a reflection of a more general principle of international investment law: claimants are only permitted to submit their own claims, held for their own benefit, not those held (be it as nominees, agents or otherwise) on behalf of third parties not protected by the relevant treaty.[116]

---

[115] Ibid. para. 260, citing D. J. Bederman, 'Beneficial Ownership of International Claims', 38 *International and Comparative Law Quarterly* 4 (1989) 936 (internal citations omitted). Indeed, this conclusion is drawn by other commentators. See, e.g., F. O. Vicuña, 'Changing Approaches to the Nationality of Claims in the Context of Diplomatic Protection and International Dispute Settlement', 15 *ICSID Review* 2 (2000) 352 ('[i]n claims to property beneficially owned by one person, the nominal title to which is vested in another person of different nationality, it was usually the nationality of the former that prevailed for the purposes of the claims'); M. M. Whiteman, *Digest of International Law*, Vol. VIII (1967) 1261 ('[w]here the beneficial owner of property, with respect to which claim was made before ... the Commission ... was a national of the United States, and where the legal owner or nominee was a non-national of the United States, the Commission allowed claims, if otherwise eligible. But where the legal owner or trustee was a national of the United States, and beneficiary or *cestui que trust* was a non-national, in claims before that Commission, the claims were denied'); R. B. Lillich and D. B. Magraw, *The Iran-United States Claims Tribunal: Its Contribution to the Law of State Responsibility* (1998) 105 ('[t]he Tribunal's precedents have made clear that beneficial owners of property are to be preferred as legitimate claimants over nominal owners').

[116] Ibid. para. 262. This finding lies in contrast to recent decisions of other tribunals. See, e.g., *Churchill Mining Plc and Planet Mining Pty Ltd v. Republic of Indonesia*, ICSID Case No. ARB/12/14, Decision on Jurisdiction, 24 February 2014, paras. 259–266; *Churchill Mining Plc and Planet Mining Pty Ltd v. Republic of Indonesia*, ICSID Case No. ARB/12/40, Decision on Jurisdiction, 24 February 2014, paras. 239–246; *Veteran Petroleum Limited v. Russian Federation*, PCA Case No. 2005-05, Interim Award on Jurisdiction and Admissibility, 30 November 2009, paras. 433–492. See also *KT Asia Investment Group BV v. Republic of Kazakhstan*, ICSID Case No. ARB/09/8, Award, 17 October 2013, paras. 140–144.

Where accepted, this principle might seem to bar a host State from bringing a claim over which it holds legal title, but where its national retains a
financial interest in the remedy. Such a defect may find cure in a textual
tool, adapted from an existing model, in order to offer foundation for the
Espousal Model within the *lex specialis* of international investment law.[117]

Further, any difficulty is overcome where the host State takes both legal
title and financial interest, and thus becomes a full successor to a claim of
its national. Such might be achieved in a model whereby the host State,
acting via the vehicle of a State insurer or other State agency, takes full
title following a disbursement event effecting payment in satisfaction of a
claim of its national, and then proceeds to prosecute the claim as opposable to the foreign investor, before the Centre if it so wishes.

Conclusion

While investment arbitration is, to repeat the metaphor, a child of diplomatic protection, the investment treaty régime imposes no inherent limitation upon either (i) the nature of the substantive rights and obligations
that may fall within its jurisdiction; or (ii) the direction in which those
rights and obligations may flow. Where a foreign investor becomes bound
by obligations[118] owing to a host State national,[119] where such host State
national sufficiently assigns a corresponding claim to the host State,[120] and

---

[117] On the power of the parties to effect such an alteration, see, e.g., *Pan American Energy
LLC and BP Argentina Exploration Company* v. *The Republic of Argentina*, ICSID Case
No. ARB/03/13, Decision on Preliminary Objections, 27 July 2006, para. 217 ('[t]he
instant case is not situated at the level of general international law but at that of treaty
law – the [applicable bilateral investment treaty] and the ICSID Convention – and the
Claimants have established that the applicable Treaty deviates from *Barcelona Traction*,
allowing, *inter alia*, claims based on direct or indirect shareholdings of nationals of one
Contracting State in companies of another Contracting State'). In similar fashion, the
parties might agree to permit claims as may be assigned to the host State, even where a
host State national remains the beneficial owner, for example by use of the following
language, adapted from Art. 28(7) of the US Model BIT (2012):

> A respondent may not assert as a defense, counterclaim, right of set-off, or
> for any other reason that the claimant [has distributed] [or] [will distribute]
> [or] [may distribute] an amount up to or equalling that of any award to any
> third party or parties.

[118] See Chapter 3.   [119] See Chapter 5.
[120] Whatever the time and form of the investor's consent to arbitration, it may be wise to
secure his express consent to an assignment of claims, in order to remove any possible
'abuse of process' or 'abuse of rights' defence at the preliminary stage. By analogy from
the contemporary position of the investor, tribunals disfavour the transfer of, for
example, an ownership share in an investment for the purpose of gaining access to

where the host State then initiates arbitration as opposable to the investor, there is a dispute between a State and a national of another State.

The *Qui Tam* Model

Like the Espousal Model, the *Qui Tam* Model is conceived to allow the host State national to participate in the prosecution of claims, in the presence of the host State as party to the dispute.

In contrast to the Espousal Model, and as in the Direct Claims (III) Model, the *Qui Tam* Model is intended to serve in those instances wherein the rights allegedly infringed by injurious conduct of the foreign investor are held by the host State itself. A useful example is found again in the realm of environmental law, where many obligations are essentially public in nature, but where private individuals or collectives may equally incur injury as a result of offending conduct.

Thus, the host State remains the right-holder and party to the dispute, with a host State national to be appointed as its representative for purposes of prosecuting its claim; see Figure 2.3. The investor's obligation owes to the host State, with the State's representative empowered to bring a claim to enforce the obligation as a private attorney general, or deputised private prosecutor.

The name of the *Qui Tam* Model derives from the Latin phrase *qui tam pro domino rege quam pro se ipso in hac parte sequitur*, referring to one who sues in a matter for the king as well as for himself.[121] The common law *qui tam* action finds kin within legal traditions reaching wide across the globe, including in the *actio popularis*, deriving from Roman law.[122]

---

arbitration once a dispute has arisen. Consent is, however, conclusive. See Z. Douglas, *The International Law of Investment Claims* (2009) 461–466. See also *Phoenix Action, Ltd.* v. *The Czech Republic*, ICSID Case No. ARB/06/5, Award, 15 April 2009, para. 144 and *Philip Morris Asia Limited* v. *The Commonwealth of Australia*, PCA Case No. 2012-12, Award on Jurisdiction and Admissibility, 17 December 2015, para. 554.

[121] See, e.g., *Black's Law Dictionary*, 10th edn. (2014) 1444.

[122] See ibid. 34 ('Roman law. An action that a male member of the general public could bring in the interest of the public welfare'). See also A. Berger, *Encyclopedic Dictionary of Roman Law* (1953) 347 ('Actiones popularis. Actions which can be brought by "any one among the people" ... They are of praetorian origin and serve to protect public interest ... They are penal, and in case of condemnation of the offender the plaintiff receives the penalty paid ... There are instances, however, established in statutes or local ordinances in which the penalty was paid to the state or municipal treasury, or divided between the aerarium and the accuser; as, e.g., provided in a decree of the Senate in the case of damage to aqueducts').

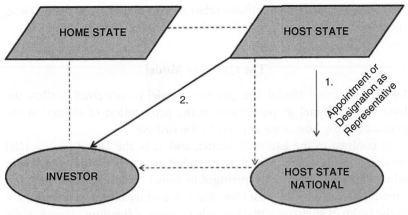

Figure 2.3   *Qui Tam* Model

Within the United States, the model is first embodied in the form of the federal False Claims Act, also known as the Lincoln Law.[123] The False Claims Act 'was enacted in 1863 by a Congress concerned that suppliers of goods to the Union Army during the Civil War were defrauding the Army',[124] with various amendments to its provisions having been adopted since that time. Under this arrangement, the private party, called a relator, is permitted to bring an action on the State's behalf. The State, not the relator, is the right-holder and party to the dispute. If the claim succeeds, the relator may receive a share of the reward.

Under the *qui tam* provisions within the False Claims Act,

> a *qui tam* complaint must be filed with the court under seal. The complaint and a written disclosure of all the relevant information known to the relator must be served on the U.S. Attorney for the judicial district where the *qui tam* was filed and on the Attorney General of the United States.[125]

Thereafter,

> [t]he government is required to investigate the allegations in the complaint . . . The government must then notify the court that it is proceeding with the action (generally referred to as 'intervening' in the action) or

---

[123] See Chapter LXVII, An Act to Prevent and Punish Frauds upon the Government of the United States, Statutes at Large 37th Cong., 3rd Sess. 696 (1863), 'Federal False Claims Act', 12 Stat. 696–699, codified as amended at 31 U.S.C. ss. 3729–3733 (2017).

[124] United States Department of Justice, *The False Claims Act: A Primer*, 1, available at: www .justice.gov/sites/default/files/civil/legacy/2011/04/22/C-FRAUDS_FCA_Primer.pdf.

[125] Ibid. 2.

declining to take over the action, in which case the relator can proceed with the action.[126]

Following this stage,

> [i]f the government intervenes in the *qui tam* action it has the primary responsibility for prosecuting the action. It can dismiss the action, even over the objection of the relator, so long as the court gives the relator an opportunity for a hearing and it can settle the action even if the relator objects so long as the relator is given a hearing and the court determines that the settlement is fair. If a relator seeks to settle or dismiss a *qui tam* action, it must obtain the consent of the government. When the case is proceeding, the government and the defendant can ask the court to limit the relator's participation in the litigation.[127]

The False Claims Act provides four statutory bars to the initiation of a *qui tam* action in the following events:

- '[t]he relator was convicted of criminal conduct arising from his or her role in the [False Claims Act] violation';
- '[a]nother *qui tam* [action] concerning the same conduct already has been filed' (the 'first to file bar');
- '[t]he government already is a party to a civil or administrative money proceeding concerning the same conduct'; or
- '[t]he *qui tam* action is based upon information that has been disclosed to the public through any of several means: criminal, civil, or administrative hearings in which the government is a party, government hearings, audits, reports, or investigations, or through the news media' (the 'public disclosure bar').[128]

As to remedy, if the government elects to intervene in the *qui tam* action, the relator is entitled to receive between fifteen and twenty-five per cent of the amount recovered by the government, whereas if the government declines to intervene, the relator's share is increased to twenty-five to thirty per cent.[129]

In England and Wales, *qui tam* actions were historically known as actions instituted by common informer procedure.[130] In Canada, the Exchequer Court Act bore language to the effect that a *qui tam* action is

---

[126] Ibid.   [127] Ibid. (citations to legislative provisions omitted).

[128] Ibid. 3 (citations to legislative provisions omitted). There is an exception to the public disclosure bar where the propounding relator is the original source of the information.

[129] Ibid.

[130] See *Tranton* v. *Astor* (1917) 33 TLR 383, 385 (where 'a private person [sues] for his own benefit to recover a statutory penalty . . . the expression "common informer" is only used

permitted in 'suits for penalties or forfeiture as where the suit is on behalf of the Crown alone'.[131]

In Singapore and Malaysia, the relator actions allowed for within their respective rules of civil procedure leave undefined both the identity of the 'relator' and the purpose of the 'relator action'.[132] However, at common law, a relator action is seen as a custom existing 'from the earliest times',[133] and originating in the traditional view that the Attorney-General, as guardian of public rights, is ideally positioned to consider and decide upon the needs of public interest, and is thus the proper plaintiff to assert

to distinguish him from a state or official informer such as His Majesty's Attorney-General'). The historical significance of *qui tam* actions lies in a lack of effective State investigation and prosecution of public wrongs. With the growth of a more accountable and reliable police force, such actions to enforce statutory law came to be viewed as less useful. See, e.g., R. W. Fischer, Comment, '*Qui Tam* Actions: The Role of the Private Citizen in Law Enforcement', 20 *UCLA Law Review* (1973); see also J. T. Boese, *Civil False Claims and* Qui Tam *Actions*, 3rd edn., vol. I (2005) 1–10. In the United Kingdom, they have since been mostly abolished by statutory intervention. See An Act to Abolish the Common Informer Procedure ('Common Informers Act 1951'), s. 1, available at: www.legislation.gov.uk/ukpga/Geo6/14-15/39. See, however, the Fraud Act 2006. See also A. Arlidge, A. Milne, and P. Sprenger, *Arlidge and Perry on Fraud*, 4th edn. (2014) para. 23-001 ('Apart from ... public agencies, private commercial interests from financial services, insurance, mobile telephone companies and film and media organisations investigate, and occasionally undertake private prosecutions') and the speech of Lord Rooker on the Animal Welfare Bill in *Hansard*, HL, vol. 683, col. GC44, 14 June 2006 ('when creating criminal offences, the presumption is that they will be common informer offences unless the contrary is provided. If we require all prosecutions to be brought only with the consent of the Crown Prosecution Service or local authorities, that would substantially fetter the existing rights of private individuals or non-state organisations to launch prosecutions').

[131] *Bank of Montreal* v. *Royal Bank of Canada* [1933] SCR 311. See also Section 30(a) of the Exchequer Court Act, *The Revised Statutes of Canada*, vol. I, Chapter 34 (1927) 624; Section 75(a) of the Supreme and Exchequer Courts Act, *The Revised Statutes of Canada: Proclaimed and Published under the Authority of the Act 49 Vict.*, vol. II, Chapter 4 (1886) 1776–1777; and *Allen Qui Tam* v. *Jarvis* (1871) 32 UCR 56, wherein a *qui tam* action was instituted to prevent intrusions into the domain of legal practice by unqualified practitioners.

[132] See RC Ord. 15, r. 11 (Singapore); RC 2012, Ord. 15, r. 11 (Malaysia). See also *The Supreme Court Practice 1999*, 2 vols. (1999), paras. 15/11/3 ('Relator actions – A relator action is one in which a person or body claiming to be entitled to restrain interference with a public right or to abate a public nuisance or to compel the performance of a public duty, is bound to bring such action in the name of the Att.-Gen. as a necessary party. The practice is to describe the plaintiff as "The Attorney-General at the relation of A B (*the relator*) ... "') and 15/11/4 ('Practice in relator actions – When an action is commenced on behalf of the Crown, or of those who enjoy its prerogative, or for a public wrong, the action may be brought by the Att.-Gen. alone, or by a relator in the name of the Att.-Gen. on the latter's authority ... if the conditions ... are satisfied').

[133] *Gouriet* v. *Union of Post Office Workers* [1978] AC 435, 477.

a public right.[134] A prospective litigant intending to enforce a public right is thus required to obtain the Attorney-General's authority, also known as *fiat*, in order to commence the action in the name of the Attorney-General.[135] English common law provides as follows regarding the role of the Attorney-General:

> His position in relator actions is the same as it is in actions brought without a relator (with the sole exception that the relator is liable for costs) . . . He is entitled to see and approve the statement of claim and any amendment in the pleadings, he is entitled to be consulted on discovery, the suit cannot be compromised without his approval; if the relator dies, the suit does not abate.[136]

A relator action may be instituted as against a private party where an individual seeks to enforce a public right in civil proceedings.[137] This procedure has been availed in cases wherein civil remedies are sought to

---

[134] Ibid. 481, 494–495. See also *The Supreme Court Practice 1999*, 2 vols. (1999), para. 15/11/3 ('The relator is bound to bring the action in the name of the Att.-Gen. as a necessary party for he is the only person recognised by public law as entitled to represent the public in a court of justice and he alone can maintain a suit *ex officio* or *ex relatione* for a declaration as to public rights . . . [O]nly the Att.-Gen. can sue on behalf of the public for the purpose of preventing public wrongs, and a private individual cannot do so on behalf of the public though he might be able to do so if he would sustain injury as a result of a public wrong').

[135] See *Singapore Law Gazette*, 'Casting the Relator Action', September 2014, available at: www.lawgazette.com.sg/2014-09/1126.htm. See also Government Proceedings Act 1956, s. 8(1) (Act 359) ('[i]n the case of a public nuisance the Attorney General, or two or more persons having obtained the consent in writing of the Attorney General, may institute a suit, though no special damage has been caused, for a declaration and injunction or for such other relief as may be appropriate to the circumstances of the case') (Malaysia).

[136] *Gouriet* v. *Union of Post Office Workers* [1978] AC 435, 478, which is applicable in Singapore under the Application of English Law Act 1993, s. 3(1) (Cap 7A) ('[t]he common law of England (including the principles and rules of equity), so far as it was part of the law of Singapore immediately before 12th November 1993, shall continue to be part of the law of Singapore') and Malaysia under the Civil Law Act 1956, s.3(1) (Act 67) ('[s]ave so far as other provision has been made or may hereafter be made by any written law in force in Malaysia, the Court shall . . . apply the common law of England and the rules of equity as administered in England on the 7 April 1956'), read in tandem with *Government of Malaysia* v. *Lim Kit Siang* [1988] 2 MLJ 12, 40 ('[t]he principle in *Boyce* v. *Paddington Borough Council* [1903] 1 Ch 109, as approved in *Gouriet* v. *Union of Post Office Workers* [1978] AC 435 is still the law applicable in this country').

[137] See *Attorney-General at and by the Relation of Pesurohjaya Ibu Kota (Commissioner of the Federal Capital), Kuala Lympur* v. *Wan Kam Fong Fo* [1967] 2 MLJ 72 and *South Johore Omnibus Sdn. Bhd.* v. *Damai Ekspres* [1983] 1 MLJ 101.

restrain the commission of a criminal or regulatory offence.[138] In particular, relator actions are available as against a private party where (i) a
plaintiff seeks to enforce a public right; and (ii) such plaintiff is not likely to
possess the requisite *locus standi* to sue on account of suffering some
special injury (or having some special interest beyond that possessed by
the public in general) from the private party's action or inaction.[139]

In New Zealand, as in England and Wales as well as Canada, the
mechanism is more deeply entrenched than a mere featuring in the laws
of procedure. Under Section 15 of the Crown Proceedings Act 1950, debt
or damages payable to the Crown (and not exceeding $500) may be sued
for and recovered, by and at the suit of any person properly appointed,[140]
with such person so appointed to sue in his name, with the addition of the
words 'suing on behalf of the Crown', or words to like effect.[141]

Across the European continent, instances of a similarly conceived
mechanism abound. In France, a taxpayer registered in the roll of the
municipality possesses the right to exercise, at his own risk and expense,
with the authorisation of the administrative court, all actions he believes to
be actions of the municipality, and which the latter, where previously called
upon to deliberate, refused or neglected to exercise.[142] In Belgium, a citizen
may bring a civil suit on behalf of the municipality wherein he resides.[143] A

---

[138] See *United Engineers (M) Bhd* v. *Lim Kit Siang* [1988] 1 MLJ 50 and *South Johore
Omnibus Sdn. Bhd.* v. *Damai Ekspres* [1983] 1 MLJ 101.

[139] *Government of Malaysia* v. *Lim Kit Siang* [1988] 2 MLJ 12, 27 and *Tan Eng Hong* v.
Attorney-General [2012] 4 SLR 476, paras. 78–84. See also *Jeyaretnam Kenneth Andrew* v.
Attorney-General [2014] 1 SLR 345, paras. 60–61.

[140] Crown Proceedings Act 1950, s. 15(1), available at: legislation.govt.nz/act/public/1950/
0054/latest/whole.html#DLM261945.

[141] Ibid. s. 15(2).

[142] Art. L2132-5 of the Code général des Collectivités Territoriales (*'Tout contribuable inscrit au
rôle de la commune a le droit d'exercer, tant en demande qu'en défense, à ses frais et risques,
avec l'autorisation du tribunal administratif, les actions qu'il croit appartenir à la commune, et
que celle-ci, préalablement appelée à en délibérer, a refusé ou négligé d'exercer'*).

[143] See Art. 271 of the Nouvelle loi communale, codifiée par l'arrêté royal du 24 juin 1988,
ratifié par la loi du 26 mai 1989 (*'§1er. – AR du 30 mai 1989, art. 56, §1er) Un ou plusieurs
habitants peuvent, au défaut du college des bourgmestre et échevins, ester en justice au
nom de la commune (... (... AR du 30 mai 1989, art. 56), en offrant, sous caution, de se
charger personnellement des frais du procès et de répondre des condamnations qui seraient
prononcées. La commune ne pourra transiger sur le procès sans l'intervention de celui ou
de ceux qui auront poursuivi l'action en son nom. (§2. Pour les communes de la région de
langue allemande, les communes énumérées à l'article 7 des lois sur l'emploi des langues en
matière administrative, coordonnées le 18 juillet 1966, ainsi que les communes de
Comines-Warneton et de Fourons, la faculté visée au §1er est subordonnée à l'autorisation
de la deputation permanente du conseil provincial, qui est juge de la suffisance de la*

similar mechanism is found in Luxembourg.[144] In Spain, a variation exists, requiring a citizen to invoke an alleged default of a local governmental entity.[145] Such invocation triggers a grace period in which the entity may act, failing which the citizen may exercise the action invoked in the name and interest of the entity.[146] Where the action is successful, the citizen is entitled to reimbursement of his costs.[147]

In some jurisdictions, a mechanism evocative of the *qui tam* action is embedded in the constitutional laws. In Brazil, the *ação popular* is an action available to any citizen of Brazil. The citizen may file an action to protect either (i) property or funds belonging to the State or to State-participated entities; (ii) the administrative morality (for example, in cases of confusion between a State officer's private and public interests or activities); (iii) the environment; or (iv) cultural or historical heritage.[148] In contrast to other

---

caution. En cas de refus, le recours est ouvert auprès du Roi, s'il s'agit de l'une des communes de la région de langue allemande, et auprès de l'Exécutif de la Région, s'il s'agit de l'une des communes énumérées à l'article 7 des lois sur l'emploi des langues en matière administrative, coordonnées le 18 juillet 1966, de la commune de Comines-Warneton ou de celle de Fourons – AR du 30 mai 1989, art. 56, §2). Art. 271bis. Le bourgmestre ou l'échevin, qui fait l'objet d'une action en dommages et intérêts devant la juridiction civile ou répressive, peut appeler à la cause l'Etat ou la commune. L'Etat ou la commune peut intervenir volontairement. – Loi du 4 mai 1999, art. 2').

[144] See Art. 85 of the Loi communale du 13 décembre 1988 (*'Un ou plusieurs habitants peuvent, à défaut du collège échevinal, ester en justice au nom de la commune, moyennant l'autorisation du ministre de l'Intérieur, en offrant, sous caution de se charger personnelle-ment des frais du procès et de répondre des condamnations qui seraient prononcées. Le ministre de l'Intérieur est juge de la suffisance de la caution. La commune ne peut transiger sur le procès sans l'intervention de celui ou de ceux qui ont poursuivi l'action en son nom. En cas de refus, un recours est ouvert auprès du Conseil d'Etat, Comité du Contentieux, statuant en dernière instance et comme juge du fond'*).

[145] See Art. 68(1), (2) of the Law 7/1985, Reguladora de las Bases del Régimen Local (*'1. Las entidades locales tienen la obligación de ejercer las acciones necesarias para la defensa de sus bienes y derechos. 2. Cualquier vecino que se hallare en pleno goce de sus derechos civiles y políticos podrá requerir su ejercicio a la Entidad interesada. Este requerimiento, del que se dará conocimiento a quienes pudiesen resultar afectados por las correspon-dientes acciones, suspenderá el plazo para el ejercicio de las mismas por un término de treinta días hábiles'*).

[146] Ibid. Art. 68(3) (*'Si en el plazo de esos treinta días la entidad no acordara el ejercicio de las acciones solicitadas, los vecinos podrán ejercitar dicha acción en nombre e interés de la entidad local'*).

[147] Ibid. Art. 68(4) (*'De prosperar la acción, el actor tendrá derecho a ser reembolsado por la Entidad de las costas procesales y a la indemnización de cuantos daños y perjuicios se le hubieran seguido'*).

[148] See, in general, *Regula a ação popular*, Section Law N.4.717/1965. See also International Association of Procedural Law, *General Report – Effective Access to Justice: The Right to Access to Justice and Public Responsibilities* (2014) 269, available at: www.ufrgs.br/caar/wp-content/uploads/2014/10/Session-3.1.pdf.

national procedures, the litigant is constitutionally shielded from judicial fees and from any risk of loss should the claim be unsuccessful, so long as the litigant does not institute such proceedings in bad faith.[149]

In India, a public interest litigation procedure exists, first allowed by the Supreme Court.[150] This doctrine allows for Indian citizens having sufficient interest in a public injury caused by a violation of legal rights to file a petition in any High Court or directly in the Supreme Court, or for the High Court or Supreme Court to initiate on its own motion a *suo moto* procedure,[151] pertaining to rights which include, amongst others, 'environmental pollution, disturbance of ecological balance, drugs, food adulteration, maintenance of heritage and culture, antiques, forest and wild life and other matters of public importance'.[152] This action is founded in Articles 32 and 226 of the Constitution of India.[153]

What is noticeably absent in these jurisdictions is compensation or reward to litigants who conduct a successful prosecution on behalf of the sovereign.[154]

---

[149] Art. 5 of the Constitution of the Federative Republic of Brazil (LXXIII) ('*qualquer cidadão é parte legítima para propor ação popular que vise a anular ato lesivo ao patrimônio público ou de entidade de que o Estado participe, à moralidade administrativa, ao meio ambiente e ao patrimônio histórico e cultural, ficando o autor, salvo comprovada má-fé, isento de custas judiciais e do ônus da sucumbência*').

[150] See *Hussainara Katoon and Others* v. *Home Secretary, State of Bihar* (1980) 1 SCC 81.

[151] See *Suo Motu* v. *Registrar, High Court of Gujarat* AIR 2002 Guj. 388.

[152] Supreme Court of India, *Compilation of Guidelines to Be Followed for Entertaining Letters/Petitions Received: In This Court as Public Interest Litigation* (2003), available at: http://supremecourtofindia.nic.in/circular/guidelines/pilguidelines.pdf. See also S. Muralidhar, 'India: Public Interest Litigation: Survey 1997–1998', 33–34 *Annual Survey of Indian Law* (1997–1998), available at: www.ielrc.org/content/a9802.pdf.

[153] *S.P. Gupta* v. *Union of India* (1982) 2 S.C.R. 365, 377 ('[w]here a legal wrong or a legal injury is caused to a person or to a determinate class of persons by reason of violation of any constitutional or legal right or any burden is imposed in contravention of any constitutional or legal provision or without authority of law or any such legal wrong or legal injury or illegal burden is threatened and such person or determinate class of persons is by reason of poverty, helplessness or disability or socially or economically disadvantaged position, unable to approach the Court for relief, any member of the public can maintain an application for an appropriate direction, order or writ in the High Court under Article 226 and in case of breach of any fundamental right of such person or determinate class of persons, in this Court under Article 32 seeking judicial redress for the legal wrong or injury caused to such person or determinate class of persons'). See also Arts. 32 and 36 of the Constitution of India.

[154] A recently adopted position of the OECD is of underlying relevance to the *Qui Tam* Model. The lack of an incentivising feature in many legal traditions may be bridged by a model derived from whistle-blower protection laws. In particular, a study on whistle-blower protection frameworks commissioned by the G20 has found that the use of incentives to encourage reporting has been employed only in the United States and

Under the *Qui Tam* Model, municipal legislation within the host State governs the relationship between the State and the prosecuting relator, in the same manner as, for example, the False Claims Act. As does the False Claims Act, such legislation may require the putative relator to request that the State first prosecute the claim.[155] Once duly appointed in accordance with the internal laws of the host State, a given host State national acts as the State itself.[156]

South Korea. See OECD, *G20 Anti-corruption Action Plan: Protection of Whistleblowers – Study on Whistleblower Protection Frameworks, Compendium of Best Practices and Guiding Principles for Legislation* (2012). The United States allows a whistle-blower to receive up to thirty per cent of the amount retrieved for fraud against the government, under the *qui tam* action provided for in its False Claims Act. See False Claims Act, 31 U. S.C. s. 3730(d). In South Korea, this amount is up to twenty per cent of the recovery, as under Arts. 11.7, 36, and 37 of the Act on Anti-corruption and the Establishment and Operation of the Anti-corruption & Civil Rights Commission (2009). The difference between the former and the latter is that whistle-blowers in the latter may be rewarded without the whistle-blower instituting proceedings. Indeed, it is only necessary for the whistle-blower to disclose acts of corruption and thus indirectly contribute to increasing the revenue of public agencies, or indirectly contribute to anti-corruption efforts in the public sector. See OECD, *Committing to Effective Whistleblower Protection* (2016) 66–7. At present, the OECD has identified that at least twenty-seven States party to its Convention on Combating Bribery of Foreign Public Officials 'do not provide effective protection to whistle-blowers who report foreign bribery in the public or private sector', ibid. 11, where the Convention has been ratified by some forty-one States. Ibid. 211. Only these two States party provide monetary incentives to affirmatively encourage whistle-blowing. The notion of incentivising whistle-blowers may serve to increase the efficacy of the *Qui Tam* Model, and to further empower host State nationals in the bringing of claims in investment arbitration. See ibid. 66 ('[d]isclosing wrongdoing can be a daunting undertaking that can lead to a loss of livelihood and professional marginalization. In addition to the stigma that may be attached to blowing the whistle, employees may also fear financial and reputational degradation. In order to curtail these potential losses and encourage individuals to come forward in the detection of wrongdoing, countries have introduced various incentives, ranging from tokens of recognition to financial rewards. While these are often considered as incentives, financial payments to whistleblowers can also provide support, for example living expenses, following retaliation').

[155] False Claims Act, 31 U.S.C. ss. 3730(b)(2) ('[a] copy of the complaint and written disclosure of substantially all material evidence and information the person possesses shall be served on the Government ... The Government may elect to intervene and proceed with the action within 60 days after it receives both the complaint and the material evidence and information') and 3730(c)(3) ('[i]f the Government elects not to proceed with the action, the person who initiated the action shall have the right to conduct the action').

[156] In labelling this model the *Qui Tam* Model, usage of the word 'agency' is studiously avoided. Where properly appointed, the prosecuting relator acts as the State itself. See, e.g., D. Anzilotti, *Corso di Diritto Internazionale*, vol. I (1912) 126 ('[t]he intent and the act of the organ, that is of the individual within his activity as an organ of the state, is the intent and the act of the state. It is the state itself that declares its intent and acts by means of these individuals. There is no distinction between organ and state: there are not two

Under the PCA Arbitration Rules 2012 and the UNCITRAL Arbitration Rules, '[e]ach party may be represented or assisted by persons chosen by it.'[157] For purposes of ICSID proceedings, it is recalled that under Article 25(3) of the ICSID Convention, '[c]onsent by a constituent subdivision or agency of a Contracting State shall require the approval of that State unless that State notifies the Centre that no such approval is required.'[158] Where given representatives act not as an 'agency', but rather as the State itself, duly empowered under the host State's internal laws, the requirement of Article 25(3) would seem not to apply. Thus, resort may be had directly to Rule 18 of the ICSID Arbitration Rules, where '[e]ach party may be represented or assisted by agents, counsel or advocates whose names and authority shall be notified by that party to the Secretary-General.'[159]

As noted, Professor Schreuer has written in regard to Article 25 that '[t]he concept of "agency" should be read not in structural terms but functionally ... What matters is that it performs public functions on behalf of the Contracting State or one of its constituent subdivisions.'[160] While it is the privilege of the host State alone to determine where the State ends and its agency begins, and while Professor Schreuer undoubtedly sought to evoke the innumerable uses of a State agency rather than to portend an extensive approval requirement, as the concept of 'agency' expands, so too does the scope of the article's mandatory prescription logically

different subjects, one of which acts for the other; there is one single subject, the state, which declares its intent and acts through its own organs. We cannot conceive the relationship between state and organ as an agency relationship: agency implies two distinct subjects, one of which declares the intention and acts for the other. But a state without its organs is nothing: it is an abstract conception; there cannot be a distinction between the state and its organ'). It is noted that municipal legislation crafted to enable a *qui tam* mechanism may conceive of the appointed representative as an agent of the State. Whatever the classification under municipal law, determinative is the appointment of the representative, and the delineation of his power.

[157] Art. 5 of the PCA Arbitration Rules 2012; Art. 5 of the UNCITRAL Arbitration Rules (as revised in 2010).

[158] Art. 25(3) of the ICSID Convention.

[159] Rule 18(1) of the ICSID Arbitration Rules. For a fuller discussion of the interplay between Article 25 of the Convention and Rule 18, as well as equivalent provisions of other arbitration rules, see A Role for the Host State, *supra*.

[160] C. Schreuer, L. Malintoppi, A. Reinisch, and A. Sinclair, *The ICSID Convention: A Commentary*, 2nd edn. (2009) 153, citing C. F. Amerasinghe, 'Jurisdiction *Ratione Personae* under the Convention on the Settlement of Investment Disputes between States and Nationals of Other States', 47 *British Yearbook of International Law* 1 (1976) 233–234.

extend, in equal measure. The designated host State national would certainly perform 'public functions' on behalf of his State.

It is posited that a direct appointment of a representative host State national is sound and unobjectionable. Where preferred, a State agency may be formed, as under the Espousal Model.[161] This agency may be duly consented to ICSID jurisdiction in satisfaction of Article 25(3), and the agency may then, in turn, notify the appointment of given host State nationals as its 'agents, counsel or advocates' in an arbitral proceeding.[162] In the same manner that the procedure of appointing a host State national as representative of the State is a matter of internal law, so too is the question of which individuals or collectives may assume this role, as the objects of such appointment. These are matters of mere municipal law with which international law is unconcerned.

A host State may, if it wishes, adopt a standard that requires any putative representative to demonstrate an injury traceable to conduct of a foreign investor alleged to violate obligations owed to the State.[163] The host State is under no obligation to do so. Thus, a host State may adopt the posture that only a showing of nationality is required, where any affront to, for example, its natural environment is an affront to each of its nationals.[164] In other words, the host State may extend *ex ante* an open-ended standing offer of

---

[161] Indeed, for convenience and efficiency, a single agency may be statutorily conceived to fill the role and to discharge the duties of the host State under all of the Direct Claims (III), Espousal, *Qui Tam*, and Hybrid Models.

[162] Rule 18(1) of the ICSID Arbitration Rules. See also See also 'ICSID Rules of Procedure for Arbitration Proceedings (Arbitration Rules)', 4 *International Tax and Business Lawyer* 2 (1986) 380.

[163] In, for example, a traditional test of *locus standi* outside of the *qui tam* context in the US federal courts, a plaintiff must make a threshold showing that he has suffered a concrete and particularised injury in fact that is actual or imminent, fairly traceable to the defendant's alleged conduct, and likely to be redressed by the court. See, e.g., *Allen* v. *Wright*, 468 U.S. 737 (1984) 752.

[164] See Annex, Model 13 (Host State Appointment of Representative). In this way, host State nationals having resources or expertise but who are not geographically proximate to an environmental harm may, if they wish, undertake an arbitration proceeding that would otherwise not be pursued, whether by the State or any other party, and secure to the State a remedy that would not otherwise be realised. It is interesting to note that such a model would reflect an inverse to the principle articulated by the Swiss jurist Emmerich de Vattel in 1758, see note 25 *supra*, with a national now acting in the cause of his injured State, and introducing yet another variety of reverse diplomatic protection. It has more recently been written that '[a]scriptions of nationality allow states to allocate control over a scarce and valuable resource: people'. M. Casas, 'Nationalities of Convenience, Personal Jurisdiction, and Access to Investor-State Dispute Settlement', 49 *New York University Journal of International Law and Politics* 1 (2016). See also W. M. Reisman et. al., *International Law in Contemporary Perspective*, 2nd edn. (2004) 357.

appointment, all objects of which are neither identified nor, in the case of the unborn, identifiable. In crafting *qui tam* legislation, the host State operates only within those constraints imposed by its own constitutional laws.

In all claims suited to the *Qui Tam* Model, the State is by definition the right holder, and thus may elect to prosecute its claim via its own machinery of State, as under the Direct Claims (III) Model, and without participation by its nationals, should it wish to do so. The *raison d'être* of the *Qui Tam* Model is to establish a mechanism which allows for participation by (and reward to) host State nationals, even where the State itself is the right-holder. Further, while the host State may predominate by requiring putative representatives to first present their case to the State (and may thereafter retain a delegated right of invocation, even where the State declines in the first instance to prosecute the claim), a benefit may be realised in an absolute right of representatives to prosecute a claim where the State declines to do so. In crafting such municipal legislation, it may be advantageous to exclude the State's power to force the abandonment of a claim outright.[165] In this way, an avenue remains to effective relief for individuals or collectives who might suffer injury flowing from breach of an obligation owed to the State, and to relief for the State itself.

The Hybrid Model

To appreciate the utility of the Hybrid Model, a cursory review of the prior two models is useful. The Espousal Model serves to secure the presence of the host State as party to the dispute by allowing the host State to accept assignment of and prosecute a claim previously held by its national, in those cases wherein the relevant rights arise in *individuals or collectives of host State nationals*. Conversely, the *Qui Tam* Model serves to allow for prosecution by the host State national of a claim opposable to the foreign investor where adverse impacts incur as a result of the investor's alleged breach of obligations owed *to the host State itself*. Under the Espousal Model, the host State accepts assignment of a claim by its national, while under the *Qui Tam* Model, the host State appoints its national as representative of the State itself for the purpose of prosecuting the State's own claim.

---

[165] See Annex, Model 13 (Host State Appointment of Representative). Furthermore, it is proposed that even where the State elects to assume control of the claim, host State nationals be afforded a right of participation or, alternatively, a right to give *amicus curiae* submissions, as under the model of, for example, Art. 4 of the UNCITRAL Rules on Transparency in Treaty-Based Investor-State Arbitration. An exception might allow the State to foreclose those claims found to be frivolous.

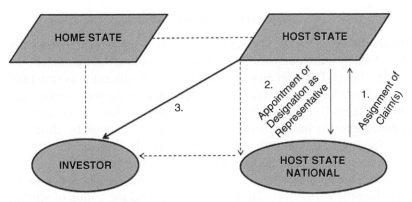

Figure 2.4   Hybrid Model

The Hybrid Model fuses these steps into a single mechanism. Under the Hybrid Model, the host State first *accepts* assignment of a claim held by its national, arising from a right alleged to be breached by a foreign investor.[166] Rather than prosecute the claim via its own machinery, the host State then *appoints* a representative to perform the role. This representative is the very national who has, in the first step, acted as assignor in conveying his claim to the State; see Figure 2.4.

As under each of the Espousal and *Qui Tam* Models where viewed in isolation,[167] the mechanics of these steps, the assignment and appointment, are matters for the municipal laws of the host State. The Hybrid Model may require more particularised statutory language, as the State's appointment of representative may not capture any or all of its nationals, but rather only the assignor of those claims to be submitted for adjudication at arbitration.

Ultimately, the Hybrid Model effectively serves to empower host State nationals to prosecute claims for the enforcement of their rights, and thus to retain a greater degree of control over arbitration proceedings than does the Espousal Model alone, while nonetheless achieving the presence of the host State as party to the dispute.

---

[166] With regard to the Espousal Model, it is noted that the investor's consent likely must extend to the assignment of a host State national's claim to the host State itself in order to remove any 'abuse of process' or 'abuse of rights' defence at the preliminary stage. See note 121 *supra*. This requirement holds equally true as to an assignment of claims in this first step of the Hybrid Model.

[167] As in the Espousal Model, the assignor host State national may retain the financial interest in any award proceeds to be procured. All requirements of each the Espousal Model and the *Qui Tam* Model, where viewed individually, must be met *mutatis mutandis* for operation of the Hybrid Model.

Summary of the Four Models

Where the rights sought to be enforced vis-à-vis the foreign investor are those held by individuals, classes, or collectives of host State nationals, the Direct Claims (I) Model may be desirable over all others for its structural simplicity. Where jurisdiction over the foreign investor is established, the Direct Claims (I) Model is the only one to afford a claim as immediately opposable to the foreign investor, without need of action by either the host State of the investment or the home State of the investor (the latter of which is required under the Direct Claims (II) Model). The choice of this model forecloses access to ICSID arbitration. Other suitable fora remain, including the Permanent Court of Arbitration and the option of arbitration under the UNCITRAL Arbitration Rules.

The Espousal Model is similarly suited to those claims wherein the rights sought to be enforced vis-à-vis the foreign investor are held by host State nationals. However, the Espousal Model enables such claims not by establishing a direct right of access to an international remedy, but rather by assignment of the relevant claims to the host State itself, with the host State to then prosecute those claims as opposable to the foreign investor via its machinery of State. The result of the assignment is an evolution of the mixed claims model and the presence of a State party to the dispute, thereby enabling the option of ICSID arbitration as amongst the available fora.

As in the Direct Claims (III) Model, the *Qui Tam* Model is suited to claims wherein the rights invoked do not arise at their origin in host State nationals, but rather in the host State itself. The host State may, if it wishes, elect to prosecute these claims via appointed representatives emerging from amongst its nationals. These duly appointed and empowered representatives may (but need not) be amongst those who are adversely impacted by the acts of the foreign investor alleged to breach obligations owed to the State.

Lastly, the Hybrid Model returns to the Direct Claims (I) and (II) Models as well as the Espousal Model insofar as here, too, the rights sought to be enforced vis-à-vis the foreign investor arise at their origin in host State nationals. The claim is first assigned to the host State, as in the Espousal Model. Rather than advance the claim via State machinery, the host State then appoints the assignor national as its representative for prosecution of the claim, thereby affording to this assignor a heightened control over the arbitration proceeding.

For an overview of the four models, see Table 2.1.

Table 2.1 *The Four Models*

Model	Original right-holder[168]	Parties to the dispute	Operation
Direct Claims (I)	Host State National	Host State National v. Investor	Host State National prosecutes his claim as directly opposable to the Investor; see Figure 2.1
Direct Claims (II)	Host State National	Host State National v. Home State	Host State National prosecutes his claim as opposable to the Home State of the Investor, where a Home State agency acts as insurer or guarantor of the Investor's obligations; see Figure 2.1
Direct Claims (III)	Host State	Host State v. Investor	Host State prosecutes its claim as directly opposable to the Investor; see Figure 2.1
Espousal	Host State National	Host State v. Investor	Host State National assigns his claim to the Host State (including, where applicable, a Host State agency that acts as insurer of its national's losses, thus becoming subrogated to his claim), which then prosecutes the claim as opposable to the Investor; see Figure 2.2
Qui Tam	Host State	Host State v. Investor	Host State appoints a representative as amongst its nationals for the prosecution of its claim, as opposable to the Investor; see Figure 2.3
Hybrid	Host State National	Host State v. Investor	Host State National assigns his claim to the Host State (as in **Espousal**), which then appoints this assignor as its representative for prosecution of the claim (as in ***Qui Tam***), as opposable to the Investor; see Figure 2.4

---

[168] The label 'original right-holder' is chosen to describe the party who holds the injured interest. In the Espousal and Hybrid Models, an injured host State national assigns his claim to the host State, which State then institutes proceedings as party to the dispute vis-à-vis the investor.

Consolidation of Models

Given the deep complexities that may arise from the particularities of any given investment dispute, it is only observed that where jurisdiction is properly obtained over each party and claim, there is no bar to consolidation of various of the models into a single arbitration proceeding.[169]

The Direct Claims (I) Model differs from all others in that the host State national is party to the dispute vis-à-vis a foreign investor. The Direct Claims (II) Model is unique in that a host State national is party to the dispute vis-à-vis the investor's home State. If either of these models were invoked alongside any other, there would result a true multiparty proceeding, with the nature of the parties thereto ensuring that the possibility of ICSID jurisdiction is foreclosed. Such cases may proceed in other *fora* such as the Permanent Court of Arbitration or in arbitration under the UNCITRAL Arbitration Rules.

It seems unlikely that the Direct Claims (I) Model would be seen in conjunction with the Espousal Model, though this combination may emerge if, for example, certain host State nationals are content for the State to carry their claims while others prefer to directly conduct the prosecution. It would seem most likely that the Direct Claims (I) Model might appear in conjunction with the *Qui Tam* Model, where host State nationals, while conducting their own claims, might additionally undertake to prosecute certain claims of the State, acting as the State's appointed representatives. Conversely, the Espousal Model might appear

---

[169] It is noted that, as in any multiparty proceeding, complexities may arise in the number and appointment of arbitrators. In the combination of, for example, the Direct Claims (I) Model with any other, there are a minimum of three parties to the dispute. One possibility is a tribunal of three arbitrators, with one to be appointed by the host State national or the host State itself, whichever is the first to file. However, this structure might give rise to the undesirable result of a 'race to the courthouse'. Another possibility is a tribunal of three arbitrators, with one to be appointed by agreement of the claimants, one to be appointed by the respondent (or by agreement of respondents), and the presiding arbitrator to be selected by an appointing authority. See, e.g., Art. 33 of the US Model BIT (2012) ('4. Unless all the disputing parties sought to be covered by the order otherwise agree, a tribunal established under this Article shall comprise three arbitrators: (a) one arbitrator appointed by agreement of the claimants; (b) one arbitrator appointed by the respondent; and (c) the presiding arbitrator appointed by the Secretary-General [of ICSID], provided, however, that the presiding arbitrator shall not be a national of either Party. 5. If, within 60 days after the Secretary-General receives a request ... the respondent fails or the claimants fail to appoint an arbitrator in accordance with paragraph 4, the Secretary-General, on the request of any disputing party sought to be covered by the order, shall appoint the arbitrator or arbitrators not yet appointed').

alongside the Direct Claims (III) Model in order for the host State to prosecute those claims assigned to it by its nationals alongside its own.

Injurious conduct by a foreign investor may often concurrently implicate rights held by individuals, classes, or collectives of host State nationals and rights of the host State itself. For example, in the case of a mass-scale event of environmental harm, the host State's environmental laws may be brought to bear while adverse impacts may also inflict compensable injury directly upon host State nationals. The *Qui Tam* Model might thus often appear in conjunction with the Hybrid Model, allowing affected host State nationals to vindicate the State's rights at the same time as their own. It seems unlikely that the *Qui Tam* Model would appear alongside the Espousal Model for, if the host State is willing to appoint its nationals as representatives for the prosecution of the State's own claims, there would seem to be no need to interpose a State agency in order to prosecute claims directly held by those same host State nationals.[170] However, this combination of the *Qui Tam* Model (or the Hybrid Model) and Espousal Model might appear once again where all host State nationals are not of the same mind, and some prefer to abdicate their direct participation in favour of resources or expertise offered by the State.

The establishment of a forum where claims by investors and host State nationals as well as the host State itself may be heard together opens new possibilities for the global resolution of all claims arising out of investment events. Further, such would permit any settlement agreement reached to be embodied in an award which is internationally enforceable, achieving a significant advantage for legal certainty and finality.

The Four Models and the International Centre for Settlement of Investment Disputes

ICSID jurisdiction is attainable as to all, with the exception of the Direct Claims (I) Model, for which the Permanent Court of Arbitration or the UNCITRAL Arbitration Rules are instead suggested. The objective requirements of the Centre's jurisdiction are established in Article 25 (1) of the ICSID Convention, reading as follows:

---

[170] Nor, for that matter, should there be any grounds for resistance to an appointment of host State nationals as representatives to prosecute the very claims that those host State nationals would have themselves assigned to the State, as under the Hybrid Model.

> The jurisdiction of the Centre shall extend to any legal dispute arising
> directly out of an investment, between a Contracting State ... and a
> national of another Contracting State, which the parties to the dispute
> consent in writing to submit to the Centre.[171]

The requirements are thus fivefold. There must be (i) an investment, out of
which there (ii) arises directly a (iii) legal dispute as between (iv) a
Contracting State and a national of another Contracting State and, lastly,
there must be (v) consent in writing of the parties. It may be said that the
first three are requirements of jurisdiction *ratione materiae*;[172] the fourth
jurisdiction *ratione personae*; and the last jurisdiction *ratione voluntatis*.

'investment'

There is a lively debate as to whether an objective definition of 'investment' exists under the ICSID Convention. On one side, observers often
rely upon the following statement from the time of its drafting:

> No attempt was made [within the Convention itself] to define the term
> 'investment' given the essential requirement of consent by the parties, and
> the mechanism through which Contracting States can make known in
> advance, if they so desire, the classes of disputes which they would or
> would not consider submitting to the Centre.[173]

In this view, it is thus left entirely to parties to supply any desired content
to a definition of the term 'investment' within the instrument (or instruments) giving rise to jurisdiction.[174]

---

[171] Art. 25(1) of the ICSID Convention.

[172] The early ICSID scholar C. F. Amerasinghe conflated these three requirements of
jurisdiction *ratione materiae* into two. See C. F. Amerasinghe, 'Jurisdiction *Ratione
Personae* under the Convention on the Settlement of Investment Disputes between
States and Nationals of Other States', 47 *British Yearbook of International Law* 1
(1976) 228 ('[t]here are two requirements concerning jurisdiction *ratione materiae*: the
dispute must be a legal dispute and it must arise directly out of an investment').

[173] *Report of the Executive Directors of the International Bank for Reconstruction and
Development on the Convention on the Settlement of Investment Disputes between
States and Nationals of Other States*, para. 27.

[174] See, e.g., Art. 1 of the Netherlands Model BIT:
For the purposes of this Agreement:

    (a) the term 'investments' means every kind of asset and more particularly, though
not exclusively:

        (i) movable and immovable property as well as any other rights in rem in
respect of every kind of asset;

        (ii) rights derived from shares, bonds and other kinds of interests in compa-
nies and joint ventures;

However, one tribunal notably defined an 'investment' under the ICSID Convention as having four elements: (i) a contribution of money or assets; (ii) a certain duration; (iii) an element of risk; and (iv) a contribution to the economic development of the host State.[175] Professor Zachary Douglas later synthesised and articulated a general rule whereby '[t]he economic materialization of an investment requires the commitment of resources to the economy of the host state by the claimant entailing the assumption of risk in expectation of a commercial return.'[176] He would thus seem to favour excluding the final contribution requirement, as well as the duration element. In this view, the existence of such an 'investment' is an absolute prerequisite to jurisdiction before the Centre.

The debate persists.[177] Regardless, in the classes of conflicts contemplated herein, the threshold of an 'investment' will typically be reached, by whatever the controlling definition. The existence of an investment is assumed.[178]

'arising directly'

The second criterion of the Convention imposes an objective requirement of vicinity to the investment. By analogy to the common law of proximate causation, separate and apart from the parties' agreement, the dispute must not only be connected to the investment but must be 'reasonably closely connected'.[179] Thus, disputes arising from 'ancillary or peripheral aspects of the investment operation' may give rise to the

> (iii) claims to money, to other assets or to any performance having an economic value;
> (iv) rights in the field of intellectual property, technical processes, goodwill and know-how;
> (v) rights granted under public law or under contract, including rights to prospect, explore, extract and win natural resources.

[175] *Salini Costruttori S.p.A. and Italstrade S.p.A* v. *Kingdom of Morocco*, ICSID Case No. ARB/00/4, Decision on Jurisdiction, 23 July 2001, para. 52.

[176] Z. Douglas, *The International Law of Investment Claims* (2009) 189.

[177] See, e.g., *Mr Patrick Mitchell* v. *Democratic Republic of the Congo*, ICSID Case No. ARB/99/7, Award, 9 February 2004, and Decision on the Application for Annulment of the Award, 1 November 2006; see also *Malaysian Historical Salvors Sdn Bhd* v. *The Government of Malaysia*, ICSID Case No. ARB/05/10, Award on Jurisdiction, 17 May 2007, and Decision on the Application for Annulment, 16 April 2009.

[178] It is noted that in practice, a possibly perverse result may obtain where the investor argues lack of an investment in seeking to foreclose jurisdiction over claims asserted by the host State or its nationals.

[179] See C. Schreuer, L. Malintoppi, A. Reinisch, and A. Sinclair, *The ICSID Convention: A Commentary*, 2nd edn. (2009) 106.

objection that they do not arise directly from the investment, and are not within the jurisdiction of the Centre.[180]

In ruling upon jurisdictional objections, various tribunals have sought to articulate indicia of the directness requirement. In the very first ICSID case, it was written as follows:

> It is well known, and it is being particularly shown in the present case, that investment is accomplished by a number of juridical acts of all sorts. It would not be consonant either with economic reality or with the intention of the parties to consider each of these acts in complete isolation from the others. It is particularly important to ascertain which is the act which is the basis of the investment and which entails as measures of execution the other acts which have been concluded in order to carry it out.[181]

Later, a tribunal similarly wrote that

> [a]n investment is frequently a rather complex operation, composed of various interrelated transactions, each element of which, standing alone, might not in all cases qualify as an investment. Hence, a dispute that is brought before the Centre must be deemed to arise directly out of an investment even when it is based on a transaction which, standing alone, would not qualify as an investment under the Convention, provided that the particular transaction forms an integral part of an overall operation that qualifies as an investment.[182]

Most pertinent to the present models, one tribunal found as follows:

> In fact, both parties agree, as does the Tribunal, that tax claims may be within ICSID's jurisdiction and that claims in relation thereto would be available to both parties to an investment dispute.
>
> The issue is therefore whether this particular claim falls within Article 25(1) of the ICSID Convention. In answering this question the Tribunal

---

[180] Ibid. Professor Schreuer has also written that the issue must be a 'central element of the investment relationship between the parties'. Ibid. 110. There is abundant authority to confirm, as is apparent from the text, that the requirement of directness refers to the relation of the dispute to the investment, and not to the nature of the investment as such. See also ibid. 107–108, citing *Fedax N.V.* v. *The Republic of Venezuela*, ICSID Case No. ARB/96/3, Decision of the Tribunal on Objections to Jurisdiction, 11 July 1997, para. 24 ('[i]t is apparent that the term "directly" relates in this Article to the "dispute" and not to the "investment." It follows that jurisdiction can exist even in respect of investments that are not direct, so long as the dispute arises directly from such transaction').

[181] *Holiday Inns S.A. and others* v. *Morocco*, ICSID Case No. ARB/72/1, Decision on Jurisdiction, 12 May 1974. For a detailed description, see P. Lalive, 'The First "World Bank" Arbitration (Holiday Inns v. Morocco) – Some Legal Problems', 51 *British Year Book of International Law* 1 (1980).

[182] *Československa Obchodní Banka, a.s.* v. *The Slovak Republic*, ICSID Case No. ARB/97/4, Decision on Objections to Jurisdiction, 24 May 1999, para. 72.

believes that it is correct to distinguish between rights and obligations that are applicable to legal or natural persons who are within the reach of a host State's jurisdiction, as a matter of general law; and rights and obligations that are applicable to an investor as a consequence of an investment agreement entered into with that host state. Legal disputes relating to the latter will fall under Article 25(1) of the Convention. Legal disputes concerning the former in principle fall to be decided by the appropriate procedures in the relevant jurisdiction unless the general law generates an investment dispute under the Convention.

The obligation not to engage in tax fraud is clearly a general obligation of law in [the host State]. It was not specially contracted for in the investment agreement and does not arise directly out of the investment.

For these reasons the Tribunal finds the claim of tax fraud beyond its competence *ratione materiae*.[183]

Thus, where 'a general obligation of law' in the host State *is* 'specially contracted for in the investment agreement', the directness requirement would tend to be satisfied.

While it is not possible to draw a definitive line to distinguish those disputes arising directly out of a given investment from those which do not, ICSID practice yields sufficient indications of the threshold. The fact that transactions that are 'ancillary but vital to the investment are made in separate form and even through separate entities does not deprive a dispute relating to them of its direct character'.[184] Similarly, the fact that a dispute yields 'important repercussions on relationships with private entities in the host State does not negate its character as arising directly out of an investment'.[185] In order to 'aris[e] directly' out of an investment, 'disputes must have distinctive features linking them to the investment that are not shared by disputes unrelated to investments'.[186]

---

[183] *Amco Asia Corporation and Others* v. *Republic of Indonesia*, ICSID Case No. ARB/81/1, Decision on Jurisdiction in Resubmitted Proceeding, 10 May 1988, paras. 124–127. This observation reflects the reality that an international tribunal remains a *juge d'exception*. Professor Schreuer rightly observes that this description of the investment relationship in terms of an investment agreement (contract) between the investor and the host State is too narrow, as such special relationship may equally emerge from the host State's investment law or from an investment treaty. See C. Schreuer, L. Malintoppi, A. Reinisch, and A. Sinclair, *The ICSID Convention: A Commentary*, 2nd edn. (2009) 110.

[184] C. Schreuer, L. Malintoppi, A. Reinisch, and A. Sinclair, *The ICSID Convention: A Commentary*, 2nd edn. (2009) 112.

[185] Ibid.

[186] Ibid. A joint stipulation that an existing dispute has arisen directly out of an investment is a useful tool in the case of a submission agreement. It may be anticipated that a tribunal will accord considerable weight to the jointly expressed intentions and expectations of the parties, though such would naturally not remove a tribunal's power to ultimately determine its own competence. On the other hand, a stipulation between the parties that

In sum, tribunals are unlikely to interpret the directness requirement restrictively. There is no great obstacle to the bringing of claims by the host State or its nationals which are within a reasonable vector of causation from the investment.

'legal dispute'

The Convention itself does not mandate or restrict the nature or content of the rights or obligations that may form the basis of a given legal dispute.[187] Rather, the Convention provides that '[t]he Tribunal shall decide a dispute in accordance with such rules of law as may be agreed by the parties', and that only '[i]n the absence of such agreement' will a tribunal 'apply the law of the Contracting State party to the dispute (including its rules on the conflict of laws) and such rules of international law as may be applicable'.[188]

The paramount principle is thus party autonomy. Where the parties have selected 'rules of law' which impose obligations upon the investor,[189] whether these rules of law originate in 'the law of the Contracting State party to the dispute', in 'rules of international law', or elsewhere, claims alleging their breach undoubtedly give rise to a 'legal dispute'.

'between a Contracting State ... and a national of another Contracting State'

The third criterion imposes a requirement as to the identity of the parties to the dispute. In the Direct Claims (II) Model, a host State national

---

any future dispute relating to their agreement arises directly out of an investment would not be meaningful. Here, too, the tribunal is not bound by such a clause, as the necessity of proximity arises from the Convention's objective requirements of jurisdiction, and it is 'futile to characterize disputes that may arise in the future'. Ibid. 107.

[187] See *Report of the Executive Directors of the International Bank for Reconstruction and Development on the Convention on the Settlement of Investment Disputes between States and Nationals of Other States*, para. 26 ('[t]he expression "legal dispute" has been used ... The dispute must concern the existence or scope of a legal right or obligation, or the nature or extent of the reparation to be made for breach of a legal obligation').

[188] Art. 42(1) of the ICSID Convention. For a view on these layers of applicable law, see E. Gaillard and Y. Banifatemi, 'The Meaning of "and" in Article 42(1), Second Sentence, of the Washington Convention: The Role of International Law in the ICSID Choice of Law Process', 18 *ICSID Review* 2 (2003). See also *Amco Asia Corporation and Others* v. *Republic of Indonesia*, ICSID Case No. ARB/81/1, Decision on Jurisdiction in Resubmitted Proceeding, para. 40; *Compañía del Desarrollo de Santa Elena S.A.* v. *Republic of Costa Rica*, ICSID Case No. ARB/96/1, Award, 17 February 2000, para. 64; and *Wena Hotels Ltd.* v. *Arab Republic of Egypt*, ICSID Case No. ARB/98/4, Decision Ad Hoc (Annulment Committee Proceeding), 5 February 2002, paras. 40–41.

[189] See Chapter 5.

claims against the investor's home State. In the Direct Claims (III) Model, the host State claims directly against the foreign investor. In the *Qui Tam* Model, the host State prosecutes its claim via a representative duly appointed under its own laws.[190] Under the Espousal and Hybrid Models, the host State accepts assignment of a claim held by its national, and prosecutes that claim either via its own machinery or via the assignor as an appointed representative.[191] Presuming that the home State of the investor and the host State of the investment are both party to the ICSID Convention, in each of these models there is, on one side, a 'Contracting State' and, on the other, 'a national of another Contracting State'.

'which the parties to the dispute consent in writing to submit to the Centre'

Where the host State (or, under the Direct Claims (II) Model, its national) seeks to avail the advantages of these mechanisms, its consent will be freely given. Thus, where the foreign investor (or, under the Direct Claims (II) Model, his home State) gives consent in writing, ICSID jurisdiction is achieved.[192]

Two Rules of Diplomatic Protection

Nationality of Claims

Within the régime of international investment law, rules concerning the nationality of claims, a traditional feature of the law of diplomatic protection, do not of their own force apply.[193] While the rule of continuous nationality is thus inapplicable,[194] its underlying rationale is present

---

[190] See The *Qui Tam* Model, supra.

[191] See The Espousal Model and The Hybrid Model, supra.

[192] See Chapter 3. It is recalled that the ICSID Convention does not require 'that the consent of both parties be expressed in a single instrument'. *Report of the Executive Directors of the International Bank for Reconstruction and Development on the Convention on the Settlement of Investment Disputes between States and Nationals of Other States*, para. 24. Professor Schreuer has observed that, for purposes of ICSID jurisdiction, '[c]onsent in writing must be explicit and not merely construed'. C. Schreuer, L. Malintoppi, A. Reinisch, and A. Sinclair, *The ICSID Convention: A Commentary*, 2nd edn. (2009) 191.

[193] See Art. 3(1) of the *Draft Articles on Diplomatic Protection with Commentaries*, ILC 2006, UN Doc. A/61/10 ('[t]he State entitled to exercise diplomatic protection is the State of nationality'); see also ibid. Art. 17 ('[t]he present draft articles do not apply to the extent that they are inconsistent with special rules of international law, such as treaty provisions for the protection of investments').

[194] The rule of continuous nationality required the injured national to hold the relevant nationality 'continuously from the date of injury to the date of the official presentation of

in cases where the host State acts to advance claims that originate in its nationals. It has been written, for instance, that '[t]he primary function of the continuous nationality rule in diplomatic protection ... is to prevent nationals from transferring their allegiance to more powerful states that might have the means to bring diplomatic (or even military) pressure to bear upon the state causing the injury.'[195]

The most critical time is *the time of the alleged injury*.[196] Thus, a variation of the nationality rule is proposed in the Espousal and Hybrid Models whereby jurisdiction vests only over claims assigned to the host State by those holding its nationality at this controlling time.[197] Such a rule imposes a simple logical restriction tailored to prevent abuse by those who would seek to convert stronger nations into 'claim agency' States.[198]

the claim'. Ibid. Arts. 5 ('Continuous nationality of a natural person') and 10 ('Continuous nationality of a corporation'). A variation of this rule is often adopted in international investment law. See, e.g., Art. 25(2)(a) of the ICSID Convention ('"National of another Contracting State" means: any natural person who had the nationality of a Contracting State other than the State party to the dispute on the date on which the parties consented to submit such dispute to conciliation or arbitration as well as on the date on which the request was registered'). In the case of treaty-born investment arbitration, these dates may fall in short succession after a dispute has arisen, as the investor's consent is often not given until such a time as he files his request for arbitration. See, e.g., *Lanco International Inc.* v. *The Republic of Argentina*, ICSID Case No. ARB/97/6, Decision on Jurisdiction, 8 December 1998, para. 40 ('[t]he investor's consent, which comes from ... its request for arbitration of OCTOBER 1, 1997 ... '). However, tribunals have articulated an 'abuse of rights' or 'abuse of process' bar to claims where ownership of the investment (and thus the claim) is transferred in an attempt to gain the requisite nationality after the time of alleged injury. See note 121 *supra*; see also Z. Douglas, *The International Law of Investment Claims* (2009) 290–297.

[195] Z. Douglas, *The International Law of Investment Claims* (2009) 459–460.

[196] It is noted that an abuse of rights or process may occur where the putative party, though not yet actually injured, may 'foresee a specific future dispute as a very high probability and not merely as a possible controversy', and thus seek to acquire the host State's nationality. *Pac Rim Cayman LLC* v. *Republic of El Salvador*, ICSID Case No. ARB/09/12, Decision on the Respondent's Jurisdictional Objections, 1 June 2012, para. 2.99.

[197] As a threshold matter, nationals of the host State are the only persons in whom the given substantive rights arise vis-à-vis the foreign investor, although States may also wish to extend the protections to permanent residents or others. See Annex, Model 1 (Definitions). Further, it may be desirable or necessary to additionally impose an explicit territoriality requirement, further restricting jurisdiction to claims for injury incurred within the territorial sovereignty of the host State, and thus expressly excluding claims for injury to host State nationals abroad.

[198] See, e.g., *Administrative Decision (No. V)* 7 RIAA 119 (1924) 141 ('[a]ny other rule would open wide the door for abuses and might result in converting a strong nation into a claim agency on behalf of those who after suffering injuries should assign their claims to its nationals or avail themselves of its naturalization laws for the purpose of procuring its

Exhaustion of Local Remedies

The rule of exhaustion of local remedies, another traditional feature of diplomatic protection,[199] similarly does not apply of its own force. A final consideration is the question of whether to impose such a requirement as to any or all of the models.[200]

Such a provision might operate to require that the host State or its nationals prosecute their claims to a final judgment in the national courts of the host State prior to initiating any claim in international arbitration. While the exhaustion requirement has a deep history in international law,[201] it has in recent times been largely abandoned in international investment law.[202] Thus, while the crafters of the governing instrument would be free to impose such a requirement if they wished to do so,

espousal of their claims'). See also H. W. Briggs, *The Law of Nations: Cases, Documents, and Notes*, 2nd edn. (1952) 733–735.

[199] See Art. 1(1) ('[a] State may not present an international claim in respect of an injury to a national . . . before the injured person has . . . exhausted all local remedies') and Art. 1(2) ('"Local remedies" means legal remedies which are open to the injured person before the judicial or administrative courts or bodies, whether ordinary or special, of the State alleged to be responsible for causing the injury') of the *Draft Articles on Diplomatic Protection with Commentaries*, ILC 2006, UN Doc. A/61/10. See also ibid. Art. 17 ('[t]he present draft articles do not apply to the extent that they are inconsistent with special rules of international law, such as treaty provisions for the protection of investments').

[200] See, e.g., Art. 26 of the ICSID Convention ('[a] Contracting State may require the exhaustion of local administrative or judicial remedies as a condition of its consent to arbitration under this Convention').

[201] See, e.g., C. F. Amerasinghe, *Local Remedies in International Law*, 2nd edn. (2003) 34–35 ('[w]hile state practice recognized the rule of local remedies in regard to diplomatic protection from the early nineteenth century and there were several instances of arbitral tribunals having to deal with diplomatic protection under treaties referring cases to them as early as 1802, the first case which can be found in which an arbitral tribunal gave judicial recognition to the rule is the Montano Case between Peru and the US. The decision in the case was handed down in 1863, i.e. in the second half of the nineteenth century. Thus, recognition in any form of judicial settlement of disputes came some time after it had been assimilated into diplomatic protection by extra-judicial, i.e. diplomatic, means').

[202] See, e.g., C. Schreuer, L. Malintoppi, A. Reinisch, and A. Sinclair, *The ICSID Convention: A Commentary*, 2nd edn. (2009) 413 ('The cases . . . show a consistent approach of ICSID tribunals not to impose an obligation to exhaust local remedies before a case is brought to international arbitration'). One example of an exhaustion-type requirement is found in Argentina's investment treaties, many of which include a provision requiring the investor to submit a dispute to the host State's courts and proscribing the commencement of arbitration under the treaty until either the competent court rules on the dispute, or eighteen months pass with no decision. For one tribunal's consideration of the merits and effects of such a provision, see, e.g., *ICS Inspection and Control Services Limited v. Argentine Republic*, PCA Case No. 2010-9, Award on Jurisdiction, 10 February 2012, paras. 243–273.

investors may often face no such hurdle in bringing their own claims, with a resulting asymmetry that may not be justifiable.

Further, one of the reasons traditionally underpinning the exhaustion requirement is not present in the case of claims by host States or host State nationals. Historically, the exhaustion requirement served in a design to allow international claims only as a final resort. If the national courts of the host State were found, in a sense, to be unsuited to the task, the tools of international justice may then be seized.[203] Thus, the international tribunal was conceived in part as a last bulwark against national courts that may be incorrigibly biased in favour of local interests, or otherwise incapable of rendering an impartial administration of justice.

As for host States and host State nationals, they may not fear their local courts.[204] Rather, they might elect to constitute an international tribunal precisely in order to avail its jurisdiction over claims which are not cognisable in the host State.[205] Furthermore, a preference for arbitration may flow from a desire for the superior international enforceability of arbitral awards.[206]

For these reasons, a fork-in-the-road or waiver provision is the better choice.[207] Such a mechanism operates to preserve the principle of *ne bis in idem*, to ensure exclusive jurisdiction to adjudicate all claims once

---

[203] See J. Paulsson, *Denial of Justice in International Law* (2005) 100–130.

[204] A similar underlying dynamic is reflected in the practice of removal to the US federal courts in the exercise of their diversity jurisdiction. See 28 U.S.C. s. 1446(a)-(c). Under the Federal Rules of Civil Procedure, where an action is filed within the courts of one of the fifty federated states, an out-of-state defendant may sometimes 'remove' a case to the federal courts which, amongst other things, typically draw their jury pools from a wider demographic, and are perceived as overcoming possible bias in favour of local litigants. However, where an out-of-state plaintiff elects to sue a local defendant in the state courts, the local defendant is not afforded the removal right, it being presumed that the local litigant need not fear such bias. It is, however, acknowledged that host State nationals may sometimes reasonably fear unfavourable treatment in their own courts, where their government might place the interests of foreign investors over their own.

[205] While the host State courts are presumably competent to hear claims for violation of, for example, the host State laws of extra-contractual liability, other obligations that may come to bind the foreign investor may have no equivalent in host State law. See Chapter 5.

[206] See Chapter 6.

[207] For an overview of the operation of these provisions, see H. Wehland, *The Coordination of Multiple Proceedings in Investment Treaty Arbitration* (2013) 86–98. The utility of such a provision will vary with the nature of the rights and obligations over which jurisdiction vests in the arbitral tribunal. There is greatest utility in a fork-in-the-road or waiver provision as to claims arising under, for example, the host State law of extra-contractual liability, as these are claims to which the investor would presumably otherwise be subject in the host State courts in any event. The utility is less clear as to claims

arbitration is commenced, to foreclose the possibility of parallel proceedings on the merits, and thus to deliver a truly final and binding result.[208]

A fork-in-the-road or waiver provision suitably serves the premise that nothing in the four models need diminish the right of the host State or its national to choose their national courts, or indeed any other forum that might accept jurisdiction, for the litigation of their disputes. Rather, the innovation lies in the premise that host States and their nationals might reasonably elect, in the exercise of their autonomy, to submit their claims to international arbitration. Where they do so, they must accept and abide by an obligation to respect the exclusivity of the tribunal.

arising from other sources, and will depend upon whether such claims are actionable in any other forum. There are three relevant categories of claims, these being (i) claims over which the arbitral tribunal (and no other forum) is vested of jurisdiction; (ii) claims over which another forum (and not the arbitral tribunal) is vested of jurisdiction; and (iii) claims over which *both* the arbitral tribunal *and* another forum enjoy a sort of concurrent jurisdiction, and thus over which the claimant may exercise a choice. In a strict sense, a fork-in-the-road or waiver provision may not serve great purpose as to the first or second categories, while being of essential utility in the third. In reality, the precise boundaries of these categories may often be a matter of vigorous dispute. Furthermore, a policy question arises as to whether a fork-in-the-road or waiver should capture only those claims that are *actually brought in arbitration*, or should additionally extend, once a claim is brought, over all claims that *could have been brought in arbitration* but were not, as under the doctrine of claim preclusion. Where seeking greater certainty, the foreign investor (or, in the case of a treaty instrument, delegations representing capital-exporting States) may reasonably insist upon a fork-in-the-road or waiver provision extending over adjudication of any and all rights and obligations that the relevant instrument introduces into the cognisance of an arbitral tribunal. See Annex, Model 11 (Waiver of Claims). Where a tribunal declines jurisdiction or declares the claims inadmissible, the would-be claimant or claimants would of course be permitted to invoke the powers of another forum, lest a denial of justice occur.

[208] See Annex, Model 11 (Waiver of Claims). For an example of a fork-in-the-road provision within an investment treaty, see Art. 8(2) of the France-Argentina BIT ('*[u]ne fois qu'un investisseur a soumis le différend soit aux juridictions de la Partie contractante concernée, soit à l'arbitrage international, le choix de l'une ou de l'autre de ces procédures reste définitif*'). A waiver provision similarly intended to achieve exclusivity (sometimes known as a 'no U-turn' provision) features within many treaty instruments conferring the State's consent to arbitration. See, e.g., Art. 26(2)(b)(i) of the US Model BIT (2012) ('[n]o claim may be submitted to arbitration under this Section unless: the notice of arbitration is accompanied . . . by the claimant's written waiver . . . of any right to initiate or continue before any administrative tribunal or court under the law of either Party, or other dispute settlement procedures, any proceeding with respect to any measure alleged to constitute a breach' of an obligation owed by the host State).

3

Jurisdiction *Ratione Personae*: The Foreign Investor

Where the host State or its nationals seek to avail the advantages of the four models, their consent will be freely given.[1] As to the foreign investor, there are various means and mechanisms to achieve jurisdiction *ratione personae*.[2]

Host State Investment Law

The host State is the gatekeeper of all investments. Where it wishes, the host State may require the investor's prospective consent to arbitration of certain categories of claims, whether by the host State itself or by its nationals, as a condition of entry. The investor's consent to arbitration may attach to the issuance of a mandatory investment licence, thus establishing arbitral jurisdiction that extends over all foreign investors legally present within the territory of the host State.[3] Licencing procedures

---

[1] As to the question of precisely which host State nationals may hold claims that are now cognisable on the international plane: this matter falls to the drafters of the relevant contractual, treaty, or statutory instruments. In other words, as with investors and investments, these claimants shall be determined either in legislative debate or in contract or treaty negotiation. As the *identity of the right-holder* is very often inextricably linked to the *definition of the right*, on this matter, see Chapter 5.

[2] In the Direct Claims (II) Model, any decision by the investor's home State to act as guarantor of obligations falling upon the investor would come as part and parcel of a policy to promote outbound investment by its nationals. See The Direct Claims (II) Model, Chapter 2.

[3] See Annex, Model 4 (Investment Licence). Professor Schreuer has observed that a host State may simply impose this requirement as a matter of its internal law and that, in this way, '[s]ubmission to arbitration may be made a condition for admission of investments in the host State'. C. Schreuer, 'Consent to Arbitration', in P. Muchlisnki, F. Ortino, and C. Schreuer (eds.), *The Oxford Handbook of International Investment Law* (2008) 837. A régime that establishes investor consent to arbitration as a requirement of licensure (and thus a prerequisite of entry) is reinforced by language featuring within most investment treaties to the effect that admission is governed by the host State's laws. See, e.g., Art. 2(1) of the China Model BIT (1997) ('[e]ach Contracting Party shall encourage investors of the other Contracting Party to make investments in its territory and admit such investments in

already form a common feature of many national laws governing the entry of foreign investment.[4] However, such need not require a blanket investment licencing scheme of general applicability. Rather, many industries – including precisely those featuring large-scale investments most liable to cause injury to the host State or its nationals – often operate within regulatory environments to which licensure requirements attach. The investor's consent to arbitration may be obtained via these processes; see Figure 3.1.

Mandatory investor commitments with respect to, for example, labour, environmental, and human rights may attach to the investment authorisation,[5] with accompanying investor consent to arbitration of disputes arising therefrom,[6] and with an agency to be designated or established for the purpose of reviewing investor applications and granting (or denying) investment licences.

In exchange for the licence, the investor now extends his own standing offer of arbitration vis-à-vis designated right-holders of and within the

---

accordance with its laws and regulations') and Art. 2(1) of the Germany Model BIT (2005) ('[e]ach Contracting State shall in its territory promote as far as possible investment by investors of the other Contracting State and admit such investments in accordance with its legislation'). The investment is only admitted (and thus the treaty's investment protections are only effective) once the investor's consent to arbitration is given. In addition to the fact that, under this model, such obligations would extend over all legally present foreign investors, even those investors who do not contract directly with the State itself, there is an additional efficiency advantage as to those who do. This structure would eliminate the need to enter the investor's substantive obligations into individual investment agreements. Rather, reference could simply be made therein to the terms of the investment licence.

[4] See, e.g., Art. 1 of the US Model BIT (2012) (defining 'investment authorization' as 'an authorization that the foreign investment authority of a Party grants to a covered investment or an investor of the other Party'). See also, e.g., Ethiopian Investment Commission, *Licensing and Registration Process in Ethiopia*, available at: www.investethiopia.gov.et/ investment-process/starting-a-business. As for incentivising the investor's assent to arbitration, the investor's home State may exert an important influence by requiring consent as a condition of its assistance in, for example, the granting of export credits. Similarly, international financial institutions or other international organisations may require consent as a condition of any assistance to the investor. It is noted that such conditionalities need not be recorded in any investment agreement or authorisation, but rather only in the governing instruments of the relevant State agency or international organisation, with the investor to present proof of his consent to arbitration in order to win the release of their aid. These tools may of course yield an impact in other means and mechanisms of gaining an investor's consent to arbitration, as well.

[5] See Chapter 5.

[6] As for the mechanics of securing the investor's consent, the terms of the investment licence would simply provide for the submission of enumerated categories of claims to final and binding resolution by arbitration. In accepting the terms of the licence *in toto*, the investor gives the requisite consent. See Annex, Model 4 (Investment Licence).

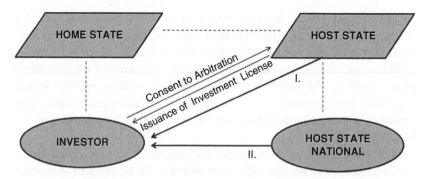

I.   Claims by the Host State, as opposable to the Investor. May be prosecuted via
      the Direct Claims (III), Espousal, *Qui Tam*, or Hybrid Models.

II.   Claims by the Host State National, as opposable to the Investor. May be
      prosecuted via the Direct Claims (I) Model, as third party beneficiary.

Figure 3.1   Jurisdiction Arising from Host State Investment Law

host State. By analogy to the common law tradition of contract formation, one might observe that a standing offer of arbitration is given in
consideration of the right of entry (which right of entry is in turn
attended by the State's own standing offer of arbitration as to the guarantees of investment protection). A standing offer of arbitration is thus
given in consideration of a standing offer of arbitration, the State's offer
in exchange for the investor's. This model thus serves to most nearly
establish reciprocity of standing offer, with unity in time.

In an alternative to the requirement of investment licensure and registration, a host State investment law may be crafted in a manner such that,
although investor consent to arbitration of certain categories of claims by
the host State and its nationals is not required as a condition of entry, such
consent is a prerequisite to enjoyment of any guarantees of investment
protection featuring within such law, including, where applicable, access to
arbitration.

It is evident that this structure affords a considerable advantage to the
investor over the more rigorous requirement of consent as an *ex ante*
condition to admission of his investment. In effect, there is no longer a
concurrent but rather a consecutive exchange of standing offers, with the
investor's offer extending if (and only if) he accepts the host State's prior
standing offer.[7] The investor may thus defer any decision regarding

---

[7] With regard to ICSID, it is recalled that the Convention does not require the consent of
both parties to be expressed in a single instrument, and that 'a host State might in its

desirability of invoking the law's protections or seizing its arbitral mechanism until such time as a dispute arises.

In effect, this model affords to the investor an opportunity to assess the particularities of a given investment conflict or dispute prior to electing whether or not to open the gate to adverse claims. Where an investor believes that he holds a viable claim for the host State's alleged breach of its obligations of investment protection, the investor may seek to weigh the potential rewards of such a claim as against the risk that he may invite claims by the host State or its nationals, and decide on balance where his preferences lie. This model is thus more favourable to the investor, as it allows the investor to retain a residual asymmetry in his unique privilege of initiation.

Contract Models

A second instrument suited to the direct attainment of the investor's consent to arbitration of claims by the host State or its nationals lies in contract, in particular those investment agreements to be concluded as between the foreign investor and the host State itself. To achieve the desired effect, in addition to delineating all rights and obligations calculated to serve the contractual purpose,[8] the contemplated instrument may establish further obligations upon the investor, with corresponding rights arising in the host State (or third party rights arising in its nationals),[9] and confer the investor's consent to the final and binding resolution of disputes arising therefrom by arbitration;[10] see Figure 3.2.

---

investment promotion legislation offer to submit disputes arising out of certain classes of investments to the jurisdiction of the Centre, and the investor might give his consent by accepting the offer in writing.' *Report of the Executive Directors of the International Bank for Reconstruction and Development on the Convention on the Settlement of Investment Disputes between States and Nationals of Other States*, para. 24. See also Rule 2(1)(c) of the ICSID Institution Rules (stating that a request for arbitration shall 'indicate the date of consent and the instruments in which it is recorded') and Rule 2(3) of the ICSID Institution Rules (stating that 'if both parties did not act on the same day, ["Date of Consent"] means the date on which the second party [consented in writing to submit the dispute to the Centre]'). The present proposal is a mere extension of a multi-instrument model.

[8] Perhaps the most significant examples of such contracts include concession agreements granting rights of exploration and development over hydrocarbon or mineral resources, contracts for the construction of State infrastructure, or contracts for the provision of State services.

[9] See Chapter 5.

[10] See Annex, Model 2 (Contractual Arbitration Agreement). On the doctrine of third party beneficiaries within the law of contract, see Chapter 2, note 6.

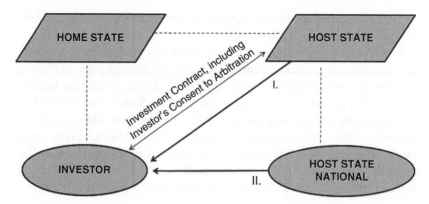

I.   Claims by the Host State, as opposable to the Investor. May be prosecuted via
     the Direct Claims (III), Espousal, *Qui Tam*, or Hybrid Models.

II. Claims by the Host State National, as opposable to the Investor. May be
     prosecuted via the Direct Claims (I) Model, as third party beneficiary.

Figure 3.2   Jurisdiction Arising from Contract

Thus, the mechanism for attaining the investor's consent to arbitration
of the designated rights is by simple assent to the contractual terms. The
host State may require the investor's consent to arbitration as a condition
to the bidding upon or the awarding or signing of the contract itself.[11]

---

[11] See Annex, Models 2 (Contractual Arbitration Agreement) and 5 (Tender Rules). A
present reform initiative within international investment law stands to dramatically
increase the importance of these contractual models. The European Commission has
proposed to eliminate investment arbitration from its treaties entirely, and for investment
disputes to instead be submitted to a permanent international investment court, to be
adjudicated by State-appointed judges offering exclusivity of function. The proposal also
includes the possibility of an appeal mechanism that allows for review of decisions on the
merits. See European Commission Press Release, *Commission Proposes New Investment
Court System for TTIP and Other EU Trade and Investment Negotiations*, 16 September
2015, available at: http://europa.eu/rapid/press-release_IP-15-5651_en.htm; see also C.
Malmström, *Proposing an Investment Court System*, 16 September 2016, available at:
https://ec.europa.eu/commission/commissioners/2014–2019/malmstrom/blog/propos
ing-investment-court-system_en. Such is likely to have the effect that investors would
increasingly prefer tailor-made contracts that allow for arbitration of their disputes by
party-appointed arbitrators. Even in the case of investments that do not entail a directly
underpinning contractual relationship with the host State itself, larger foreign investors
may nonetheless respond by seeking from the host State guarantees that reflect their
preferred obligations of investment protection, and including a customised arbitration
agreement. As Judge Crawford has observed, 'the market will find ways of resolving these
problems irrespective of what governments think the right ways to resolve them is.' J.
Crawford, 'The Ideal Arbitrator: Does One Size Fit All?', 11th Washington College of Law

The *clause compromissoire* may feature in the original investment contract, and thus yield its effect prospectively as to any dispute that might
later arise in the course of performance.[12] Alternatively, consent might be
given in a submission agreement, which operates to submit an existing
dispute to arbitration, following the time that a dispute has arisen.[13]

Treaty Models

The Host State's Contingent Consent

As the foreign investor lacks treaty-making capacity, treaty-born instruments for the attainment of jurisdiction over the investor offer a more
circuitous path. They are no less legally sound. Further, in a manner similar
to host State investment laws, there is the added benefit that, where consented and availed, treaty-born arbitral jurisdiction may extend over all
investor-nationals of the relevant State (or States) that are present within
the territory of the host State, and not only those investors who contract
directly with the State itself.[14]

Under the prevailing treaty model, the host State typically extends to the
foreign investor (i) certain substantive guarantees of investment protection;[15] and, via the standing offer,[16] (ii) the procedural right to bring a
claim in international arbitration for their enforcement. With the addition
of carefully crafted language, the investor no longer holds these privileges
as of right, but rather conditionally, upon his own consent to (i) be bound

Annual International Commercial Arbitration Lecture (2016). Thus, contrary to a stated
objective of harmonisation, the European Commission proposal risks fuelling a further
fragmentation of international investment law.

[12] See Annex, Model 2 (Contractual Arbitration Agreement).

[13] It is preferred that the arbitration agreement be concluded at the time of original
contracting, as the emergence of a dispute may yield a distorting effect upon either party's
willingness to accept arbitration.

[14] At the outset, it is noted that these treaty models require the arbitration provision to
permit commencement of proceedings by the host State (or, in the case of the Direct
Claims (I) and (II) Models, the host State national). With regard to the host State, such
provision is present in many investment treaties. See, e.g., Art. 8(3) of the UK Model BIT
(2005) ('[i]f any such dispute should arise ... then, if the national or company affected
also consents in writing to submit the dispute to the Centre ... either party may institute
proceedings') and Art. 9(2) of the Switzerland-Pakistan BIT ('[e]ach party may start the
procedure'). See also Introduction, note 1.

[15] See Chapter 1, note 29.

[16] See, e.g., *Lanco International Inc.* v. *The Argentine Republic*, ICSID Case No. ARB/97/6,
Decision on Jurisdiction, 8 December 1998, para. 40 ('the consent of the State ... comes
directly from the ARGENTINA U.S. Treaty').

by certain obligations owing towards the host State or its nationals;[17] and (ii) submit to arbitration, as may be initiated by these designated right-holders, for the enforcement of such rights.[18]

In one mechanism, Professor Schreuer has suggested that '[bilateral investment treaties] may provide specifically that their benefits will extend only to investors that have consented to arbitration.'[19] In a first step, while the investor need not give his consent to arbitration in order to gain admission of his investment, the investor must give consent to arbitration of certain categories of claims by the host State or its nationals as a condition to the enjoyment of any treaty guarantees of investment protection.

In one step further, the investor's consent to arbitration of claims by the host State or its nationals may gain for the investor not only the treaty's substantive investment protections, but also the host State's consent to arbitration of disputes arising therefrom, and thus the pathway to the investor's own initiation of a treaty-born claim.[20] By this mechanism, the host State gives its assent to arbitration in a contingent consent clause, whereby '[i]n addition to the acquisition of an investment in the host contracting state ... the claimant must have satisfied any conditions precedent to the consent of the host contracting state party to the arbitration of investment disputes as stipulated in the investment treaty';[21] see Figure 3.3.

---

[17] See Chapter 5; see also Annex, Model 10 (Jurisdiction *Ratione Materiae*).

[18] See Annex, Model 6 (Contingent Consent Clause). Such consent may be conferred by various media, for example (i) in an investment agreement; (ii) in an application for (or on acceptance of) an investment licence; or indeed (iii) in any other properly recorded and legally effective instrument to be delivered to a designated authority of the host State.

[19] See C. Schreuer, 'Consent to Arbitration', in P. Muchlisnki, F. Ortino, and C. Schreuer (eds.), *The Oxford Handbook of International Investment Law* (2008) 837.

[20] While legally distinct, these two models may ultimately yield the same effect in practice, as an investor may hold limited options for the effective policing of the host State's treaty obligations outside of arbitration, causing the investor to place little or no value upon the substantive protections alone, and thus to insist upon an accompanying arbitral mechanism. Even where, for example, the investor might maintain a meaningful prospect to seek his home State's diplomatic protection, such residual opening may run counter to the end of a more unified régime for the settlement of international investment disputes. Further, such gives rise to a newly asymmetrical space, wherein host States and host State nationals alone enjoy a right to arbitrate. For these reasons, this latter model is to be preferred. See Annex, Model 6 (Contingent Consent Clause).

[21] Z. Douglas, *The International Law of Investment Claims* (2009) 151. In crafting the controlling language, the difference between jurisdiction and admissibility must be heeded. If the host State's consent is truly made conditional upon the investor's, then such reaches to the jurisdiction of the tribunal. If, however, the provision is differently styled or structured, such may reach rather to admissibility. This distinction carries a consequence. One tribunal has explained the 'subtle distinction' as follows:

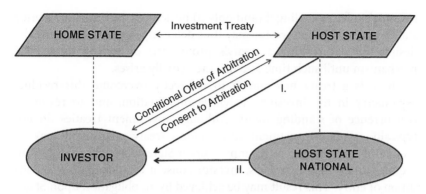

I.   Claims by the Host State, as opposable to the Investor. May be prosecuted via
     the Direct Claims (III), Espousal, *Qui Tam*, or Hybrid Models.

II. Claims by the Host State National, as opposable to the Investor. May be
     prosecuted via the Direct Claims (I) Model, as third party beneficiary.

Figure 3.3   Jurisdiction Arising from Treaty

This model is structurally akin to one noted previously, but for the fact
that the host State's conditional offer of arbitration now flows from a
treaty instrument, rather than its own investment law. There is not a
concurrent but rather a consecutive exchange of standing offers, with the

> A decision that a Tribunal lacks jurisdiction and a decision that a claim is
> not arbitrable both prevent the claim proceeding. However, the former is
> only a determination that the chosen Tribunal cannot hear the claim. In
> contrast, a decision of lack of admissibility is a decision that the claim
> should not be heard at all. Inadmissibility, therefore, encompasses those
> situations where the Tribunal possesses jurisdiction (as it does here) but
> where there is a substantive obstacle to the enforcement of the claim, such
> as illegality, or a procedural obstacle such as where a mandatory pre-
> condition to enforcing the claim, such as the giving of notice, has not
> been complied with.

Philippine International Air Terminals Co., Inc. v. *The Government of the Republic of the
Philippines*, ICC Case No. 12610, Award, 22 July 2010, para. 572, citing J. Paulsson,
'Jurisdiction and Admissibility', in G. Aksen et al. (eds.), *Global Reflections on International
Law, Commerce and Dispute Resolution, Liber Amicorum in Honour of Robert Briner* (2005)
601, 617. See also *Hochtief AG* v. *Argentine Republic*, ICSID Case No. ARB/07/31, Decision on
Jurisdiction, 24 October 2011, para. 90 ('jurisdiction is an attribute of a tribunal and not of a
claim, whereas admissibility is an attribute of a claim but not of a tribunal') and Z. Douglas,
The International Law of Investment Claims (2009) 469 (writing that '[a] jurisdictional
requirement must be positively established by the claimant', whereas, for example, '[a] "denial
of benefits" provision must be positively invoked by the respondent [host State]', with the host
State to bear the burden of proof).

investor's offer extending if (and only if) he accepts the host State's prior standing offer.[22] The investor may thus defer any decision regarding the desirability of invoking a treaty's protections or seizing its arbitral mechanism until such time as a dispute actually arises.

There is a treaty mechanism to indirectly overcome this residual asymmetry in the investor's privilege of initiation, and to restore a concurrence of standing offers. Although investment treaties do not typically regulate investment admission, a treaty instrument may be crafted in a manner so as to impose upon States party an obligation to require, under their own laws, investor consent to arbitration as a condition of entry. This result may be achieved by an obligation upon States party to enact implementing legislation within their own national investment codes.

Jurisdiction without Privity

Although foreign investors, lacking treaty-making capacity, may not be party to a treaty instrument, and while treaty obligations traditionally fall upon States for the regimenting of State behaviour, treaties may nonetheless yield direct effect upon individuals where the relevant provision so indicates.[23] Jurisdiction over the foreign investor may be established (which is to say that arbitration, where properly elected by the host State

---

[22] With regard to ICSID, it is recalled that the Convention does not require the consent of both parties to be expressed in a single instrument, and that 'a host State might in its investment promotion legislation offer to submit disputes arising out of certain classes of investments to the jurisdiction of the Centre, and the investor might give his consent by accepting the offer in writing.' *Report of the Executive Directors of the International Bank for Reconstruction and Development on the Convention on the Settlement of Investment Disputes between States and Nationals of Other States*, para. 24. In latter days, a host State's standing offer may come not only in 'its investment promotion legislation', but also in an investment treaty. The present proposal, with its contingent consent clause or conditional offer of arbitration, is a mere extension of a multi-instrument model.

[23] See, e.g., R. Portmann, *Legal Personality In International Law* (2010) 277–278 ('[t]he direct effect of treaties upon individuals (or other municipal legal persons) is affirmed in the present framework whenever this follows from interpreting the relevant provision according to general rules of treaty interpretation', and '[a]s a matter of general international law, international treaties have direct effect upon individuals whenever the provision in question so indicates'). See also *Lagrand Case* (Germany v. United States), Judgment, 2001 ICJ Reports 466, para. 77; *Case Concerning Avena and Other Mexican Nationals* (Mexico v. United States), 2004 ICJ Reports 12, para. 40; and Commentary to Article 33(2) of the *Articles on Responsibility of States for Internationally Wrongful Acts, with Commentaries*, Yearbook of the International Law Commission, vol. II(2) (2001).

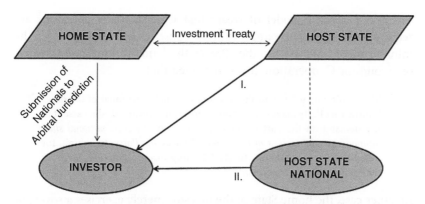

I.   Claims by the Host State, as opposable to the Investor. May be prosecuted via the Direct Claims (III), Espousal, *Qui Tam*, or Hybrid Models.

II. Claims by the Host State National, as opposable to the Investor. May be prosecuted via the Direct Claims (I) Model, as third party beneficiary.

Figure 3.4   Jurisdiction without Privity

or its national, may be compelled) by direct effect of a treaty instrument concluded by the investor's home State;[24] see Figure 3.4.

A first possibility lies in the adoption of model treaty language in the vein proposed by the International Institute for Sustainable Development, model language which draws an implied consent to arbitration by the investor:

> Each investor and investment, by virtue of establishing or continuing to operate or own an investment subject to this Agreement, consents to the submission of a claim to arbitration under this Agreement.[25]

[24] Such an exercise of sovereign power by the home State is akin to that effected by States in acceding to, for example, the Rome Statute. See Art. 12(2) of the Rome Statute of the International Criminal Court, 2187 UNTS 90, 37 ILM 1002 (1998) ('[t]he Court may exercise its jurisdiction if one or more of the following States are Parties to this Statute . . . (a) The State on the territory of which the conduct in question occurred . . . (b) The State of which the person accused of the crime is a national'). The exercise of this power may encounter challenge under the constitutional laws of national jurisdictions. See, e.g., Chapter 4, notes 28, 29.

[25] Art. 4 at Annex A of the International Institute for Sustainable Development Model International Agreement on Investment for Sustainable Development (2005), available at: www.iisd.org/pdf/2005/investment_model_int_agreement.pdf. In this model text, American-trained lawyers might see a standard that is evocative of the US Supreme Court's foundational 'minimum contacts' test establishing the constitutional threshold for jurisdiction of one state's courts over defendants hailing from another. See

There is a second model of treaty text which equally abandons any requirement of the investor's express consent, and perhaps even his minimum contacts. Within the 1968 Netherlands-Indonesia Agreement on Economic Cooperation, it was provided that

> [t]he Contracting Party in the territory of which a national of the other Contracting Party makes *or intends to make* an investment, shall assent to any demand on the part of such national and *any such national shall comply with any request of the former Contracting Party*, to submit, for conciliation or arbitration, to [ICSID] *any dispute that may arise in connection with the investment.*[26]

In either case, the home State of the investor merely exercises a sovereign prerogative, in particular its privilege to submit its own nationals to an international tribunal.[27] Under these models, the home State of the investor elects to offer its investor-nationals to a properly invoked arbitral jurisdiction.[28]

International Shoe Co. v. *Washington*, 326 U.S. 310 (1945). The Court interpreted and applied the Due Process Clause of the Fourteenth Amendment of the Constitution to hold that 'due process requires only that, in order to subject a defendant to a judgment *in personam*, if he be not present within the territory of the forum, he have certain minimum contacts with it such that the maintenance of the suit does not offend traditional notions of fair play and substantial justice.' Ibid. 316.

[26] Art. 11 of the Netherlands-Indonesia Agreement on Economic Cooperation (with Protocol and Exchanges of Letters dated 17 June 1968), signed on 7 July 1968 (entered into force on 17 July 1971), 799 UNTS 13 (emphasis added).

[27] In tandem, the investor's home State may, if it wishes, promulgate implementing legislation to give force and effect to the treaty's dictation within its internal laws, though this step may be unnecessary if the express language of the treaty to which the home State accedes is evidently self-executing. Even where a treaty is designed to be self-executing, a State may consider that implementing legislation is useful in clarifying the manner of a treaty's application within the structure of its own laws.

[28] By removing the requirement of express investor consent, the mechanism is transformed by force of international law into a machinery that more resembles a forum of compulsory jurisdiction. In other words, this forum is evocative of a court in the sense that a properly pleaded complaint is not an offer or invitation. These texts are akin to provisions for deemed or compelled consent, such as those that exist in many national regulatory contexts. See, e.g., 18 U.S.C. s. 3261(a) (by obtaining employment or accompanying US Armed Forces outside of the United States an individual consents to US jurisdiction for criminal matters and the application of US criminal law); 14 C.F.R. s. 91.703(a) (by operating an aircraft registered in the United States an individual agrees to comply with US aviation regulations, even when within a foreign jurisdiction); 18 U.S.C. s. 7(6) (by operating a spacecraft registered in the United States an individual submits to US federal jurisdiction, even when in space). As to jurisdiction *ratione materiae*, such a tribunal remains restricted to the adjudication of those rights and obligations of the parties as are indicated within the treaty instrument itself. See Chapter 5. A compulsion to arbitration may face challenge under the constitutional laws of the relevant State. See, e.g., Chapter 4,

Because such treaty instruments would almost certainly foreclose the possibility of ICSID jurisdiction,[29] it is suggested that reversion may be had to the Direct Claims (I) Model, in order to afford to host State nationals most direct control over their claims.[30] However, certain host State nationals may prefer to abdicate direct participation in favour of resources or expertise offered by the State.

It is finally noted that, while a treaty instrument may establish arbitral jurisdiction over the foreign investor without his express consent, whether by direct effect or via implementing legislation within the investor's home State, new questions may later arise in the enforcement of a resulting award.[31]

A Harmonisation Mechanism

Prominent amongst the present criticisms of international investment law is its disembodied manifestation in a proliferation of more than 3,000 treaties, the majority of these mere bilateral instruments. This fractured landscape quite predictably impacts upon consistency in substantive and procedural norms, with attendant losses for lack of legal certainty.

Professor Gabrielle Kaufmann-Kohler and Dr. Michele Potestà have proposed that the United Nations Convention on Transparency in Treaty-Based Investor State Arbitration (whereby States may opt into an expanded application of the UNCITRAL Rules on Transparency in Treaty-Based

notes 28, 29. Under international law, a treaty obligation supersedes mere municipal law wherever they may conflict. See Art. 27 of the Vienna Convention on the Law of Treaties, 1155 UNTS 331, 8 ILM 679 (1969) ('[a] party may not invoke the provisions of its internal law as justification for its failure to perform a treaty'); see also M. E. Villiger, *Commentary on the 1969 Vienna Convention on the Law of Treaties* (2009) 375 ('[o]n the whole, it can be said that Article 27 amounts to codification of a long-standing principle of customary international law'). Nonetheless, consideration of the constitutional laws of the putative States party is advised.

[29] It is recalled that, for purposes of ICSID jurisdiction, '[c]onsent in writing must be explicit and not merely construed.' C. Schreuer, L. Malintoppi, A. Reinisch, and A. Sinclair, *The ICSID Convention: A Commentary*, 2nd edn. (2009) 191. Further, in an ICSID proceeding, '[t]he Secretary-General shall register [a request for arbitration] unless he finds, on the basis of the information contained in the request, that the dispute is manifestly outside the jurisdiction of the Centre.' Art. 36(3) of the ICSID Convention. Due to the lack of 'consent in writing' by the investor, a claim brought under the model offered by either the International Institute for Sustainable Development's model treaty or the early Netherlands-Indonesia treaty would likely not withstand even this superficial level of inquiry in the Secretary General's exercise of *prima facie* control over the jurisdiction of the Centre.

[30] See The Direct Claims (I) Model, Chapter 2.   [31] See Chapter 6.

Investor-State Arbitration, commonly known as the Mauritius Convention) may serve as a model for a multilateral treaty instrument whereby States would opt into participation in a permanent international investment court or appellate mechanism, as proposed by the European Commission.[32] In like fashion, an opt-in convention may be availed to harmonise and unify international investment law by enabling multilateral adoption of mechanisms to arbitrate the conduct of international investors.[33]

The Mauritius Convention is drafted in a manner to yield an altering effect upon all prior investment treaties existing as between acceding States.[34] In so doing, it is conceived to evade the necessity of tedious renegotiation and amendment procedures as to the prohibitively large number of investment treaties presently in effect.[35] In tandem with the

---

[32] G. Kaufmann-Kohler and M. Potestà, 'Can the Mauritius Convention Serve as a Model for the Reform of Investor-State Arbitration in Connection with the Introduction of a Permanent Investment Tribunal or an Appeal Mechanism? Analysis and Roadmap', *CIDS-Geneva Center for International Dispute Settlement* (2016). On the European Commission's proposal, see note 11 *supra*. The Mauritius Convention entered into force in October 2017 after Switzerland became the third State to ratify it, following Mauritius and Canada.

[33] The contractual models of negotiating and attaining an investor's consent to arbitration of certain categories of claims by the host State or its nationals remain outside the ambit of such a treaty instrument. The role of contractual arbitration agreements is likely to endure, or even to augment. See note 11 *supra*.

[34] See Art. 1(1) ('[t]his Convention applies to arbitration between an investor and a State or a regional economic integration organization conducted on the basis of an investment treaty concluded before 1 April 2014') and Art. 1(2) ('[t]he term "investment treaty" means any bilateral or multilateral treaty, including any treaty commonly referred to as a free trade agreement, economic integration agreement, trade and investment framework or cooperation agreement, or bilateral investment treaty, which contains provisions on the protection of investments or investors and a right for investors to resort to arbitration against contracting parties to that investment treaty') of the United Nations Convention on Transparency in Treaty-Based Investor State Arbitration, UNGA Res. 69/116, 10 December 2014.

[35] An opt-in convention tailored to serve the purpose of arbitrating investor conduct might reach beyond the opt-in convention conceived by Professor Kaufmann-Kohler and Dr. Potestà in one critical regard: to address the matter of substantive rights and obligations, namely obligations of the investor. Professor Kaufmann-Kohler and Dr. Potestà have foreseen this eventuality. See G. Kaufmann-Kohler and M. Potestà, 'Can the Mauritius Convention Serve as a Model for the Reform of Investor-State Arbitration in Connection with the Introduction of a Permanent Investment Tribunal or an Appeal Mechanism? Analysis and Roadmap', *CIDS-Geneva Center for International Dispute Settlement* (2016) 85 n 435 ('[i]f future treaties were to provide for *obligations of the investor* and *host State claims against the investor's breach of these obligations*, the dispute resolution clause of the future [investment treaty] will have to be tailored accordingly') (emphasis added). Under the presently proposed opt-in convention, it is the convention itself that would operate, in effect, to tailor both the substantive obligations and the dispute settlement provisions of

model requiring an investor's consent to arbitration as an *ex ante* condition to admission of his investment, although entry is governed by the laws of the host State, an opt-in convention may be crafted to impose upon States party an obligation to require, under their own laws, investor consent to arbitration as a condition of entry.

Perhaps a more natural fit for an opt-in convention lies in the treaty models requiring the investor's consent to arbitration as a condition to his enjoyment of a treaty's investment protections.[36] This is so because a treaty's provisions (including those establishing a right of arbitration), being by their nature creatures of treaty, may be altered by effect of treaty alone. Such structure thus obviates the need of intervention into the complex codes of national law that traditionally govern the admission of foreign investments. Thus, a State's contingent consent may be born by effect of an opt-in convention, with prior investment treaties of the acceding State to be altered in their effect such that a standing offer of arbitration is no longer unconditional vis-à-vis admitted investors, but is rather conditioned upon the investor's own consent to arbitration of given categories of claims by the host State or its nationals;[37] see Figure 3.5.

existing investment treaties of acceding States. Further, as the best-developed bodies of law for the imposition of obligations upon the investor may often arise in the municipal laws of the host State, in addition to stating any other agreed-upon rules of law, the opt-in convention might facilitate the inclusion of an annex whereby acceding States may indicate their own laws (or selected provisions thereof) to be applicable in those disputes to which they (or their nationals) are party. See Chapter 5. Further, whether by a fork-in-the-road or waiver provision featuring within the original investment treaty or the opt-in convention, the principle of *ne bis in idem* must be respected. See Chapter 2, notes 208, 209. Lastly, as in the Mauritius Convention, in order for an opt-in convention to be effective, it may require a provision barring invocation of any most-favoured-nation status as granted in any other treaty. See Art. 2(5) of the United Nations Convention on Transparency in Treaty-Based Investor State Arbitration, UNGA Res. 69/116, 10 December 2014 ('[t]he Parties to this Convention agree that a claimant may not invoke a most favoured nation provision to seek to apply, or avoid the application of, the UNCITRAL Rules on Transparency under this Convention').

[36] See The Host State's Contingent Consent, Chapter 3.

[37] It is noted that this model does not redress the residual asymmetry that persists where the investor holds the unique privilege of initiation. See The Host State's Contingent Consent, Chapter 3. Further, proper effect requires that both the host State and the investor's home State in the given instance have acceded to the opt-in convention, for where the investor's home State has not acceded, any earlier offer by the host State remains outstanding and unaltered. Professor Kaufmann-Kohler and Dr. Potestà observe that although some might regard an opt-in convention as effecting an amendment of a State's existing investment treaties (with an accompanying necessity of any amendment formalities stipulated therein), the 'more correct view' is that the relationship between existing investment treaties and an opt-in convention is regarded as one of 'subsequent treaties having the same subject-matter'. G. Kaufmann-Kohler and M. Potestà, 'Can the

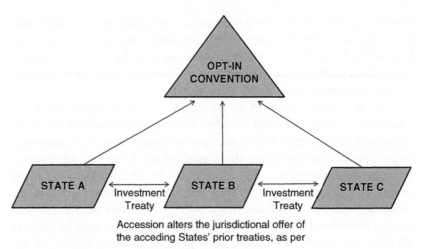

Figure 3.5   The Opt-In Convention

A further possibility lies in employing an opt-in convention as a
vehicle to achieve the treaty methods of jurisdiction without privity.[38] An opt-in convention may require that each acceding State
submit its own investor-nationals to properly invoked arbitral

Mauritius Convention Serve as a Model for the Reform of Investor-State Arbitration in
Connection with the Introduction of a Permanent Investment Tribunal or an Appeal
Mechanism? Analysis and Roadmap', *CIDS-Geneva Center for International Dispute
Settlement* (2016) 79. The authors also note that this view is 'consistent with the view
held by the [European] Commission in respect of the Mauritius Convention and it reflects
the position taken in [an OECD] study with regard to the development of a multilateral
instrument to modify bilateral tax treaties'. Ibid., citing OECD, *Developing a Multilateral
Instrument to Modify Bilateral Tax Treaties, Action 15 – 2015 Final Report*, OECD/G20
Base Erosion and Profit Shifting Project (2015) 31, para. 15 (noting that 'the term
"modification" is better adapted to this project than the term "amendment." There is
no need for a formal "amendment" of each one of the existing bilateral tax treaties. Rather,
these treaties will be "modified" automatically by the multilateral instrument') and para.
18 ('[i]n the silence of the multilateral treaty, the applicable customary rule, codified in
Article 30(3) of the [Vienna Convention on the Law of Treaties], is that when two rules
apply to the same matter, the later in time prevails (*lex posterior derogat legi priori*).
Accordingly, earlier (i.e. previously concluded) bilateral treaties would continue to apply
only to the extent that their provisions are compatible with those of the later multilateral
treaty'). Even if an opt-in convention were considered to effect an amendment of previous
treaties, the instruments to be amended are a State's own investment treaties (which
originate consent, and thus jurisdiction), and not (even in a case where an ICSID tribunal
is ultimately seized) the ICSID Convention (carrying, as it does, a requirement of
unanimity for amendment; see Art. 66(1) of the ICSID Convention).

[38] See Jurisdiction without Privity, Chapter 3.

jurisdiction over given claims by host States with which the acceding State has an investment treaty in effect, and including claims by host State nationals. In a further step, such a provision may be structured by reciprocity, whereby the submission of the acceding State's investor-nationals to arbitral jurisdiction is operative only vis-à-vis host States having also acceded to the opt-in convention, and thus having similarly submitted their own investor-nationals.[39]

By usage of an opt-in convention, a greater harmonisation of international investment law may be achieved in the course of reform from within to arbitrate the conduct of international investors across existing investment treaties.[40]

---

[39] See Annex, Model 8 (Opt-In Convention).

[40] The pursuit of harmonisation has become a matter of heightened international concern in recent times. See, e.g., *The Addis Ababa Action Agenda of the Third International Conference on Financing for Development*, endorsed by UNGA Res. 69/313, 27 July 2015, para. 87 ('[w]e will strengthen coherence and consistency among bilateral and regional trade and investment agreements') and para. 91 (requesting UNCTAD 'to continue its existing programme of meetings and consultations with Member States on investment agreements' for this and other purposes).

4

Mass Proceedings and Settlement Agreements

An effective mechanism for arbitrating the conduct of international investors must be equipped to enable methods of collective redress, and thus to contend with the possibility of a large number of injured claimants via multiparty or mass arbitration. As a threshold matter, reference to collective redress evokes two distinct eventualities: a claim that is held uniquely by a *collective*, separate and apart from its individual members, or *a summation of factually and legally similar individual claims*. The two are fundamentally different in the nature of the implicated rights, and thus in the character of the concerned claimant or claimants.

A true collective, such as an indigenous people, may be the beneficiary of given rights, whether under municipal or international law.[1] The legal personality of a collective, and thus its power to prosecute a claim, is less certain.[2] The collective must enjoy the capacity to act via its executive organs in order to avail any right.[3] By contrast, the use of the term 'collective redress' to reference a (perhaps very large) number of factually and legally similar individual claims raises very different matters. Where

[1] See Chapter 5.

[2] In an interesting recent development, see Art. VI of the American Declaration on the Rights of Indigenous Peoples, AG/RES.2888 (XLVI-O/16) 167, available at: http://cdn7.iitc.org/wp-content/uploads/AG07150E06_web.pdf ('[i]ndigenous peoples have collective rights that are indispensable for their existence, well-being, and integral development as peoples', and '[i]n this regard, the states recognize and respect the right of the indigenous peoples to their collective action'). See also ibid. Art. IX ('[t]he states shall recognize fully the juridical personality of the indigenous peoples, respecting indigenous forms of organization and promoting the full exercise of the rights recognized in this Declaration').

[3] One example of a collective mechanism is found in a 1995 additional protocol to the European Social Charter. Under this protocol, the contracting States recognise the right of various international organisations (as well as of certain representative national organisations) of, for example, employers or trade unions to submit complaints alleging unsatisfactory application of the Charter. Council of Europe Additional Protocol to the European Social Charter Providing for a System of Collective Complaints, 9 November 1995, CETS 158.

the term 'collective' refers not to the character of the right-holder, but rather to the numerosity of the claimants, such primarily raises practical questions as to how the claims process is best administered.[4]

The International Bar Association has defined 'collective redress' as 'a procedure designed to allow a group of individuals with similar claims to combine their claims in a single action, rather than require each individual to file his or her own lawsuit', reflecting the conception of a summation of individual claims.[5] Two common forms of such action are 'representative proceedings, in which a named representative acts on behalf of a class of unnamed claimants, and aggregate proceedings, in which a group of individually named claimants jointly files a claim'.[6] In the case of representative proceedings, these may be further classified into 'opt-in' and 'opt-out' actions, depending upon whether putative unnamed claimants are required to expressly consent to the arbitration of their rights ('opting in'), or whether such putative claimants are presumed to have joined the proceeding, and whose position will thus be decided with *res judicata* effect vis-à-vis the respondent, unless they expressly withdraw any implied consent by notifying their non-participation ('opting out').[7]

The case that has brought most attention to these questions within the investment arbitration régime is *Abaclat and others* v. *Argentine Republic*.[8] The controversy surrounding that case stems from Argentina's submission that it did not consent, via the standing offer of an investment treaty, to arbitrate a dispute with an entire class of claimants who held factually and legally similar claims. Where the relevant

---

[4] For a guide of best practices as discerned from past experiences, see International Organization for Migration, *Property Restitution and Compensation: Practices and Experiences of Claims Programmes* (2008), available at: http://publications.iom.int/sys tem/files/pdf/property_restitution_compensation.pdf.

[5] IBA Legal Practice Division, *Guidelines for Recognising and Enforcing Foreign Judgments for Collective Redress* (2008), para. 2.

[6] C. Lamm, E. Hellbeck, et al., 'Mass Claims in Investment Arbitration: Jurisdiction and Admissibility', in B. Hanotiau and E. A. Schwartz (eds.), *Class and Group Actions in Arbitration*, Dossiers of the ICC Institute of World Business Law (2016), citing *Abaclat and Others* v. *Argentine Republic*, ICSID Case No. ARB/07/5, Decision on Jurisdiction and Admissibility, 4 August 2011, para. 483 and S. I. Strong, *Class, Mass, and Collective Arbitration in National and International Law* (2013) 6.

[7] It is noted that the ICSID Convention's express requirement of 'consent in writing' of all parties to the dispute almost certainly bars any 'opt-out' representative proceeding from its jurisdiction. Art. 25(1) of the ICSID Convention. Rather, in order for ICSID jurisdiction to vest, an 'opt-in' model is required.

[8] *Abaclat and Others* v. *Argentine Republic*, ICSID Case No. ARB/07/5, Decision on Jurisdiction and Admissibility, 4 August 2011.

instruments fell silent, the *Abaclat* majority found that it had the power, under Article 44 of the ICSID Convention and Rule 19 of the ICSID Arbitration Rules, to adjudicate mass or collective claims,[9] over a vociferous dissent.[10]

In reverse fashion, one may question whether an investor must expressly consent to mass or collective claims by the host State or its nationals in order for arbitral jurisdiction to vest.[11] Express consent may, in any event, be sought or given in order to establish greater certainty.[12]

---

[9] Ibid. para. 551. It has been written that

> [t]he *Abaclat* majority, which to date has remained the only investment tribunal to rule on a mass claim, decided to qualify the proceedings as 'mass proceedings' based on 'the high number of Claimants appearing together as one mass'. The tribunal found that 'the present proceedings seem to be a sort of a hybrid kind of collective proceedings, in that it starts as aggregate proceedings, but then continues with features similar to representative proceedings due to the high number of Claimants involved'. In reaching this conclusion the *Abaclat* tribunal considered that each individual claimant was aware of, consented to, and was identified in the arbitration, thus distinguishing the proceeding from a class action. It also considered, however, that each claimant's participation in the proceeding was passive in that each claimant had delegated the right to make all decisions relating to the conduct of the proceeding to an agent who, due to the high number of claimants could not take into account the particular interests of individual claimants, but was limited to representing the interests that were common to all claimants as a group.

C. Lamm, E. Hellbeck et al., 'Mass Claims in Investment Arbitration: Jurisdiction and Admissibility', in B. Hanotiau and E. A. Schwartz (eds.), *Class and Group Actions in Arbitration*, Dossiers of the ICC Institute of World Business Law (2016), citing *Abaclat and Others* v. *Argentine Republic*, ICSID Case No. ARB/07/5, Decision on Jurisdiction and Admissibility, 4 August 2011, paras. 480, 486–488. In contrast, two other tribunals have found that lower numbers of claimants before them did not cross the threshold of mass claims, as opposed to a simple multiparty proceeding. See *Ambiente Ufficio S.p.A. and others* v. *Argentine Republic*, ICSID Case No. ARB/08/9, Decision on Jurisdiction and Admissibility, 8 February 2013, paras. 119–121; *Giovanni Alemanni and others* v. *Argentine Republic*, ICSID Case No. ARB/07/8, Decision on Jurisdiction and Admissibility, 17 November 2014, para. 267.

[10] Whereas the majority wrote of a 'gap' in the ICSID instruments, *Abaclat and Others* v. *Argentine Republic*, ICSID Case No. ARB/07/5, Decision on Jurisdiction and Admissibility, 4 August 2011, para. 551, such was, in dissent, described as a 'qualified silence'. Ibid. Dissenting Opinion of Professor Georges Abi-Saab, 28 October 2011, paras. 160–169.

[11] For a view favouring the findings of the *Abaclat* majority, see R. Kabra, 'Has *Abaclat v Argentina* Left ICSID with a 'Mass'ive Problem?', 31 *Arbitration International* 3 (2015).

[12] In the event, a body of arbitration rules that is purposely suited to the adjudication of mass claims will be a useful innovation. See ibid. 29 ('given the vast number of investment disputes that can potentially require (or abuse) such a mechanism, and the fact-specific

Tribunals, commissions, and other bodies for the adjudication of mass claims have historically been established to redress the consequences upon individuals of wars or other international crises, such as the Iran-United States Claims Tribunal, the United Nations Compensation Commission (established following Iraq's ejection from Kuwait in 1991), the Commission for Real Property Claims of Displaced Persons and Refugees in Bosnia and Herzegovina, and the Eritrea-Ethiopia Claims Commission.[13] In like manner, where stakeholders of an investment are not able to avail an antecedent arbitration agreement or other arbitral jurisdiction for the resolution of investment conflicts and where harm has already incurred, the matter may be submitted to arbitration via a settlement agreement.[14] An agreement may establish an arbitral tribunal or claims commission mandated to hear claims of persons affected by the investment who fall within a delineated definition.[15] For instance, a host State may conclude a settlement agreement which establishes a claims body where an environmental impact has occurred with consequent harm to its nationals. The settlement amount paid by the investor may then be held for the purpose of satisfying claims and covering costs of the claims process. The terms of a settlement may

nature of the determination of procedural adaptations required, it is suggested that the Administrative Council of the ICSID adopt Additional Facility Rules, to define and confirm the boundaries within which such claims can be adjudicated by ICSID tribunals'). It is noted that within the 2004 US Model BIT, prior to the time of the controversial *Abaclat* jurisdictional finding, the drafters incorporated what might be availed as a mass claims mechanism, evidently inspired by the provisions that govern class action lawsuits within Rule 23 of the US Federal Rules of Civil Procedure. See Art. 33(6) of the US Model BIT (2004) ('[w]here a tribunal established under this Article is satisfied that two or more claims that have been submitted to arbitration under Article 24(1) have *a question of law or fact in common*, and *arise out of the same events or circumstances*, the tribunal *may*, in the interest of fair and efficient resolution of the claims, and after hearing the disputing parties, by order: (a) assume jurisdiction over, and hear and determine together, all or part of the claims; (b) assume jurisdiction over, and hear and determine one or more of the claims, the determination of which it believes would assist in the resolution of the others; or (c) instruct a tribunal previously established under Article 27 [Selection of Arbitrators] to assume jurisdiction over, and hear and determine together, all or part of the claims.') (emphasis added). An identical provision features at Art. 33(6) of the more current US Model BIT (2012).

[13] H. Das, 'The Concept of Mass Claims and the Specificity of Mass Claims Resolution', in *Redressing Injustices through Mass Claims Processes: Innovative Responses to Unique Challenges* (2005) 6–7. See also H. M. Holtzmann and E. Kristjànsdòttir, *International Mass Claims Processes: Legal and Practical Perspectives* (2007) and V. Heiskanen, 'Arbitrating Mass Investor Claims: Lessons of International Commissions', in *Multiple Party Actions in International Arbitration* (2009).

[14] See Annex, Model 9 (Mass Claims Settlement Agreement).

[15] As the *identity of the right-holder* is very often inextricably linked to the *definition of the right*, on this matter, see Chapter 5.

allow for direct pursuit of claims by host State nationals, for the host State to act as representative of its nationals, or for use of the Espousal Model,[16] provided that any necessary machinery is established within the host State's internal laws.[17]

The oil pollution in Nigeria's Ogoniland offers one emblematic instance of the numerous conflicts that may be ripe for such a resolution.[18] In this case, oil extraction activities dating from the 1950s caused widespread environmental harm in the delta region of the Niger River, with severe consequences for the livelihood of local peoples. These affected nationals later commenced court proceedings against a consortium including the Royal Dutch Shell oil major and its affiliate entities within various national jurisdictions, including Nigeria, the United States, the Netherlands, and the United Kingdom. Despite one 2009 settlement agreement[19] and another in 2015,[20] these efforts have not met with great success.[21] A collaborative effort between Shell and the Nigerian State to redress the harms caused by the investment activity appears more promising. Upon the request of the Nigerian government, the United Nations Environment Programme issued an extensive report in 2011 in which it offered a detailed plan to remediate the environmental harm and proposed an

---

[16] See The Espousal Model, Chapter 2.

[17] It is possible to entrust the Permanent Court of Arbitration or another international institution with the administration of this sort of mass claims process. The Permanent Court of Arbitration 'continues to gather information concerning various mass claims tribunals and processes to create a conveniently accessible source of useful information for those involved in existing mass claims tribunals as well as those responsible for the design of future ones'. Permanent Court of Arbitration, *116th Annual Report* (2016) 16. While this type of settlement agreement may be instrumental in securing compensation for past harms incurred and, in certain cases, in enabling stalled investment projects to proceed, this sort of *ex post* dispute resolution mechanism may not achieve the goal of prospectively influencing stakeholder conduct.

[18] For a general discussion of the Ogoni case, see, e.g., G. Pentassuglia, 'Indigenous Groups and the Developing Jurisprudence of the African Commission on Human and People's Rights: Some Reflections', 3 *UCL Human Rights Review* (2010).

[19] See, e.g., *The Guardian*, 'Shell Pays Out $15.5m over Saro-Wiwa Killing', 9 June 2009, available at: www.theguardian.com/world/2009/jun/08/nigeria-usa.

[20] See, e.g., *Bloomberg*, 'Shell to Pay $83 Million Settlement for Nigeria Oil Spills', 6 January 2015, available at: www.bloomberg.com/news/articles/2015–01–07/shell-agrees-83-million-settlement-for-nigeria-bodo-oil-spills.

[21] In January 2013, for instance, four out of five claims against Shell arising out of spills in Nigeria were quashed by a Dutch court. See *The Guardian*, 'Shell Acquitted of Nigeria Pollution Charges', 30 January 2013, available at: www.theguardian.com/environment/2013/jan/30/shell-acquitted-nigeria-pollution-charges.

initial sum of US$ 1 billion for the first five years of operations.[22] Shell has voluntarily committed to cooperate in the implementation of the report's recommendations.

The implications of a host State entering into a settlement agreement with an investor have also arisen in the *Chevron* v. *Ecuador* arbitration, in the context of the host State's power to waive claims. A decision of the tribunal noted that Ecuador had in a 1995 agreement waived those *collective* or 'diffuse' rights conferred upon the affected group by virtue of a given article of the Ecuadorean Constitution, though this waiver remained without prejudice to *individual* claims arising from the same events.[23] If the State's waiver of 'diffuse' rights is indeed effective, a question arises as to whether this waiver also forecloses claims by collectives of individuals which find their legal basis in another source. These considerations lead to broader questions as to the definition of the viable claim or claims as well as the identification of the relevant right-holder.[24]

A conflict may be submitted to arbitration by virtue of an agreement as directly between a foreign investor and affected host State nationals, as between two or more disputing private parties.[25] In another step, and in order to reduce the danger of the investor's unrestricted liability across multiple fora, an escrow fund might be established to hold a settlement

---

[22] United Nations Environment Programme, *Environmental Assessment of Ogoniland* (2011), available at: http://postconflict.unep.ch/publications/OEA/UNEP_OEA.pdf.

[23] *Chevron Corporation and Texaco Petroleum Corporation* v. *The Republic of Ecuador*, PCA Case No. 2009–23, First Partial Award on Track I, 17 September 2013, para. 112(3).

[24] See Chapter 5. Difficulties thus arise where questions are posed as to the State's power to dispose over given rights. It would seem to be fundamental that in order for the State to dispose over a right, it must effectively be the right-holder, whether by origination (as under, for example, Article 19(2) of the Ecuadorean Constitution, leading to the possibility of claims by the host State under the Direct Claims (III) or *Qui Tam* Models) or by assignment or transfer (as under the Espousal or Hybrid Model). This proposition is not absolute. In known cases, the relevant right-holder's State of nationality has acted not to extinguish his claims outright, but to compel those claims to adjudication in an exclusive international forum. The relevant right-holder is thus able to initiate a claim in a court of competent jurisdiction *until such time* as the State forecloses its own courts from hearing the matter, without necessity of any transfer or assignment of any right to the State, and indeed without need of the right-holder's consent at all. Such action is naturally not immune from constitutional challenge. See notes 28, 29 *infra*. The extent (if any) of the State's power to dispose over given rights ultimately remains a question of the laws of the host State. This principle has been implicitly recognised by the *Chevron* tribunal. *Chevron Corporation and Texaco Petroleum Corporation* v. *The Republic of Ecuador*, PCA Case No. 2009–23, Decision on Track 1B, 12 March 2015, para. 186.

[25] See The Direct Claims (I) Model, Chapter 2.

payment against which claimants may recover via a claims process that forms the exclusive recourse of all claimants who do not expressly opt out of the mechanism. Though it did not arise in an investment context, perhaps the most successful settlement agreement of this type was reached in 1999 to bring an end to a class action lawsuit filed in US federal court against a number of Swiss banks. The plaintiffs had sought to recover assets held in accounts which had been dormant since the end of the Second World War. Under the settlement agreement, the action was dismissed and the banks agreed to create a US$ 1.25 billion settlement fund. A 'world-wide notification program was implemented ... to inform the potential beneficiaries of their eligibility to participate', and '[p]ursuant to a Plan of Allocation and Distribution that was proposed by a Special Master ... [a specially created claims resolution tribunal] decides claims to assets deposited with Swiss banks by victims or targets of Nazi persecution in accounts that were open or opened during the period 1933 to 1945'.[26]

Finally, although not immune to constitutional challenge,[27] certain mass claims processes offer precedent for the proposition

---

[26] H. M. Holtzmann and E. Kristjànsdòttir, *International Mass Claims Processes: Legal and Practical Perspectives* (2007) 26. In an instance that arises within the investment and environmental domains, a similar settlement agreement was successfully reached to bring an end to class action litigation following the 2010 oil spill which resulted from a well blowout at the site of the Deepwater Horizon drilling rig in the Gulf of Mexico. A comprehensive settlement agreement which provides for the establishment of a mass claims process to be funded by British Petroleum and includes a detailed definition of the class as well as various damages categories was approved by a federal judge on 21 December 2012. See *In re: Oil Spill by Oil Rig Deepwater Horizon in Gulf of Mexico, on April 20, 2010*, 910 F. Supp. 2d 891, E.D. La. (2012). In accordance with US procedural rules governing class action lawsuits, this mass claims process is not an exclusive one insofar as all putative class members were afforded an opportunity to opt out of the class at an early stage, and thereby to reserve all rights to proceed against British Petroleum in a court or other forum. Unlike in the case of the dormant Swiss accounts, in accepting this settlement agreement, the court emphasised the fact that the 'uncapped compensation' available via the claims process would 'ensure that a benefit paid to one member of the class will in no way reduce or interfere with a benefit obtained by another member'. Ibid. 918. Thus, a comprehensive settlement agreement was firmly in place within two and a half years of the initial pollution event, striking a contrast to the state of affairs in Ecuador, where the matter has been protracted for decades without conclusive resolution via a durable mechanism. For an innovative proposal that might have achieved a successful result, see B. Neuborne, 'A Plague on Both Their Houses: A Modest Proposal for Ending the Ecuadorean Rainforest Wars', 1 *Stanford Journal of Complex Litigation* 2 (2013).

[27] Under international law, a treaty obligation supersedes mere municipal law wherever they may conflict. See Art. 27 of the Vienna Convention on the Law of Treaties, 1155 UNTS 331, 8 ILM 679 (1969) ('[a] party may not invoke the provisions of its internal law as

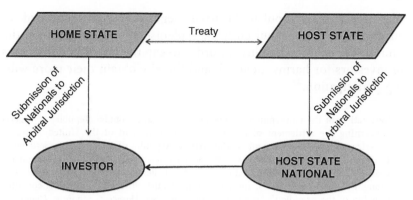

Figure 4.1   Exclusive Jurisdiction

that, by treaty instrument, two or more States may compel the exclusivity of an arbitral forum for the resolution of defined disputes;[28] see Figure 4.1. Further, where wished, the States party to

justification for its failure to perform a treaty'); see also M. E. Villiger, *Commentary on the 1969 Vienna Convention on the Law of* Treaties (2009) 375 ('[o]n the whole, it can be said that Article 27 amounts to codification of a long-standing principle of customary international law'). Nonetheless, consideration of the constitutional laws of the putative States party is advised.

[28] See Annex, Model 12 (Exclusivity of Remedy). The Iran-United States Claims Tribunal was established by and derives its jurisdiction from a Claims Settlement Declaration concerning the settlement of claims by the Government of the United States of America and the Government of the Islamic Republic of Iran. Article II of the Claims Settlement Declaration states as follows:

1. An international arbitral tribunal (the Iran-United States Claims Tribunal) is hereby established for the purpose of deciding claims of nationals of the United States against Iran and claims of nationals of Iran against the United States, and any counterclaim which arises out of the same contract, transaction or occurrence that constitutes the subject matter of that national's claim, if such claims and counterclaims are outstanding on the date of this Agreement, whether or not filed with any court, and arise out of debts, contracts (including transactions which are the subject of letters of credit or bank guarantees), expropriations or other measures affecting property rights, excluding claims described in Paragraph 11 of the Declaration of the Government of Algeria of 19 January, 1981, and claims arising out of the actions of the United States in response to the conduct described in such paragraph, and excluding claims arising under a binding contract between the parties specifically providing that any disputes thereunder shall be within the sole jurisdiction of the competent Iranian courts, in response to the Majlis position.

2. The Tribunal shall also have jurisdiction over official claims of the United States and Iran against each other arising out of contractual arrangements between them for the purchase and sale of goods and services.

that treaty may stipulate 'a fixed negotiated sum deposited in advance that is not required to be replenished and is, therefore, the limit of the debtor's liability' in order to cap the financial obligations of investors for harms incurred, and thereby obtain their more willing participation.[29]

> Declaration of the Government of the Democratic and Popular Republic of Algeria concerning the settlement of claims by the Government of the United States of America and the Government of the Islamic Republic of Iran (Claims Settlement Declaration), 19 January 1981, available at: www.iusct.net/General%20Documents/2-Claims%20Settlement%20Declaration.pdf. A challenge to the Declaration was brought in the United States, and its Supreme Court ultimately upheld the constitutionality of the president's 'executive agreement'. See *Dames & Moore* v. *Donald T. Regan, Secretary of the Treasury, et al.*, 453 U.S. 654 (1981) 657, 679 ('[t]he United States has repeatedly exercised its sovereign authority to settle the claims of its nationals against foreign countries ... Although those settlements have sometimes been made by treaty, there has also been a longstanding practice of settling such claims by executive agreement without the advice and consent of the Senate, and this practice continues at the present time'). Under an exclusivity model, in a marked difference from the fork-in-the-road or waiver provision, the claimant is not afforded a choice of forum. See Chapter 2, notes 208, 209.

[29] H. M. Holtzmann and E. Kristjànsdòttir, *International Mass Claims Processes: Legal and Practical Perspectives* (2007) 132. See also Art. 2(1) of the Agreement between the Government of the United States of America and the Government of the Federal Republic of Germany concerning the Foundation 'Remembrance, Responsibility and the Future':

>> The United States shall, in all cases in which the United States is notified that a claim [against German companies arising from the National Socialist era and World War II] has been asserted in a court in the United States, inform its courts through a Statement of Interest, in accordance with Annex B [entitled Elements of U.S. Government Statement of Interest], and, consistent therewith, as it otherwise considers appropriate, that it would be in the foreign policy interests of the United States for the Foundation to be the exclusive remedy and forum for resolving such claims asserted against German companies ... and that dismissal of such cases would be in its foreign policy interest.

> Agreement between the Government of the United States of America and the Government of the Federal Republic of Germany concerning the Foundation 'Remembrance, Responsibility and the Future', signed 17 July 2000 (entered into force 19 October 2000), 2130 UNTS 249. Challenges to the Agreement were brought in the United States and Germany. In the United States, the Supreme Court ultimately found a state insurance commissioner to be pre-empted from establishing a parallel claims mechanism by the clearly intended exclusivity of the Foundation. See *American Insurance Association et al.* v. *Garamendi, Insurance Commissioner, State of California*, 539 U.S. 396 (2003) 422–423 ('[t]he approach taken serves to resolve the several competing matters of national concern apparent in the German Foundation Agreement: the national interest in maintaining amicable relationships with current European allies; survivors' interests in a "fair and prompt" but non-adversarial resolution of their claims

In a final version of this option, it may be possible to submit invest-ment disputes or conflicts to adjudication at the Permanent Court of Arbitration in a manner that both caps the liability of the foreign investor and compels the exclusivity of the forum via the Convention for the Pacific Settlement of International Disputes of 1907. Article 81 of that instrument states that awards issued within the scope of the Convention 'settle[] the dispute definitively and without appeal'.[30] In lieu of crafting an entirely new treaty or modifying an existing one – either of which may be subject to parliamentary ratification processes in given States – two or more States party to the Convention may, by executive act, conclude a *compromis* by which they submit a given dispute to arbitration, and establish a fund for this purpose.[31]

---

so as to "bring some measure of justice . . . in their lifetimes"; and the companies' interest in securing "legal peace" when they settle claims in this fashion'); see also ibid. 421 ('[t]he foregoing account of negotiations toward the three settlement agreements is enough to illustrate that the consistent Presidential foreign policy has been to encourage European governments and companies to volunteer settlement funds in preference to litigation or coercive sanctions'). A constitutional challenge was similarly rejected by Germany's Federal Constitutional Court. See BVerfG, Order of the First Senate of 7 December 2004 – 1 BvR 1804/03, para. 52 ('[i]n legislating on property rights pursuant to Article 14.1, sentence 2 of the Basic Law and enacting the (challenged) provisions of the Foundation Act, the legislature has achieved an overall settlement whose objective it is to deal with conflicting interests fairly. This is not constitutionally objectionable') and para. 64 ('[t]he purposes of the Foundation Act are according to § 2.1 on the one hand "to make financial compensation available to former forced labourers and to those affected by other injustices from the National Socialist period" and according to the Preamble on the other hand "to provide adequate legal certainty for German enterprises and the Federal Republic of Germany in particular in the United States of America". Neither of these goals is constitutionally objectionable').

[30] Art. 81 of the Convention for the Pacific Settlement of International Disputes of 1907.

[31] See Arts. 46 and 52 of the Convention for the Pacific Settlement of International Disputes of 1907. The Permanent Court of Arbitration has accumulated significant institutional experience in the administration of mass claims processes during the course of the Eritrea-Ethiopia Claims Commission, amongst others. For an in-depth view into the operation of the Eritrea-Ethiopia War and Claims Commission, see S. D. Murphy, W. Kidane, and T. Snider, *Litigating War: Mass Civil Injury and the Eritrea-Ethiopia Claims Commission* (2013). Further, the Permanent Court of Arbitration has formed a Steering Committee on International Mass Claims to further pursue the development of this particular institutional capacity. It is noted that such executive acts are governed by the internal laws of the relevant States, and are subject to diverse constitutional laws.

5

Jurisdiction *Ratione Materiae*:
The Substantive Rights

Despite the focus of this volume, the imbalanced and unidirectional nature of the current system of international investment law is not purely a procedural matter. The current generation of international investment instruments focuses almost exclusively upon the obligations of host States vis-à-vis foreign investors, leaving a vacuum of substantive obligations of the investor. Even where the obligations of investors towards the host State or other stakeholders are addressed in some manner, such obligations are rarely made directly binding and enforceable. As Judge Crawford has famously observed, 'the treaty commitments of the host state towards the investor are unilateral, and ... the agreement to arbitrate, though it incorporates by reference the jurisdictional requirements of the [bilateral investment treaty], does not incorporate its substantive provisions nor does it make them applicable bilaterally.'[1]

As explored in earlier chapters, the moral and practical arguments in favour of bilateral obligations not only owed *to* but also *by* foreign investors are clear, but the legal means to achieve this are wanting. Restrictions imposed by the *rationae materiae* scope of jurisdictional clauses, as well as by the specific wording of applicable law provisions, may be overcome in some cases through more sophisticated approaches to treaty interpretation[2] or the re-conceptualisation of certain investment law standards.[3] However, this may not always be enough. As the ILC has

---

[1] J. Crawford, 'Treaty and Contract in Investment Arbitration', 24 *Arbitration International* 3 (2008) 363.

[2] See, e.g., V. Prislan, 'Non-investment Obligations in Investment Treaty Arbitration: Towards a Greater Role for States?', in F. Baetens (ed.), *Investment Law Within International Law: Integrationist Perspectives* (2013).

[3] See, e.g., F. Francioni, 'Access to Justice, Denial of Justice and International Investment Law', 20 *European Journal of International Law* 3 (2009) 739 ('[o]ne could argue that a progressive interpretation of the "fair and equitable standard", which has been systematically adopted in [bilateral investment treaty] practice and in regional agreements such as NAFTA, entails that the investor who seeks equity for the protection of his investment must also be accountable, under principles of equity and fairness, to the host state's

noted, '[n]ormative conflicts do not arise as "technical mistakes" that could be "avoided" by a more sophisticated way of legal reasoning. New rules and legal regimes emerge as responses to new preferences, and sometimes out of conscious effort to deviate from preferences as they existed under old regimes. They require a legislative, not a legal-technical response.'[4] An attempt to provide effective recourse to affected host State nationals may thus require adjustments to the substantive law – or at least to the definition thereof – which is to be applied by international investment tribunals. Beyond their procedural components, this is the further challenge that the models set forth in this volume seek to meet.

Choice of Law as the Starting Point

While the aforementioned challenge should not be minimised, a distinct advantage of the present proposal is its versatility. In principle, all it does is to place the institution of international arbitration at the disposal of host States and host State nationals for the resolution of disputes that may arise with foreign investors, and to do so in situations where those same foreign investors (or their home States on their behalf) share the same interest in creating a centralised, neutral, and effective forum for the resolution of such disputes. Indeed, the silver lining to the challenges proposed by the largely consent-based models developed herein is the emphasis upon party autonomy, which renders the uses of the present models potentially limitless.

None of the sets of arbitral rules envisaged for use with the models imposes any significant limits upon the choice of applicable law in a given case. In particular, the ICSID Convention provides as follows:

> The Tribunal shall decide a dispute in accordance with such rules of law as may be agreed by the parties. In the absence of such agreement, the Tribunal shall apply the law of the Contracting State party to the dispute (including its rules on the conflict of laws) and such rules of international law as may be applicable.[5]

---

population affected by the investment. It is hard to conceive of equity as a one-sided concept: equity always requires fair and equitable balancing of competing interests, in this case the interests of the investor and the interest of individuals and social groups who seek judicial protection against possible adverse impacts of the investment on their life or their environment').

[4] International Law Commission, *Conclusions of the Work of the Study Group on the Fragmentation of International Law: Difficulties Arising from the Diversification and Expansion of International Law* (2006), para. 484.

[5] Art. 42(1) of the ICSID Convention.

As is readily apparent from its text, this provision 'grant[s] maximum autonomy' in the choice of applicable law,[6] and even the default choice of law – including both the host State's law and international law – should not exclude any of the sources envisaged. The UNCITRAL Arbitration Rules provide similarly, where

> [t]he arbitral tribunal shall apply the rules of law designated by the parties as applicable to the substance of the dispute. Failing such designation by the parties, the arbitral tribunal shall apply the law which it determines to be appropriate.[7]

As in the ICSID Rules, this again expresses the 'overriding principle of party autonomy in choosing the applicable rules of law'.[8] The PCA Environmental Rules are nearly identical to the UNCITRAL Arbitration Rules in this respect.[9] Meanwhile, the PCA Arbitration Rules 2012 contain a somewhat more complex choice of law provision, which applies different laws depending upon the identity of the parties to the arbitration.[10] For the purposes of arbitrations between private parties or mixed arbitrations

---

[6] C. Schreuer, L. Malintoppi, A. Reinisch, and A. Sinclair, *The ICSID Convention: A Commentary*, 2nd edn. (2009) 550.

[7] Art. 35(1) of the UNCITRAL Arbitration Rules (as revised in 2010).

[8] D. Caron and L. Caplan, *The UNCITRAL Arbitration Rules: A Commentary*, 2nd edn. (2013) 111. See also *Report of the Sectary-General on the Revised Draft Set of Arbitration Rules*, UNCITRAL, 9th Session, Addendum 1 (Commentary), UN Doc. A/CN.9/112/Add.1 (1975).

[9] Article 33(1) of the PCA Environmental Rules provides as follows:

> In resolving the dispute, the arbitral tribunal shall apply the law or rules of law designated by the parties as applicable to the substance of the dispute. Failing such designation by the parties, the arbitral tribunal shall apply the national and/or international law and rules of law it determines to be appropriate.

To the extent of the differences vis-à-vis the UNCITRAL Arbitration Rules underlined previously, the PCA Environmental Rules ensure even greater flexibility on account of the particular circumstances of environmental disputes. See D. Ratliff, 'The PCA Optional Rules for Arbitration of Disputes Relating to Natural Resources and/or the Environment', 14 *Leiden Journal of International Law* 4 (2001) 894:

> Article 33(1), requires the tribunal to apply 'the law or rules of law designated by the parties as applicable to the substance of the dispute'. Further, failing such designation by the parties, the tribunal shall apply 'the national and/or international law and rules of law it determines to be appropriate'. This is an especially important innovation considering that in international environmental law, issues often arise in a national context and become transnational at a later stage. Thus, the arbitrators are given the broadest possible scope in determining the applicable law.

[10] The purpose of the provision is to preserve the application of the proper sources of international law in cases between States (per Article 38 of the ICJ Statute) and cases

between a State and a private party, they are identical to the UNCITRAL Arbitration Rules.[11]

In all cases, these arbitration rules allow recourse to 'rules of law', rather than imposing any obligation upon parties or a tribunal to identify a particular system of law which must be deemed applicable in its entirety, and to the exclusion of other sources of law.[12] This is important in enabling the models set forth in this volume, since it allows for the application of a-national law which does not form part of any defined legal system or which does not give rise to obligations except by agreement.[13] Even more fundamentally, the flexibility to designate 'rules of law' permits parties to freely select from the menu below: they hold total discretion as to which substantive obligations they wish to subject to the present mechanism. They may 'choose certain pieces of legislation from a particular legal system'[14] or even 'designate as applicable to their case rules of more than one legal system, including rules of law which have been elaborated on the

---

involving intergovernmental organisations (per Article 33 of the PCA State/International Organization Rules 1996 and Article 33 of the PCA International Organization/Private Party Rules 1996). B. Daly, E. Goriatcheva, and H. Meighen, *A Guide to the PCA Arbitration Rules* (2014) 138. In respect of cases involving intergovernmental organisations, see also Art. 5 of the Vienna Convention on the Law of Treaties, 1155 UNTS 331, 8 ILM 679 (1969), as well as the Vienna Convention on the Law of Treaties between States and International Organizations or between International Organizations, 25 ILM 543 (1986).

[11] Article 35(1) of the PCA Arbitration Rules 2012 provides as follows:

> The arbitral tribunal shall apply the rules of law designated by the parties as applicable to the substance of the dispute. Failing such designation by the parties, the arbitral tribunal shall: ... (d) In all other cases, apply the law which it determines to be appropriate. In such cases, the arbitral tribunal shall decide in accordance with the terms of the agreement and shall take into account relevant trade usages.

[12] C. Schreuer, L. Malintoppi, A. Reinisch, and A. Sinclair, *The ICSID Convention: A Commentary*, 2nd edn. (2009) 563; D. Caron and L. Caplan, *The UNCITRAL Arbitration Rules: A Commentary*, 2nd edn. (2013) 114; D. Ratliff, 'The PCA Optional Rules for Arbitration of Disputes Relating to Natural Resources and/or the Environment', 14 *Leiden Journal of International Law* 4 (2001) 894; B. Daly, E. Goriatcheva, and H. Meighen, *A Guide to the PCA Arbitration Rules* (2014) 136.

[13] This is often analysed in the context of choosing to apply 'general principles', the *lex mercatoria*, or transnational instruments such as the UNIDROIT Principles of International Commercial Contracts, Art. 1.6(2) UNIDROIT Principles (2010). D. Caron and L. Caplan, *The UNCITRAL Arbitration Rules: A Commentary*, 2nd edn. (2013) 114–116; B. Daly, E. Goriatcheva, and H. Meighen, *A Guide to the PCA Arbitration Rules* (2014) 136.

[14] C. Schreuer, L. Malintoppi, A. Reinisch, and A. Sinclair, *The ICSID Convention: A Commentary*, 2nd edn. (2009) 563.

international level'.[15] Indeed, international investment law has already been described as summoning the image of a 'mosaic of applicable laws'.[16]

Given no limit on choice of law under any of the relevant arbitration frameworks, the only limits which might attach in this respect would arise from external sources. In particular, it may be that under certain national laws particular subject matters are 'not capable of settlement by arbitration', rendering invalid both the arbitration agreement and any resulting arbitral award.[17] Such usually does not, however, pose a problem in the context of foreign investment activities. Where the State is directly involved in the conclusion of the arbitration agreement, such questions do not often arise, and the State may be precluded from relying upon a violation of its own law.[18] In addition, where the arbitration agreement is contained in or arises out of a treaty instrument, that arbitration agreement will be governed in principle by international law, where the rule of preclusion is even clearer.[19]

Moreover, international law generally does not contain any analogous rules restricting the scope of disputes *ratione materiae* which may be

---

[15] UNCITRAL Working Group II, *Settlement of Commercial Disputes: Revision of the UNCITRAL Arbitration Rules*, 45th Session, UN Doc. A/CN.9/WG.II/WP.143/Add.1 (2006), para. 30, citing UNCITRAL, *Analytical Commentary on Draft Text of a Model Law on International Commercial Arbitration*, 18th Session, UN Doc. A/CN.9/264 (1985) 61–62. In regard to Article 42(3) of the ICSID Convention, Professor Schreuer notes that the parties' choice of law 'may extend beyond legal rules *stricto sensu* to principles of equitable justice'. C. Schreuer, L. Malintoppi, A. Reinisch, and A. Sinclair, *The ICSID Convention: A Commentary*, 2nd edn. (2009) 554. Further, Professor Schreuer has written that the parties are even 'free to declare applicable the rules of a treaty that is not in force or of a non-binding code of conduct such as the World Bank's 1992 Guidelines on the Treatment of Foreign Direct Investment ... The 1992 Guidelines may be seen as a suitable blueprint for a set of "rules of law" to be agreed by the parties under Art. 42(1)'. Ibid. 564. See also A. Broches, 'Convention on Settlement of Investment Disputes between States and Nationals of Other States of 1965, Explanatory Notes and Survey of its Application', 18 *Yearbook Commercial Arbitration* (1993) and M. Hirsch, 'The Arbitration Mechanism of the International Centre for the Settlement of Investment Disputes', 10 *Arbitration International* 2 (1994).

[16] Z. Douglas, *The International Law of Investment Claims* (2009) 40.

[17] See Arts. II(1) and V(2)(a) of the New York Convention and Art. 34(2)(b)(i) of the UNCITRAL Model Law on International Commercial Arbitration of 1985 (as amended in 2006).

[18] J. Paulsson, 'May a State Invoke its Internal Law to Repudiate Consent to International Commercial Arbitration?: Reflections on the *Benteler* v. *Belgium* Preliminary Award', 2 *Arbitration International* 2 (1986).

[19] See Arts. 27 and 46 of the Vienna Convention on the Law of Treaties, 1155 UNTS 331, 8 ILM 679 (1969).

submitted to arbitration.[20] In fact, despite the many varied and sensitive subject matters that are dealt with in investor-State arbitration, there is no known instance where it has been sought to set aside or challenge the enforcement of an investor-State award on the basis of the non-arbitrability of the underlying subject matter.

It is nevertheless likely that certain subject matters may remain beyond the reach of even the most liberal users of these mechanisms. The evaluation of the legality of certain purely criminal behaviour and certain exercises of police powers will, for example, surely remain the exclusive purview of the State apparatus, and thus beyond the reach of the present mechanism, even if it is recognised that its use may serve to grant greater recourse to victims of such criminality. However, such restrictions are more likely to be the product of conscious policy choices by the actors involved – in their autonomy not to consent to the arbitration of such disputes – rather than any external prohibition.

General Considerations Favouring a Broad Substantive Scope

As a result of this largely unconstrained party autonomy, the application of the present mechanism could easily span the entirety of national laws of extra-contractual obligations, human rights, indigenous rights, environmental law, and labour protections. It could also capture other forms of improper conduct by foreign investors, as well as other significant

[20] Under general international law, even disputes regarding peremptory norms (*jus cogens*) may be submitted to any of the means of pacific settlement of disputes set forth in Article 33(1) of the United Nations Charter. See, e.g., *Armed Activities on the Territory of the Congo* (New Application: 2002) (Democratic Republic of the Congo v. Rwanda), Jurisdiction and Admissibility, 3 February 2006, 2006 ICJ Reports 6, para. 125; see also J. Crawford, 'Chance, Order, Change: The Course of International Law, General Course on Public International Law', 365 *Hague Recueil des Cours* 9 (2013), para. 333 ('[t]he majority of the Court affirmed that the mere fact that obligations erga omnes or peremptory norms are at issue "cannot in itself constitute an exception to the principle that its jurisdiction always depends on the consent of the parties"'). Restrictions on the submission of disputes to arbitration may arise from States' other treaty obligations (see, e.g., *MOX Plant Case* (Ireland v. United Kingdom), PCA Case No. 2002-01, Procedural Order No. 3, 24 June 2003, 126 ILR 310, 42 ILM 1187, paras. 20–22) or from prohibitions on the adjudication of third party rights and obligations (see, e.g., *Larsen v. Hawaiian Kingdom*, PCA Case No. 1999-01, Award, 5 February 2001, paras. 12.6–12.19), but not general international law. Highly sensitive questions such as the violation of the prohibition on the use of force under Article 2(4) of the United Nations Charter (and the *jus ad bellum*) have been validly submitted to arbitration. See *Eritrea-Ethiopia Claims Commission*, PCA Case No. 2001-02, Partial Award, *Jus Ad Bellum*, Ethiopia's Claims 1–8, 19 December 2005, 2006 ILM 430.

areas of public and private law where the conduct of an investor is scrutinised for its impact upon local populations.[21]

The limitless possibilities which may be contemplated nevertheless come with a corresponding challenge: how to limit – or at least define – the substantive scope of disputes which may be submitted to arbitration in accordance with any of the models. The question that thus presents itself is *what substantive rights* would be in the interests of States, host State nationals, investors, and other stakeholders to adjudicate under these mechanisms. A simple answer might be that the greatest substantive scope of application is desirable. After all, the peaceful resolution of disputes is a salutary end unto itself, and there is every reason for States to grant their nationals the largest possible scope for effective recourse and redress in their disputes with foreign investors. The history of international investment law reflects the progressive evolution of this ideal away from an exclusively inter-State sphere. Gunboat diplomacy gave way in the early twentieth century to claims in diplomatic protection,[22] which later gave way to mixed arbitration involving direct claims by private parties against States[23] and eventually to the modern legal and institutional framework governing investor-State relations.[24] The dominant feature of this trend has been States' desire to afford an effective forum for the resolution of disputes between States and foreign investors, while progressively depoliticising and removing disputes from the

[21] To the extent that it would see such broad application, the resulting instrument may prove akin to a 'bilateral arbitration treaty' that operates as a default mechanism to submit a large class of disputes arising between the nationals of contracting States to international arbitration, where the disputants do not specify another *modus* of dispute settlement. See G. Born, *BITs, BATs, and Buts: Reflections on International Dispute Resolution* (2014), available at: www.wilmerhale.com/uploadedFiles/Shared_Content/Editorial/News/Documents/BITs-BATs-and-Buts.pdf.

[22] Convention on the Limitation of the Employment of Force for the Recovery of Contract Debts (Hague Convention II of 1907), signed 18 October 1907 (entered into force 26 January 1910), 36 Stat 2241, 1 Bevans 607; W. Benedek, 'Drago-Porter Convention (1907)', *Max Planck Encyclopedia of Public International Law* (2007). The Drago-Porter Convention was a response to the decision authorising the use of force in order to obtain compensation for pecuniary injury to nationals which was made by the arbitral tribunal in the case of *Preferential Treatment of Claims of Blockading Powers against Venezuela* (Germany, Great Britain, and Italy v. Venezuela), Permanent Court of Arbitration, Award, 22 February 1904, IX UNRIAA 99.

[23] For the first mixed arbitration, administered by the Permanent Court of Arbitration, see *Radio Corporation of America* v. *The National Government of the Republic of China*, PCA Case No. 1934–01, Award, 13 April 1935 (1935) 3 UNRIAA 1621, 8 ILR 26, (1936) 30 AJIL 535.

[24] The institutional structure of ICSID and its first set of arbitration rules were in fact modelled upon the Permanent Court of Arbitration and its 1962 rules for arbitration of mixed disputes. A. R. Parra, *The History of ICSID* (2012) 16.

sphere of inter-State relations.[25] While the investment promotion objective of the current system has been questioned,[26] as have the conventional explanations for the proliferation of investment treaties,[27] the rationale of de-politicisation remains. The de-politicisation of disputes between foreign investors and host State nationals, by reducing the role of the host State as an unnecessary intermediary, would thus seem a logical further extension of this trend.[28] Indeed, a principal *raison d'être* of the models is as a means to resolve those impasses often created by social conflict surrounding specific investment projects.

A suggested broad scope of application may encounter resistance in view of States' general reticence towards unconstrained jurisdiction, as well as from those who recall trite statements from the jurisprudence to the effect that the scope of jurisdiction created under investment instruments is always carefully negotiated and circumscribed.[29] However, the reasons for affording only limited jurisdiction over host States do not necessarily apply to jurisdiction created in favour of host State nationals. States' reticence to accept jurisdiction over a larger class of disputes is intimately linked to the substantive obligations created by investment treaties. Host States generally seek to extend the advantages of

---

[25] See André von Walter, 'Le contentieux à l'investissement: entre dépolitisation et repolitisation', in *L'arbitrage relatif aux investissements: nouvelles dynamiques internationales*, 4 March 2011, available at: http://convention-s.fr/wp-content/uploads/2015/07/CNV_journ%C3%A9e04032011_-arbitrage_dossier.pdf; I. F. I. Shihata, 'Towards a Greater Depoliticization of Investment Disputes: The Roles of ICSID and MIGA', 1 *ICSID Review* 1 (1986); M. Doe Rodríguez and J. L. Aragón Cardiel, 'Cause and Coincidence: The Renaissance of the Permanent Court of Arbitration in Latin America in the Field of Foreign Investment', in A. Tanzi, A. Asteriti, R. Polanco Lazo, and P. Tuirini, *International Investment Law in Latin America* (2016).

[26] See, e.g., S. D. Franck, 'Foreign Direct Investment, Investment Treaty Arbitration and the Rule of Law', 19 *McGeorge Global Business and Development Law Journal* (2007).

[27] See generally L. S. Poulsen, *Bounded Rationality and Economic Diplomacy: The Politics of Investment Treaties in Developing Countries* (2015) and L. S. Poulsen, 'Diplomats Want Treaties: Diplomatic Agendas and Perks in the Investment Regime', 7 *Journal of International Dispute Settlement* 1 (2016). See also *Wintershall Aktiengesellschaft* v. *Argentine Republic*, ICSID Case No. ARB/04/14, Award, 8 December 2008, para. 85 (quoting comments by Professor Christoph Schreuer in his cross-examination as an expert witness).

[28] See Direct Claims (I) Model, Chapter 2.

[29] See, e.g., *Plama Consortium Limited* v. *Republic of Bulgaria*, ICSID Case No. ARB/03/24, Decision on Jurisdiction, 8 February 2005, paras. 207–209; see also J. Kurtz, 'Building Legitimacy through Interpretation in Investor-State Arbitration: On Consistency, Coherence, and the Identification of Applicable Law', in Z. Douglas, J. Pauwelyn, and J. E. Viñuales (eds.), *The Foundations of International Investment Law: Bringing Theory into Practice* (2014) 274.

investment protection only in circumstances where associated economic and social policy objectives are met. A number of restrictions on the *ratione personae, ratione materiae,* and *ratione temporis* application of the investment instrument or its dispute settlement clause are used to ensure this result. To the extent that the analogy applies to users of the present mechanism – where additional rights and obligations are created for investors, host States, or host State nationals – there may be sound reasons to limit who may claim, and on what grounds.

On the other hand, where use of the present mechanisms would only serve to offer an additional forum for existing disputes, or recourse to vindicate existing rights, the reasons for imposing constraints do not exist. In fact, one may presume that many States would wish generally to expand their nationals' access to recourse for existing rights, and to promote avenues for the effective resolution of existing disputes. The case for a broad substantive scope of application is stronger still in areas where access to recourse is currently missing or has proven ineffective.

The Uncertain Status of Host State Counterclaims

One of the major lacunae of the current investment treaty arbitration régime is that an investor's conduct is at best only taken into account in relation to excluding or reducing compensation (or jurisdiction or admissibility with respect to claims for compensation). This situation has been described as unsatisfactory for a number of reasons. In particular, this system is prone to producing an 'all-or-nothing' approach, which requires a decision-maker to assign priority as between the rights of the investor and the rights of the host State and its nationals, and give effect to only one right over another.[30] One of the major suggested means to overcome this deficiency is through counterclaims brought against an investor by the host State.

However, three major impediments undermine the effectiveness of host State counterclaims. First, the jurisdiction of an investor-State tribunal to entertain counterclaims by the host State is uncertain. Depending upon vicissitudes of the wording of the relevant dispute

---

[30] See *Spyridon Roussalis* v. *Romania*, ICSID Case No. ARB/06/1, Declaration of Michael Reisman, 28 November 2011, Chapter 1, Note 32. Similar dynamics have also been the object of criticism by Professor Bernardo Cremades in the context of the adjudication of claims of corruption and other serious illegality. See *Fraport AG Frankfurt Airport Services Worldwide* v. *The Republic of the Philippines*, ICSID Case No. ARB/03/25, Dissenting Opinion of Mr. Bernardo M. Cremades, 19 July 2007.

settlement clause, such claims may fall within the tribunal's jurisdiction[31] or be wholly excluded,[32] especially where the amount of the counterclaim exceeds the amount of compensation claimed by the investor. Moreover, even where a broadly worded dispute settlement clause encompasses counterclaims in a general manner, it may not countenance claims for the alleged breach of obligations other than those enumerated in the investment treaty. In addition, in ICSID cases, the terms of Article 25 of the ICSID Convention may pose a further obstacle.[33]

Second, even if a host State counterclaim falls within the jurisdiction of the tribunal, the State may not enjoy standing to bring a claim where the rights in question are not vested in the State itself. For example, the State (or the investor) may not be privy to the agreement that is alleged to have been breached by the investor,[34] or the State may not (in the absence of an applicable *parens patriae* doctrine) be the relevant right-holder under the applicable law.[35] Such will necessarily exclude a further significant proportion of potential counterclaims.

Finally, most tribunals require a close connection to exist as between the counterclaim and the primary claim. However, the strictness with

---

[31] See *Saluka Investments B.V.* v. *The Czech Republic*, PCA Case No. 2001–04, UNCITRAL, Decision on Jurisdiction over the Czech Republic's Counterclaim, 7 May 2004, paras. 38–39; *Sempra Energy International* v. *Argentine Republic*, ICSID Case No. ARB/02/16, Award, 28 September 2007, para. 289; *Sergei Paushok, CJSC Golden East Company and CJSC Vostokneftegaz Company* v. *Government of Mongolia*, UNCITRAL, Award on Jurisdiction and Liability, 28 April 2011, para. 689; *Inmaris Perestroika Sailing Maritime Services GmbH and Others* v. *Ukraine*, ICSID Case No. ARB/08/8, Award, 1 March 2012; *Hesham Talaat M. Al-Warraq* v. *The Republic of Indonesia*, UNCITRAL, Final Award, 15 December 2014, para. 660; and *Urbaser S.A. and Consorcio de Aguas Bilbao Biskaia Ur Partzuergoa* v. *Argentine Republic*, ICISD Case No. ARB/07/26, Award, 8 December 2016, para. 1143.

[32] See *Limited Liability Company Amto* v. *Ukraine*, SCC Arbitration No. 080/2005, Final Award, 26 March 2008, para. 118; *Spyridon Roussalis* v. *Romania*, ICSID Case No. ARB/06/1, Award, 7 December 2011, para. 869; *Vestey Group Ltd* v. *Bolivarian Republic of Venezuela*, ICSID Case No. ARB/06/4, Award, 15 April 2016; and *Rusoro Mining Ltd.* V. *Bolivarian Republic of Venezuela*, ICSID Case No. ARB(AF)/12/5, Award, 22 August 2016.

[33] See The Four Models and the International Centre for Settlement of Investment Disputes, Chapter 2.

[34] See *Saluka Investments B.V.* v. *The Czech Republic*, PCA Case No. 2001–04, UNCITRAL, Decision on Jurisdiction over the Czech Republic's Counterclaim, 7 May 2004, paras. 44, 49–50; *Gustav F W Hamester GmbH & Co KG* v. *Republic of Ghana*, ICSID Case No. ARB/07/24, Award, 18 June 2010, para. 356; and *Hesham Talaat M. Al-Warraq* v. *The Republic of Indonesia*, UNCITRAL, Final Award, 15 December 2014.

[35] See *Genin* v. *Estonia*, ICSID Case No. ARB/99/2, Award, 25 June 2001, 94 n 101 and *Limited Liability Company Amto* v. *Ukraine*, SCC Arbitration No. 080/2005, Final Award, 26 March 2008, para. 118.

which this requirement is applied may vary considerably.[36] As a result, only a few host State counterclaims have been assessed on their merits, and often on the assumption (without actually deciding) that the counterclaim is within the tribunal's competence to consider.[37]

Counterclaims are in any event limited in their usefulness. They are by definition *ex post facto* remedies whereby affected parties may only obtain redress if the host State halts the investment activity, and thus the harming conduct. No redress is offered unless and until the investor brings a claim (and even then, a successful counterclaim only provides redress to any host State national indirectly through the host State). To suggest counterclaims as a generalised tool would invite host States to seek conflict with investors.

Nevertheless, there are recent cases in which investors have chosen to consent to counterclaims brought by the host State.[38] These cases provide an empirical basis to believe that investors may see fit to accept the use of the present models.

Promoting Access to Recourse

As seen, truly effective recourse is lacking, both as a matter of substance and procedure. From the perspective of host States and their nationals,

---

[36] See *Saluka Investments B.V.* v. *The Czech Republic*, PCA Case No. 2001–04, UNCITRAL, Decision on Jurisdiction over the Czech Republic's Counterclaim, 7 May 2004, para. 62; *Sergei Paushok, CJSC Golden East Company and CJSC Vostokneftegaz Company* v. *Government of Mongolia*, UNCITRAL, Award on Jurisdiction and Liability, 28 April 2011, paras. 693–694; *Hesham Talaat M. Al-Warraq* v. *The Republic of Indonesia*, UNCITRAL, Final Award, 15 December 2014, para. 667; and *Oxus Gold plc* v. *Republic of Uzbekistan, the State Committee of Uzbekistan for Geology & Mineral Resources, and Navoi Mining & Metallurgical Kombinat*, UNCITRAL, Award, 17 December 2015.

[37] See, e.g., *Genin* v. *Estonia*, ICSID Case No. ARB/99/2, Award, 25 June 2001, para. 376. See also *Mr. Patrick Mitchell* v. *Democratic Republic of the Congo*, ICSID Case No. ARB/99/7, Award, 9 February 2004; *Desert Line Projects LLC* v. *The Republic of Yemen*, ICSID Case No. ARB/05/17, Award, 6 February 2008; and *Inmaris Perestroika Sailing Maritime Services GmbH and Others* v. *Ukraine*, ICSID Case No. ARB/08/8, Award, 1 March 2012. In the case of *Urbaser S.A. and others* v. *Argentine Republic*, the tribunal expressly considered and accepted jurisdiction over the host State's counterclaim, only to dismiss it on its merits. See *Urbaser S.A. and Consorcio de Aguas Bilbao Bizkaia, Bilbao Biskaia Ur Partzuergoa* v. *The Argentine Republic*, ICISD Case No. ARB/07/26, Award, 8 December 2016, paras. 1110–1221.

[38] See, e.g., *Perenco Ecuador Ltd.* v. *The Republic of Ecuador et al.*, ICSID Case No. ARB/08/6, Interim Decision on the Environmental Counterclaim, 11 August 2015; see also *Burlington Resources Inc.* v. *Republic of Ecuador*, ICSID Case No. ARB/08/5, Decision on Counterclaims, 7 February 2017, paras. 60–62.

this is what the present mechanism seeks to address. This is a principal concern in the area of multinational business activities. The Third Pillar of Professor John Ruggie's 'Protect, Respect, and Remedy Framework' adopted by the UNHRC holds that, in addition to States' obligations to protect against infringements of human rights and business enterprises' responsibility to respect human rights, all actors have a responsibility to ensure that victims of business-related human rights abuses are able to access effective remedies, judicial and non-judicial.[39]

The UNGP, subsequently elaborated by Professor Ruggie, further develop and 'operationalise' this idea.[40] For instance, Principle 25 provides the following as a 'foundational principle':

> As part of their duty to protect against business-related human rights abuse, States must take appropriate steps to ensure, through judicial, administrative, legislative or other appropriate means, that when such abuses occur within their territory and/or jurisdiction those affected have access to effective remedy.[41]

The corollary for investors is found in Principle 22:

> Where business enterprises identify that they have caused or contributed to adverse impacts, they should provide for or cooperate in their remediation through legitimate processes.[42]

Principle 28 then seeks to leverage non-State-based grievance mechanisms, including 'those administered by a business enterprise alone or with stakeholders, by an industry association or a multi-stakeholder group', as well as 'regional and international human rights bodies', as a means for both States and enterprises to satisfy their respective responsibilities and facilitate access to effective

---

[39] UNHRC Res. A/HRC/RES/8/7, passed on 18 June 2008, available at: http://ap.ohchr.org/documents/E/HRC/resolutions/A_HRC_RES_8_7.pdf. The full text of the Framework is available at: www.reports-and-materials.org/sites/default/files/reports-and-materials/Ruggie-report-7-Apr-2008.pdf.

[40] Ibid.; UNHRC Resolution A/HRC/RES/17/4, passed on 6 July 2011, available at: http://daccess-dds-ny.un.org/doc/RESOLUTION/GEN/G11/144/71/PDF/G1114471.pdf?OpenElement; J. G. Ruggie, *Just Business: Multinational Corporations and Human Rights* (2013) 81 ('[t]he Framework addresses what should be done; the Guiding Principles how to do it').

[41] Principle 25 of the UNGP. As the commentary to Principle 25 explains, '[u]nless States take appropriate steps to investigate, punish and redress business-related human rights abuses when they do occur, the State duty to protect can be rendered weak or even meaningless.'

[42] Principle 22 of the UNGP.

recourse in the case of business-related human rights harms.[43] In many ways, the present models seek to actuate these principles, and to grant them concrete application within a sphere that already sees significant interaction between business and human rights objectives.[44]

Duplication, Fragmentation, or Excessive Burden

Given that it seeks to grant effect to the UNGP and other similar soft law (or State-based) frameworks in a circumscribed but binding manner, directly upon foreign investors, the mechanism set forth may raise questions regarding overlap with possible future multilateral conventions and the rise of international tribunals on such issues as business and human

[43] Principle 28 of the UNGP ('States should consider ways to facilitate access to effective non-State based grievance mechanisms dealing with business-related human rights harms'). Principle 31 of the UNGP provides that, to be effective, non-judicial grievance mechanisms should be:

(a) Legitimate: enabling trust from the stakeholder groups for whose use they are intended, and being accountable for the fair conduct of grievance processes;
(b) Accessible: being known to all stakeholder groups for whose use they are intended, and providing adequate assistance for those who may face particular barriers to access;
(c) Predictable: providing a clear and known procedure with an indicative time frame for each stage, and clarity on the types of process and outcome available and means of monitoring implementation;
(d) Equitable: seeking to ensure that aggrieved parties have reasonable access to sources of information, advice and expertise necessary to engage in a grievance process on fair, informed and respectful terms;
(e) Transparent: keeping parties to a grievance informed about its progress, and providing sufficient information about the mechanism's performance to build confidence in its effectiveness and meet any public interest at stake;
(f) Rights-compatible: ensuring that outcomes and remedies accord with internationally recognized human rights;
(g) A source of continuous learning: drawing on relevant measures to identify lessons for improving the mechanism and preventing future grievances and harms.

[44] The commentary to Principle 9 of the UNGP speaks to States' maintaining 'adequate domestic policy space to meet their human rights obligations when pursuing business-related policy objectives with other States or business enterprises, for instance through investment treaties or contracts', and explicitly references investment treaty arbitration:

[T]he terms of international investment agreements may constrain States from fully implementing new human rights legislation, or put them at risk of binding international arbitration if they do so. Therefore, States should ensure that they retain adequate policy and regulatory ability to protect human rights under the terms of such agreements, while providing the necessary investor protection.

rights, indigenous rights, environmental and labour protections, and others.

To start, some may argue that the present mechanism is duplicative of those existing efforts to create robust binding norms and institutionalised dispute resolution mechanisms. However, insofar as the establishment of universal recourse through centralised bodies such as the proposed Tribunal for Business and Human Rights[45] or the International Court for the Environment[46] remains elusive, the present efforts are complementary to such longer-term objectives. One must also recall that the third pillar of the UNGP seeks greater access to recourse for affected individuals and populations, precisely through a complementary web of State and non-State, judicial and non-judicial mechanisms. It is a field in which systemic gaps in recourse for affected individuals and populations are unfortunately all too common. Additional and complementary avenues for such recourse are undoubtedly beneficial and to be greeted positively.

On the other side, foreign investors and multinational enterprises (as well as States that are not inclined to support new dispute resolution fora) may object on the basis of excessive burden or potential liability implied by new obligations. The answer to such objections is found once again in party autonomy. Under the contractual or licensing models, investors will not be subjected to any obligations that they have not undertaken by

---

[45] See C. Cronstedt and R. C. Thompson, *An International Arbitration Tribunal on Business and Human Rights*, Version Five, 13 April 2015, available at: https://business-human rights.org/sites/default/files/documents/Tribunal%20Version%205.pdf and C. Cronstedt and R. C. Thompson, 'A Proposal for an International Arbitration Tribunal on Business and Human Rights', 57 *Harvard International Law Journal* (2016). See also UNHRC, *Elaboration of an International Legally Binding Instrument on Transnational Corporations and Other Business Enterprises with Respect to Human Rights*. Draft Resolution by Bolivia (Plurinational State of), Cuba, Ecuador, South Africa, Venezuela (Bolivarian Republic of), UN Doc. A/HRC/26/L.22/Rev.1 (2014).

[46] See International Bar Association Climate Change Justice and Human Rights Task Force, *Achieving Justice and Human Rights in an Era of Climate Disruption* (2014) 15, 85–86 ('[i] In summary, despite the many advantages of establishing an [International Court for the Environment], and the various efforts made already, particularly in the ICJ itself, an [International Court for the Environment] has been an elusive political goal'); see also T. Stephens, *International Courts and Environmental Protection* (2009) 56–62; E. Hey, *Reflections on an International Environmental Court* (2000); P. Riches and S. A. Bruce, 'Building an International Court for the Environment: A Conceptual Framework', Center for Governance and Sustainability, Issue Brief Series (2013); M. Vespa, 'An Alternative to an International Environmental Court? The PCA's Optional Arbitration Rules for Natural Resources and/or the Environment', 2 *The Law and Practice of International Courts and Tribunals* (2003).

express consent.[47] Under the treaty-based models, such obligations are agreed by both the home State of the investor and host State of any investment,[48] as part of the regulatory régime to which an investor has subjected himself, and whether in exchange for bringing an investment claim of his own[49] or by the mere act of investing in a given jurisdiction.[50]

Finally, an objection might be made on the basis of desire to avoid the further 'fragmentation of international law'.[51] Upon closer inspection, however, this doubt would appear to be misguided. Existing investment tribunals and other fora are currently compelled to decide normative conflicts between investors' treaty rights and rights held by host State nationals by resort to hierarchy in order to decide which holds priority. The models proposed herein, however, would expand the harmonisation toolset of investment tribunals, allowing the social costs of foreign investment to be effectively internalised, while the benefits remain to be weighed against them.[52]

Moreover, to the extent that a broad scope of application is adopted, the use of the models would yield a significant harmonising effect, as they would serve to centralise the resolution of disputes arising out of the adverse effects of investment activities. Such is a highly desirable end,

---

[47] There are numerous examples of voluntary assumption of obligations by the private sector, analogous to contractual models. The most well-known of these is the United Nations Global Compact, albeit that it is precisely criticised for its lack of monitoring, compliance, and enforcement mechanisms.

[48] See Treaty Models, Chapter 3.   [49] See Annex, Model 6 (Contingent Consent Clause).

[50] See Annex, Model 7 (Jurisdiction without Privity).

[51] As the International Law Commission has observed, 'existing international law does not consist of one homogenous legal order, but mostly of different partial systems, producing an "unorganized system".' G. Hafner, 'Risks Ensuing from Fragmentation of International Law', *Report of the International Law Commission on the Work of its Fifty-Second Session* (2000) 143–144. The ILC's solution to the fragmentation of international law is 'harmonisation', which is the 'generally accepted principle that when several norms bear on a single issue they should, to the extent possible, be interpreted so as to give rise to a single set of compatible obligations', in particular through Arts. 31–33 (and especially Article 31(3)(c)) of the Vienna Convention on the Law of Treaties, 1155 UNTS 331, 8 ILM 679 (1969). ILC, *Conclusions of the Work of the Study Group on the Fragmentation of International Law: Difficulties Arising from the Diversification and Expansion of International Law* (2006), paras. 4–8. For further discussion on the principle of systemic integration, see C. McLachlan, 'The Principle of Systemic Integration and Article 31(3)(c) of the Vienna Convention', 53 *International and Comparative Law Quarterly* 2 (2005). The 'fragmentation' concern, of course, does not apply to national laws, whose principal sources and decision-makers remain unaffected.

[52] As already noted, the models herein would hold several advantages over even an established system of host State counterclaims. See The Uncertain Status of Host State Counterclaims, *supra*.

considering that the adverse effects of investment activities are highly transactional and cross-cutting by nature.[53] Claims brought on the basis of multiple sources of host States' and host State nationals' rights may thus be efficiently adjudicated in tandem with investors' own claims. No equivalent clearinghouse forum currently exists. The use of this mechanism could thus be a means for harmonisation of various different systems and sources of rights insofar as it brings them all within a single coherent framework.

On the other hand, to the extent that users choose not to give the models a broad scope of application, and thereby raise the risk of fragmentation, such would be a result of conscious exercises of party autonomy. Thus, the discourse over fragmentation concerns would seem to present another argument in favour of a broad substantive scope of application of the models, especially insofar as other means of harmonisation are persistently lacking.

Thresholds and Due Diligence Obligations

In addition to questions of which standards might be subjected to the use of the models, there arises a question as to whether those standards are to be made directly applicable without modification or modulation. Users of the models may wish to consider applying a threshold criterion as to the gravity or materiality of violations, so that not every minor or technical instance of non-compliance would trigger a claim.[54] Equally, different levels of involvement by the investor in adverse impacts may be used to modulate the resulting remedial obligations. For example, the UNGP and OECD Guidelines for Multinational Enterprises impose

---

[53] Human rights are 'universal, indivisible, interdependent and interrelated', Article I(5) of the Vienna Declaration and Programme of Action, adopted by the World Conference on Human Rights in Vienna on 25 June 1993. Professor Ruggie considers that '[c]ompanies can affect virtually the entire spectrum of internationally recognized rights. Therefore, the corporate responsibility to respect applies to all such rights'. UNHRC, *Protect, Respect and Remedy: A Framework for Business and Human Rights: Report of the Special Representative of the Secretary-General on the Issue of Human Rights and Transnational Corporations and Other Business Enterprises*, UN Doc. A/HRC/8/5, 7 April 2008, para. 24.

[54] A similar idea has been suggested in respect of provisions explicitly allowing for potential host State counterclaims or civil liability, so as to avoid such actions being used 'to harass investors on the basis of trivial violations of treaty standards'. J. A. VanDuzer, P. Simons, and G. Mayeda, 'Integrating Sustainable Development into International Investment Agreements: A Guide for Developing Countries', *Commonwealth Secretariat* (2012) 289, 390.

different obligations depending upon whether enterprises 'cause', 'contribute', or are 'directly linked' to adverse human rights impacts.[55]

A due diligence approach might also be preferred in lieu of strict adherence to stipulated norms. This is a common practice. Even where environmental harm is not itself fully proscribed, customary international law imposes the obligation to conduct an environmental impact assessment.[56] In similar fashion, there is a growing practice requiring due diligence to avoid adverse human rights impacts through a human rights impact assessment.[57] While such would materially reduce the obligations upon the investor, a due diligence approach of this kind presents the added benefit of 'privileg[ing] a logic of prevention' over after-the-fact liability.[58]

Various instruments, including those already identified, likewise proscribe investors' 'complicity' in grave abuses of human rights by other actors, whether public or private. Complicity as a legal standard implicates yet another level of remoteness in the investor's involvement, requiring only some form of direct affiliation or deliberate failure to act in the face of human rights abuses.[59] It is thus often restricted to impacts described with the adjective 'grave' or some other indicator of severity, so

---

[55] Companies that *cause* an adverse human rights impact are expected to cease, prevent, and remedy the impact. Companies that *contribute* to an adverse human rights impact are expected to cease, prevent, and remedy the impact to the extent of their contribution. Companies *directly linked* to adverse human rights impacts are expected only to use or seek leverage to mitigate the adverse impact. Enodo Rights & Debevoise Business Integrity Group, 'Practical Definitions of Cause, Contribute, and Directly Linked to Inform Business Respect for Human Rights', Discussion Draft, 9 February 2017, 3; International Bar Association, *IBA Practical Guide on Business and Human Rights for Business Lawyers*, 28 May 2016, 21.

[56] *Case Concerning Pulp Mills on the River Uruguay* (Argentina v. Uruguay), Judgment, 2010 ICJ Reports 14, para. 204; *Indus Waters Kishenganga Arbitration* (Pakistan v. India), PCA Case No. 2011–01, Partial Award, 18 February 2013, para. 450.

[57] International Bar Association, *IBA Practical Guide on Business and Human Rights for Business Lawyers*, 28 May 2016, 19; J. A. VanDuzer, P. Simons, and G. Mayeda, 'Integrating Sustainable Development into International Investment Agreements: A Guide for Developing Countries', *Commonwealth Secretariat* (2012) 294.

[58] International Chamber of Commerce, Oral Statement, 'The Relation between the United Nations Guiding Principles and the Elaboration of an International Legally Binding Instrument on TNCs and Other Business Enterprises', UNHRC, Open-Ended Intergovernmental Working Group on Transnational Corporations and Other Business Enterprises with Respect to Human Rights, Second Session, 27 October 2016, 2.

[59] J. A. VanDuzer, P. Simons, and G. Mayeda, 'Integrating Sustainable Development into International Investment Agreements: A Guide for Developing Countries', *Commonwealth Secretariat* (2012) 312–317.

as not to unduly create vicarious liability for acts outside of enterprises' sphere of control (if not wholly outside their sphere of influence). It is nevertheless a well-defined and workable conceptual standard derived from analogous national and international contexts:

> As a legal matter, most national jurisdictions prohibit complicity in the commission of a crime, and a number allow for criminal liability of business enterprises in such cases. Typically, civil actions can also be based on an enterprise's alleged contribution to a harm, although these may not be framed in human rights terms. The weight of international criminal law jurisprudence indicates that the relevant standard for aiding and abetting is knowingly providing practical assistance or encouragement that has a substantial effect on the commission of a crime.[60]

The 'non-complicity' standard is also linked directly to the practice of conducting appropriate human rights due diligence, since this is the vehicle by which enterprises would be expected to identify risks of complicity and take reasonable steps to avoid involvement in an alleged abuse.

Defining the Right-Holder

As explored earlier, the various models seek to establish *ratione personae* jurisdiction over the host State or host State nationals. While a variation of the Direct Claims Model may be used regardless of who the original right-holder may be, the latter three models (the Espousal, *Qui Tam*, and Hybrid Models) are specific as to who the original right-holder must be in order to allow for their use. In the case of rights originally vested in host State nationals, the Espousal or Hybrid Model may be used. In the case of rights vested directly in the host State, the *Qui Tam* Model may be used.[61]

While this structure makes it essential to identify the right-holder, the models start from the premise that defining the rights in question will itself provide sufficient definition as to the right-holders, and thereby drive the choice of model. In most cases, the nature of the right, whether it be vested in an individual, a collective, or the State itself, is apparent (or discernible) in the same source of law from which that right is drawn. This expectation holds true especially for claims which might be brought on the basis of the host State's laws.

It is also possible to combine use of the various models in a single consolidated proceeding in a manner that largely obviates this question, at least as a question of jurisdiction *ratione personae*. Under consolidation of

[60] Commentary to Principle 17 of the UNGP.   [61] See Table 2.1 (The Four Models).

models, the arbitral tribunal would have jurisdiction to adjudicate all rights, whether held by the host State or its nationals, even if the distinction may remain relevant in determining which is entitled to any relief ordered. Achieving further precision of the right-holder could then be left to tribunals in individual cases insofar as may be relevant to the merits of specific claims. A growing jurisprudence, together with other secondary regulation mechanisms – such as joint interpretation committees, the legislative processes of international organisations responsible for the relevant instruments, and the jurisprudence of other courts and tribunals (both domestic and international) – may be sufficient to achieve certainty.

Yet, there are situations where this issue cannot be avoided. For instance, the UNDRIP lacks an official definition of who is 'indigenous', giving rise to some concerns about the risk of certain groups seeking to 'exploit' this ambiguity.[62] A definition of 'indigenous peoples', or a method for their identification, may therefore be desirable in any instrument foreseeing the application of UNDRIP.

Ambiguity in the definition of rights and right-holders may also be problematic where it precludes the orderly settlement of potential claims against an investor, or leaves unclear the effects of a settlement to which not all stakeholders have directly subscribed.[63] This ambiguity in the holder of rights arises in various fields of law where rights vested in individuals may overlap with rights held by collectives or the State itself. The establishment of a forum where claims by host State nationals, host State collectives, and the host State itself may be heard together opens new possibilities for global settlements relating to all claims arising out of certain unlawful events. Moreover, it would permit such a settlement agreement to be embodied in an award which is internationally enforceable.[64] Such would represent a significant boon in terms of legal certainty and finality, especially for the investor.

---

[62] 'United States Joins Australia and New Zealand in Criticizing Proposed Declaration on Indigenous Peoples' Rights', 101 *American Journal of International Law* 1 (2007).

[63] For a prime example, see the successive decisions on these issues in the *Chevron-Texaco* v. *Ecuador* case: *Chevron Corporation and Texaco Petroleum Corporation* v. *The Republic of Ecuador*, PCA Case No. 2009–23, UNCITRAL, Decision on Track 1B, 12 March 2015; *Chevron Corporation and Texaco Petroleum Corporation* v. *The Republic of Ecuador*, PCA Case No. 2009–23, UNCITRAL, First Partial Award on Track I, 17 September 2013.

[64] An attempt to recreate this precise advantage in the context of settlement agreements arising out of mediation or conciliation processes is currently being pursued by UNCITRAL. See *Settlement of Commercial Disputes: Enforceability of Settlement Agreements Resulting from International Commercial Conciliation/Mediation*, UN Doc.

Areas of Law for Possible Incorporation

Having addressed certain preliminary questions, we turn to the bodies of law that might be entered into the models. The five areas explored appear to be those best suited for inclusion in the instruments. However, in keeping with the principle of party autonomy, these are put forward as mere possibilities – a non-exclusive list from which drafters might draw inspiration. The survey is not intended to be exhaustive; further consideration of each may be warranted in view of the specific circumstances of a given case or context.

Human Rights

The first category of substantive rights and obligations is that of human rights, including civil and political rights.[65] The simplest and most direct

A/CN.9/WG.II/WP.187 ('one obstacle to greater use of conciliation was that settlement agreements reached through conciliation might be more difficult to enforce than arbitral awards . . . Consequently, it was proposed that the Working Group develop a multilateral convention on the enforceability of international commercial settlement agreements reached through conciliation, with the goal of encouraging conciliation in the same way that the [New York Convention] had facilitated the growth of arbitration'). If such efforts are successful, there is no reason why the models herein cannot be equally applied to mediation and conciliation processes.

[65] The interaction between human rights and international investment law has been addressed by a number of arbitral tribunals and scholars. See, for arbitral decisions, *Biloune and Marine Drive Complex* v. *Ghana*, Award on Jurisdiction, 27 October 1989; *Mondev International Ltd* v. *United States of America*, ICSID Case No. ARB(AF)/99/2, Award, 11 October 2002, paras. 139–144; *Técnicas Medioambientales, TECMED S.A.* v. *The United Mexican States*, ICSID Case No. ARB(AF)/00/2, NAFTA, Award, 29 May 2003, para. 116; *Azurix Corp.* v. *Argentine Republic*, ICSID Case No. ARB/01/12, Award, 14 July 2006, paras. 311–312; *Fireman's Fund Insurance Company* v. *United Mexican States*, ICSID Case No. ARB(AF)/02/01, Award, 17 July 2006, paras. 171–173; *Sempra Energy International* v. *Argentine Republic*, ICSID Case No ARB/02/16, Award, 28 September 2007, para. 332; and *Copper Mesa Mining Corporation* v. *The Republic of Ecuador*, PCA Case No. 2012–02, UNCITRAL, Award, 15 March 2016, paras. 5.60–5.67, 6.97–6.102. For scholarly analysis, see T. Weiler, 'Balancing Human Rights and Investor Protection: A New Approach for a Different Legal Order', 27 *Boston College International and Comparative Law Review* 2 (2004); S. Leader, 'Human Rights, Risks, and New Strategies for Global Investment', 9 *Journal of International Economic Law* 3 (2006); J. D. Fry, 'International Human Rights Law in Investment Arbitration: Evidence of International Law's Unity', 18 *Duke Journal of Comparative & International Law* 77 (2007); P-M. Dupuy, E-U. Petersmann, and F. Francioni (eds.), *Human Rights in International Investment Law and Arbitration* (2009); J. L. Černič, 'Corporate Human Rights Obligations and International Investment Law', 3 *Anuario Colombiano de Derecho Internacional* 243 (2010); M. Jacob, *International Investment Agreements and Human Rights*, Institute for Development and Peace, University of Duisburg-Essen, INEF Research Paper Series on Human Rights, Corporate Responsibility and Sustainable

manner to incorporate enforceable human rights norms into an agreement implementing the models is to stipulate such norms (or the instruments containing them). A second approach would set a common
denominator at treaties ratified by both the home State and host State.
Both approaches are eminently workable. However, they suffer a common flaw afflicting the international investment sphere, which is that
such standards may quickly become outdated or under-inclusive in the
light of rapid developments in the field of corporate social responsibility
and business and human rights. Standards, or references to standards,
which allow for progressive evolution consistent with State practice and
intention would be highly preferred.

A better approach to defining applicable human rights norms might be
through a general reference to a category of broadly accepted instruments. This is the approach taken in both the UNGP and the OECD
Guidelines for Multinational Enterprises. Both instruments define 'internationally recognized human rights' as those

> contained in the International Bill of Human Rights (consisting of the
> Universal Declaration of Human Rights and the main instruments
> through which it has been codified: the International Covenant on Civil
> and Political Rights and the International Covenant on Economic, Social
> and Cultural Rights), coupled with the principles concerning fundamental
> rights in the eight ILO core conventions as set out in the Declaration on
> Fundamental Principles and Rights at Work.[66]

The UN Office of the High Commissioner for Human Rights also considers the following additional instruments to constitute core international human rights instruments:

Development (2010); J. E. Alvarez, 'Are Corporations "Subjects" of International Law?', 9
Santa Clara Journal of International Law 1 (2011); B. Simma, 'Foreign Investment
Arbitration: A Place for Human Rights?', 60 *International and Comparative Law
Quarterly* 3 (2011); P. Dumberry and G. Dumas-Aubin, 'When and How Allegations of
Human Rights Violations Can Be Raised in Investor-State Arbitration', 13 *Journal of
World Investment & Trade* 3 (2012); P. Dumberry and G. Dumas-Aubin, 'How to Impose
Human Rights Obligations on Corporations under Investment Treaties?', *Yearbook on
International Investment Law and Policy* (2011–2012); M. Pentikäinen, 'Changing
International "Subjectivity" and Rights and Obligations under International Law –
Status of Corporations', 8 *Utrecht Law Review* 1 (2012); L. G. Garcia, 'The Role of
Human Rights in International Investment Law', in *The Future of ICSID and the Place
of Investment Treaties in International Law* (2013); S. Hang, 'Investing in Human Rights:
Using Bilateral Investment Treaties to Hold Multinational Corporations Liable for Labor
Rights Violations', 37 *Fordham International Law Journal* 4 (2014).

[66] Commentary to Principle 12 of the UNGP; OECD Guidelines for Multinational
Enterprises, para. 39.

- International Convention on the Elimination of All Forms of Racial Discrimination (CERD, 1965);
- Convention on the Elimination of All Forms of Discrimination against Women (CEDAW, 1979), together with its Optional Protocol (1999);
- Convention against Torture and Other Cruel, Inhuman or Degrading Treatment or Punishment (CAT, 1984), together with its Optional Protocol (2002);
- Convention on the Rights of the Child (CRC, 1989), together with the Optional Protocol on the involvement of children in armed conflict (2000), the Optional Protocol on the sale of children, child prostitution, and child pornography (2000), and the Optional Protocol on a communications procedure (2014);
- International Convention on the Protection of the Rights of All Migrant Workers and Members of Their Families (1990);
- International Convention for the Protection of All Persons from Enforced Disappearance (2006); and
- Convention on the Rights of Persons with Disabilities (2006), together with its Optional Protocol (2006).

Additionally, two further instruments may be of relevance to security practices adopted by an investor in the context of investment projects:

- UN Basic Principles on the Use of Force and Firearms by Law Enforcement Officials; and
- UN Code of Conduct for Law Enforcement Officials.

The phrase 'internationally recognized human rights' is evocative of customary international law. A reference to customary international law is in fact an obvious touchstone for evolving norms in this field. However, the difficulty of identifying customary international law with sufficient precision counsels against the use of a bare reference. While the UDHR is recognised as customary international law, other major human rights instruments such as the ICCPR and the ICESCR are not universally so accepted. Customary international law therefore remains at risk of being under-inclusive.[67]

---

[67] The phrase 'internationally recognized human rights' is also reminiscent of general principles of law, which, as stated in Article 38(1)(c) of the ICJ Statute, must be 'recognized by civilized nations'. The significance and suitability of general principles of law as sources of international human rights has been analysed in the literature. In particular, Philip Alston and Bruno

Unfortunately, there is only a modest amount of treaty practice to rely upon in this area for inspiration. While it has become somewhat common for investment treaties to include a preambular reference to human rights,[68] references in the body of the treaty are a far more recent phenomenon. Within treaties that do include reference to human rights or corporate social responsibility within the body, most refer to the contracting States' own responsibilities to establish national frameworks for corporate social responsibility, to not encourage investment by lowering human rights standards,[69] to discuss such matters in periodic reviews[70] or joint committees,[71] to encourage voluntary adherence by investors to the UNGP, OECD Guidelines for Multinational Enterprises, and UN Global Compact,[72] or to exhort investors 'to voluntarily incorporate internationally recognised standards of corporate social responsibility'.[73] Only Brazil's recently concluded investment treaties can be said to impose direct obligations upon investors to 'employ their best efforts' to comply with corporate social responsibility standards, as defined using the aforementioned 'internationally recognised standards' formulation.[74] Only the SADC Model BIT and a model text proposed by the Commonwealth Secretariat would establish a direct duty

Simma have argued that general principles of law may afford a more suitable basis for the creation of international human rights law than custom, given the requirements for the formation of the latter. B. Simma and P. Alston, 'The Sources of Human Rights Law: Custom, *Jus Cogens*, and General Principles', in 12 *Australian Yearbook of International Law* (1988).

[68] UNCTAD reports 187 investment instruments containing such a reference in their preamble. Of investment instruments signed since 2010, 46 out of 121 contain such preambular references. See UNCTAD, IIA Mapping Project, available at: http://invest mentpolicyhub.unctad.org/IIA/mappedContent#iiaInnerMenu.

[69] Such provisions are rapidly increasing in prevalence, being found consistently in recent treaties concluded by Austria, Brazil, the Belgium-Luxembourg Economic Union, Canada, the European Free Trade Area, the Eurasian Economic Union, India, Japan, South Korea, Mexico, Turkey, and the United States, among others.

[70] See, e.g., Art. 30 of the Japan-Uruguay BIT (2015).

[71] See, e.g., Art. 23(3) of the Norway Model BIT (2007) and Art. 7(2)(d) of the COMESA Investment Agreement (2007).

[72] See, e.g., Art. 31 of the Norway Model BIT (2015).

[73] This appears to be the current treaty practice of Canada and Colombia, among others. See, e.g., Benin-Canada BIT (2013); Burkina Faso-Canada BIT (2015); Cameroon-Canada BIT (2014); Canada-Côte d'Ivoire BIT (2014); Canada-Mali BIT (2014); Canada-Nigeria BIT (2014); Canada-Republic of Korea FTA (2014); Canada-Senegal BIT (2014); Canada-Serbia BIT (2014); Canada-Honduras FTA (2013); Colombia-Costa Rica FTA (2013); Colombia-France BIT (2014); Colombia-Panama FTA (2013). This same approach is also reflected in the new India Model BIT (2016).

[74] See Annex II of the Angola-Brazil BIT (2015); Art. 15 of the Brazil-Chile BIT (2015); Art. 9 of the Brazil-Malawi BIT (2015); Art. 13 of the Brazil-Mexico BIT (2015); Annex II of the Brazil-Mozambique BIT (2015).

of investors to respect human rights, including obligations of human rights
due diligence and non-complicity.[75]

Nevertheless, borrowing from these latter two instruments, the ideal
approach where parties wish to render human rights standards directly
binding upon investors would seem to be a general reference to 'internationally recognized human rights' or 'internationally recognised standards of corporate social responsibility', accompanied by an enumerated
list of instruments establishing a standard that is reflective of the prevailing state at the time of conclusion of the instrument in question.

Labour Rights

The same issues of defining enforceable rights arise in the context
of labour rights, although they are more attenuated.[76] The main

---

[75] Art. 15.1 of the SADC Model BIT (2012) ('[i]nvestors and their investments have a duty to
respect human rights in the workplace and in the community and State in which they are
located. Investors and their investments shall not undertake or cause to be undertaken
acts that breach such human rights. Investors and their investments shall not assist in, or
be complicit in, the violation of the human rights by others in the Host State, including by
public authorities or during civil strife'); J. A. VanDuzer, P. Simons, and G. Mayeda,
'Integrating Sustainable Development into International Investment Agreements: A
Guide for Developing Countries', *Commonwealth Secretariat* (2012) 308–309, 317.

[76] See generally J. Augusti-Panareda and S. Puig, 'Labor Protection and Investment
Regulation: Promoting a Virtuous Circle', 51 *Stanford Journal of International Law* 1
(2015); J. S. Vogt, 'Trade and Investment Arrangements and Labor Rights', in L. Blecher,
N. K. Stafford, and G. C. Bellamy (eds.), *Corporate Responsibility for Human Rights
Impacts: New Expectations and Paradigms* (2014); L. Bartels, 'Social Issues: Labour,
Environment and Human Rights', in S. Lester and B. Mercurio (eds.), *Bilateral and
Regional Trade Agreements: Commentary, Analysis and Case Studies* (2009); K. Gordon,
'International Investment Agreements: A Survey of Environmental, Labour and Anti-
corruption Issues', in OECD, *International Investment Law: Understanding Concepts and
Tracking Innovations* (2008); R. Grynberg and V. Qalo, 'Labour Standards in US and EU
Preferential Trading Arrangements', 40 *Journal of World Trade* 4 (2006); P. Alston, 'Core
Labour Standards and the Transformation of the International Labour Rights Regime', 15
European Journal of International Law 3 (2004). On the World Trade Organization, see, e.
g., D. K. Brown, A. V. Deardorff, and R. M. Stern, 'Labor Standards and Human Rights:
Implications for International Trade and Investment', in Z. Drabek and P. C.
Mavroidis (eds.), *Regulation of Foreign Investment: Challenges to International
Harmonization* (2013). For a case directly invoking labour standards in an investment instrument, see Office of the United States Trade Representative, *In the
Matter of Guatemala – Issues Relating to the Obligations under Article 16.2.1(a)
of the CAFTA-DR* (United States of America v. Guatemala), available at: https://
ustr.gov/issue-areas/labor/bilateral-and-regional-trade-agreements/guatemala-sub
mission-under-cafta-dr. An arbitration agreement has also been included at clause
5 of the *Accord on Fire and Building Safety in Bangladesh* concluded following the

source of international labour law is the work of the ILO, which already sees broad subscription to international labour standards adopted within a legislative process that brings together representatives of governments, employers, and workers (the tripartite constituents).[77] In addition, the UDHR (Articles 23[78] and 24[79]) and the ICCPR (Articles 8[80] and

---

Rana Plaza incident, available at: www.bangladeshaccord.org/wp-content/uploads/2013/10/the_accord.pdf.

[77] The ILO, which was founded in 1919 and which became a specialised agency of the United Nations in 1946, has 187 member States and a ratification rate of its fundamental conventions exceeding ninety per cent.

[78] Art. 23 of the UDHR provides as follows:

1. Everyone has the right to work, to free choice of employment, to just and favourable conditions of work and to protection against unemployment.
2. Everyone, without any discrimination, has the right to equal pay for equal work.
3. Everyone who works has the right to just and favourable remuneration ensuring for himself and his family an existence worthy of human dignity, and supplemented, if necessary, by other means of social protection.
4. Everyone has the right to form and to join trade unions for the protection of his interests.

[79] Art. 24 of the UDHR provides that '[e]veryone has the right to rest and leisure, including reasonable limitation of working hours and periodic holidays with pay.'

[80] Art. 8 of the ICCPR provides as follows:

1. No one shall be held in slavery; slavery and the slave-trade in all their forms shall be prohibited.
2. No one shall be held in servitude.
3. (a) No one shall be required to perform forced or compulsory labour;
   (b) Paragraph 3 (a) shall not be held to preclude, in countries where imprisonment with hard labour may be imposed as a punishment for a crime, the performance of hard labour in pursuance of a sentence to such punishment by a competent court;
   (c) For the purpose of this paragraph the term 'forced or compulsory labour' shall not include:
      (i) Any work or service, not referred to in subparagraph (b), normally required of a person who is under detention in consequence of a lawful order of a court, or of a person during conditional release from such detention;
      (ii) Any service of a military character and, in countries where conscientious objection is recognized, any national service required by law of conscientious objectors;
      (iii) Any service exacted in cases of emergency or calamity threatening the life or well-being of the community;
      (iv) Any work or service which forms part of normal civil obligations.

22^{81}) already consecrate labour rights within the broader human rights context, as do the UNGP and the OECD Guidelines for Multinational Enterprises in their references to 'the principles concerning fundamental rights in the eight ILO core conventions as set out in the Declaration on Fundamental Principles and Rights at Work'.[82] These instruments already effectively include (i) freedom of association and the effective recognition of the right to collective bargaining; (ii) the elimination of forced or compulsory labour; (iii) the effective abolition of child labour; and (iv) the elimination of discrimination in respect of employment and occupation.[83] As a result, the suggested references to 'internationally recognized human rights' can be expected to capture core international labour standards as well.

Yet the ambit of ILO instruments is far broader. There are numerous additional ILO conventions which may bear particular relevance to a given investment project. For example, the ILO Indigenous and Tribal Peoples Convention (1989) (the ILO Convention No. 169) might be particularly relevant to investments in the exploitation of natural resources on indigenous

---

[81] Art. 22 of the ICCPR provides as follows:

1. Everyone shall have the right to freedom of association with others, including the right to form and join trade unions for the protection of his interests.
2. No restrictions may be placed on the exercise of this right other than those which are prescribed by law and which are necessary in a democratic society in the interests of national security or public safety, public order (ordre public), the protection of public health or morals or the protection of the rights and freedoms of others. This article shall not prevent the imposition of lawful restrictions on members of the armed forces and of the police in their exercise of this right.
3. Nothing in this article shall authorize States Parties to the International Labour Organisation Convention of 1948 concerning Freedom of Association and Protection of the Right to Organize to take legislative measures which would prejudice, or to apply the law in such a manner as to prejudice, the guarantees provided for in that Convention.

[82] Commentary to Principle 12 of the UNGP; OECD Guidelines for Multinational Enterprises, para. 39.

[83] The eight ILO core conventions are as follows:

C029 – Forced Labour Convention, 1930 (No. 29) (including P029 – Protocol of 2014 to the Forced Labour Convention, 1930);
C087 – Freedom of Association and Protection of the Right to Organise Convention, 1948 (No. 87);
C098 – Right to Organise and Collective Bargaining Convention, 1949 (No. 98);
C100 – Equal Remuneration Convention, 1951 (No. 100);
C105 – Abolition of Forced Labour Convention, 1957 (No. 105);
C111 – Discrimination (Employment and Occupation) Convention, 1958 (No. 111);
C138 – Minimum Age Convention, 1973 (No. 138); and
C182 – Worst Forms of Child Labour Convention, 1999 (No. 182).

lands. In addition, the ILO international labour standards may also take the form of 'recommendations', which serve as non-binding guidelines.

Parties seeking broader incorporation of international labour standards may thus opt to stipulate additional instruments that shall be deemed applicable in the light of their relevance to a given investor or investment. Alternatively, this may be an area where it is advisable to adopt the approach of rendering applicable those ILO conventions to which both the home State and host State are party (or even those to which only the host State is a party). Such formulas may be further supplemented by an obligation to take into account any relevant ILO recommendations, as well as other ILO conventions in the guise of recommendations.[84]

Apart from the universal instruments set out previously, there are also numerous regional instruments which contain labour rights, including the following:

- 1969 American Convention on Human Rights and its Additional Protocol in the Area of Economic, Social and Cultural Rights (1988);
- European Social Charter (1961) and Additional Protocol to the Charter (1988);
- European Convention for the Protection of Human Rights and Fundamental Freedoms (1950);
- African Charter on Human and Peoples' Rights (1981); and
- African Charter on the Rights and Welfare of the Child (1990).

Depending on the context in which a given dispute might arise, regional human rights instruments may also be appropriate to include within the substantive ambit of an investor's obligations to host State nationals.

A growing number of trade agreements, both bilateral and multilateral, as well as regional economic integration arrangements contain references to or provisions on workers' rights.[85] The first free trade agreements to

---

[84] See, e.g., Art. 1(d) of the Belgium-Luxembourg Economic Union-Barbados BIT (2009) (which defines 'labour legislation' as 'any legislation of the Contracting Parties in force at the date of the signature of this Agreement or passed after the date thereof or any provision of such legislation that purports to give effect to the following international labour standards as defined by the International Labour Organisation: (i) the right of association; (ii) the right to organise and bargain collectively; (iii) a prohibition on the use of any form of forced or compulsory labour; (iv) a minimum age for the employment of children; (v) acceptable conditions of work with respect to minimum wages, hours of work, and occupational safety and health').

[85] See International Institute for Labour Studies, ILO, *Social Dimensions of Free Trade Agreements* (2013).

incorporate references to labour rights in the mid-1990s did so in hortatory language within the treaty's preamble, without elaboration.[86] States continue to resort to this mechanism to include references to labour rights in their international trade and investment agreements. Yet, nowadays it is more common to see references to 'international core standards' or 'international labour rights',[87] or to include explicit references to ILO instruments.[88]

Further developments in this area have subsequently led to the conclusion of side deals to free trade agreements for social issues where trade and investment promotion is linked to cooperation and upward harmonisation on labour matters. Such agreements generally include a set of remedies for individuals, unions, and corporations, should they believe there has been a breach of their rights under the side deal.[89] The NAALC, a side deal to NAFTA, is the prime example.[90] Although the eleven principles that it lists are in line with those included in the ILO's Declaration on Fundamental Principles and Rights at Work, the NAALC does not explicitly reference international labour standards, and presents its principles as 'guiding principles' rather than binding 'common minimum standards'.[91]

As regards provisions in the body of treaties, investment agreements also regularly include clauses prohibiting States from relaxing labour standards

---

[86] This was also the model followed in some US treaties. See, e.g., the Preamble and Art. 13 of the US Model BIT (2004) and K. J. Vandevelde, *U.S. International Investment Agreements* (2009) 747 ('[c]laims for violation of the labor provision may not be brought under either the investor-state or the state-state disputes provision. The rationale is that, ultimately, the primary purpose of the labor provision is to promote labor rights rather than to protect U.S. investors, and it was not intended that the provision would provide the basis of a claim by an investor against a host state. Because prior to 2004 the treaties did not contain a labor provision, this decision was not regarded as weakening traditional [bilateral investment treaty] protections for investment'). Although this practice was subsequently abandoned by the United States in favour of substantive and actionable labour provisions, it remains a common approach for other States.

[87] See Art. 13 of the US-Uruguay BIT (2005) for a reference to international labour rights, but without mention of the ILO.

[88] See the Preamble to the European Community-CARIFORUM Economic Partnership Agreement (2008) for a reference to the ILO ('basic labour rights in line with the commitments [the signatories] have undertaken within the International Labour Organisation').

[89] Canada has used this format on several occasions. See, e.g., Canada-Costa Rica FTA (2002) and Canada-Chile FTA (1996).

[90] See Arts. 1(a) and 1(b) of NAALC. NAALC sets as objectives, amongst others, improving working conditions and living standards in each party's territory and promoting, to the maximum extent possible, the eleven labour principles set out in its Annex 1 (Labor Principles).

[91] Annex 1 of the NAALC (Labor Principles).

in order to attract investment. This approach can be seen, for example, in a number of Mexico's free trade agreements signed in the 1990s,[92] in the Economic Partnership Agreement between the European Community and CARIFORUM,[93] in the US Model BIT as well as several US free trade agreements,[94] in the Austrian Model BIT,[95] and in the EU-Republic of Korea FTA.[96] In addition, a number of bilateral investment treaties and free trade agreements in the early and mid-2000s also include an affirmation of the parties' commitments under the ILO Declaration on Fundamental Principles and Rights at Work (1998) and as ILO members, these being recognition of the right of the parties to establish their own labour standards, a requirement to either maintain high levels of labour standards or endeavour to ensure that domestic labour standards are consistent with certain listed international labour standards, and a requirement to strive to improve all such standards.[97] Finally, various treaties also contain general exception clauses disallowing claims by investors relating to measures to ensure labour rights.[98]

---

[92] See, e.g., Bolivia-Mexico FTA (1994); Nicaragua-Mexico FTA (1997); and Chile-Mexico FTA (1998).

[93] See Arts. 73 and 193 of the European Community-CARIFORUM Economic Partnership Agreement (2008).

[94] See, e.g., Art. 13 of the US Model BIT (2012); Chapter 18 of the Australia-United States FTA (2004); Art. 16.2 of the United States-Dominican Republic-Central America FTA (2004); Art. 18.2 of the United States-Chile FTA (2003); Art. 6 of the United States-Jordan FTA (2000); and Art. 16.2 of the United States-Morocco FTA (2004).

[95] Art. 5 of the Austrian Model BIT (2008). See also Art. 5 of the Austria-Tajikistan BIT (2010); Art. 5 of the Kosovo-Austria BIT (2010).

[96] Arts. 13.4 and 13.7 of the EU-Republic of Korea FTA (2010). See also Art. 6 of the Belgium-Luxembourg Economic Union-Ethiopia BIT (2006) and Arts. 1601–1604 of the Canada-Colombia FTA (2008), which references the obligations between the parties set out in the Canada-Colombia Agreement on Labour Cooperation (2008).

[97] See Arts. 1(6) and 6 of the Belgium-Luxembourg Economic Union-Ethiopia BIT (2006); Art. 13 of the US Model BIT (2012); Arts. 18.1 and 18.7 of the Australia-United States FTA (2004); Arts. 16.1 and 16.8 of the United States-Dominican Republic-Central America FTA (2004); Arts. 18.1 and 18.8 of the United States-Chile FTA (2003); Art. 6 of the United States-Jordan FTA (2000); and Arts. 16.1 and 16.7 of the United States-Morocco FTA (2004). Article 13.4 of the EU-Republic of Korea FTA (2010) goes slightly further than the US Model BIT and other US agreements by recognising the parties' commitments to the 2006 Ministerial Declaration of the UN Economic and Social Council on Full Employment and Decent Work and the importance of 'full and productive employment and decent work for all' for sustainable development. Art. 192 of the European Community-CARIFORUM Economic Partnership Agreement (2008) provides that 'each Party and Signatory CARIFORUM State shall ensure that its own social and labour regulations and policies provide for and encourage high levels of social and labour standards' consistent with ILO Conventions.

[98] See, e.g., Art. 13(3) of the US-Uruguay BIT (2005).

Again, the aforementioned provisions aim to prevent a 'race to the bottom' in regard to labour standards, but do not offer a remedy to affected host State nationals. The NAALC and other side agreements do include compliance mechanisms and State-to-State dispute settlement options. The United States has in fact brought a case against Guatemala under the United States-Dominican Republic-Central America FTA over concerns that Guatemala was not effectively enforcing labour laws relating to the right of association, the right to organise and bargain collectively, and the right to acceptable conditions of work.[99] However, even where such compliance mechanisms may be triggered by complaints regarding an investor's conduct,[100] the processes they envisage target the States' compliance with their own labour standards or those existing at international law, as opposed to the behaviour of the investor.[101]

As a result, it remains largely those instruments that enshrine human rights obligations for investors which do the same in respect of labour obligations, whether in a unified category of rights encompassing both areas or separately as to each.[102] In addition to these, the Ghana Model BIT also requires investors to comply with local and international labour

---

[99] Office of the United States Trade Representative, *Standing Up for Workers: Ensuring that the Benefits of Trade Are Broadly Shared*, Fact Sheet, September 2014, available at: https://ustr.gov/about-us/policy-offices/press-office/fact-sheets/2014/September/ Standing-Up-for-Workers-Ensuring-that-the-Benefits-of-Trade-are-Broadly-Shared; Office of the United States Trade Representative, *In the Matter of Guatemala – Issues Relating to the Obligations under Article 16.2.1(a) of the CAFTA-DR*, available at: https:// ustr.gov/issue-areas/labor/bilateral-and-regional-trade-agreements/guatemala-submis sion-under-cafta-dr.

[100] See, e.g., Art. 16(3) of the NAALC (National Administrative Officer Complaints).

[101] J. A. VanDuzer, P. Simons, and G. Mayeda, 'Integrating Sustainable Development into International Investment Agreements: A Guide for Developing Countries', *Commonwealth Secretariat* (2012) 320 ('[t]hese types of provisions do not oblige state parties to ensure minimum standards are met in their domestic law in compliance with their international labour obligations, and they target investor behaviour only indirectly and weakly').

[102] See, e.g., Arts. 15.2 ('[i]nvestors and their investments shall act in accordance with core labour standards as required by the ILO Declaration on Fundamental Principles and Rights of Work, 1998') and 15.3 ('[i]nvestors and their investments shall not [establish,] manage or operate Investments in a manner inconsistent with international environ-mental, labour, and human rights obligations binding on the Host State or the Home State, whichever obligations are higher') of the SADC Model BIT (2012); see also J. A. VanDuzer, P. Simons, and G. Mayeda, 'Integrating Sustainable Development into International Investment Agreements: A Guide for Developing Countries', *Commonwealth Secretariat* (2012) 332–333 (including enumerated labour standards to be complied with).

standards, including 'in accordance with relevant guidelines'.[103] The Asian-African Legal Consultative Committee Model Agreements further contain a mechanism by which to enshrine such rights in an investment licensing process, as envisaged in one model herein for jurisdiction arising from host State investment law (but which could also be envisaged in treaty-based instruments).[104] Finally, there are numerous examples of jurisdiction arising from contract, most recently and prominently in the labour field in the Accord on Fire and Building Safety in Bangladesh that followed from the Rana Plaza incident, where a building collapse resulted in the deaths of more than a thousand people.[105]

Once again, borrowing from these instruments, parties wishing to provide for broad labour standards directly enforceable upon investors might easily combine a general reference to 'internationally accepted labour standards as defined by the International Labour Organisation' with an enumerated list of further ILO conventions of specific relevance, an obligation to 'take into account relevant ILO recommendations', and any desired reference to national or regional labour standards.[106]

---

[103] Art. 12 of the Ghana Model BIT (2008) ('1. [n]ationals and companies of one Contracting Party in the territory of the other Contracting Party shall be bound by the laws and regulations in force in the host State, including its laws and regulations on labour, health and the environment ... 3. Nationals and companies of one Contracting Party in the territory of the other Contracting Party shall behave in accordance with relevant guidelines and other internationally accepted standards applicable to foreign investors').

[104] Art. 3(ii) of Model B of the Asian-African Legal Consultative Committee Model Agreements (1985) ('[t]he investment shall be received subject to the terms and conditions specified in the letter of authorization. Such terms and conditions may include the obligation or requirement concerning employment of local personnel and labour in the investment projects, organisation of training programmes, transfer of technology and marketing arrangements for the products'). See Host State Investment Law, Chapter 3; see also Annex, Model 4 (Investment License).

[105] See clause 5 of the *Accord on Fire and Building Safety in Bangladesh*, available at: www.bangladeshaccord.org/wp-content/uploads/2013/10/the_accord.pdf.

[106] Where further precision is desired as to the ambit of applicable national laws, a definition such as the one given at Art. 13 of the US Model BIT (2012) could be used. That provision provides as follows: For purposes of this Article, 'labor laws' means each Party's statutes or regulations, or provisions thereof, that are directly related to the following:

  (a) freedom of association;
  (b) the effective recognition of the right to collective bargaining;
  (c) the elimination of all forms of forced or compulsory labor;
  (d) the effective abolition of child labor and a prohibition on the worst forms of child labor;
  (e) the elimination of discrimination in respect of employment and occupation; and

Environmental Rights

Concerns regarding adverse environmental impacts of investors' activities are long-standing, and exemplified in many investor-State disputes.[107] All of the previously described means to ensure recognition of and regulatory space for non-discriminatory measures in investment treaties have been employed in the environmental sector as well. As with labour standards,

(f) acceptable conditions of work with respect to minimum wages, hours of work, and occupational safety and health.

Art. 5 of the Austrian Model BIT (2008) contains a nearly identical definition. Both definitions are themselves based upon Art. 2 of the ILO Declaration on Fundamental Principles and Rights at Work (1998).

[107] See, e.g., *Compañía del Desarrollo de Santa Elena S.A.* v. *Republic of Costa Rica*, ICSID Case No. ARB/96/1, Award, 17 February 2000, para. 121; *Metalclad Corp.* v. *United Mexican States*, ICSID Case No. ARB(AF)/97/1, Award, 30 August 2000; *Methanex Corp.* v. *United States of America*, NAFTA/UNCITRAL, Final Award, 3 August 2005; *Biwater Gauff (Tanzania) Ltd.* v. *United Republic of Tanzania*, ICSID Case No. ARB/05/22, Award, 24 July 2008, paras. 57–68, 356–392; *Glamis Gold Ltd.* v. *United States of America*, NAFTA/UNCITRAL, Award, 8 June 2009; *Chemtura Corporation* v. *Government of Canada*, PCA Case No. 2008-01, Award, 2 August 2010; *Chevron Corporation and Texaco Petroleum Corporation* v. *The Republic of Ecuador*, PCA Case No. 2009-23, Decision on Track 1B, 12 March 2015; *Perenco Ecuador Ltd.* v. *The Republic of Ecuador et al.*, ICSID Case No. ARB/08/6, Interim Decision on the Environmental Counterclaim, 11 August 2015; *Bilcon of Delaware et al.* v. *Government of Canada*, PCA Case No. 2009-04, Award, 10 March 2015; *Pac Rim Cayman LLC* v. *Republic of El Salvador*, ICSID Case No. ARB/09/12, Award, 14 October 2016; *Burlington Resources Inc.* v. *Republic of Ecuador*, ICSID Case No. ARB/08/05, Decision on Counterclaims, 7 February 2017. For scholarly commentary in this area, see, e.g., J. M. Wagner, 'International Investment, Expropriation and Environmental Protection', 29 *Golden Gate University Law Review* 3 (1999); D. Ong, 'The Impact of Environmental Law on Corporate Governance: International and Comparative Perspectives', 12 *European Journal of International Law* 4 (2001); S. Baughen, 'Expropriation and Environmental Regulation: The Lessons of NAFTA Chapter Eleven', 18 *Journal of Environmental Law* 2 (2006); D. Bodansky, J. Brunnée, and E. Hey (eds.), *The Oxford Handbook of International Environmental Law* (2007); A. van Aaken, 'Defragmentation of Public International Law through Interpretation: A Methodological Proposal', 16 *Indiana Journal of Global Legal Studies* 2 (2009); P. Birnie, A. E. Boyle, and C. Redgwell, *International Law and the Environment*, 3rd edn. (2009); P. Aerni et al., 'Climate Change and International Law: Exploring the Linkages between Human Rights, Environment, Trade and Investment', 53 *German Yearbook of International Law* 139 (2010); J. E. Viñuales, 'Foreign Investment and the Environment in International Law: An Ambiguous Relationship', 80 *British Yearbook of International Law* 1 (2010); Å. Romson, *Environmental Policy Space and International Investment Law*, Department of Law, Stockholm University (2012); J. E. Viñuales, *Foreign Investment and the Environment in International Law* (2012); Z. Douglas, 'The Enforcement of Environmental Norms in Investment Treaty Arbitration', in P-M. Dupuy and J. E. Viñuales (eds.), *Harnessing Foreign Investment to Promote Environmental Protection: Incentives and Safeguards* (2013).

preambular references[108] and clauses prohibiting the relaxing of environmental standards in order to attract investment[109] have been a regular
feature of investment treaties since the 1990s. NAFTA and other free trade
agreements also include side deals on environmental cooperation.[110]
Insofar as public health is concerned, general exception clauses date back
to the very first bilateral investment treaty ever.[111] These provisions now
feature frequently, and in combination with each other, in a number of
States' model treaties.[112] In addition, a number of more recent treaties
address environmental standards within broader corporate social responsibility standards.[113]

Despite this widespread practice, environmental obligations for investors beyond the national sphere remain difficult to define with precision.
Out of the aforementioned instruments, only the US Model BIT refers in
explicit terms to 'multilateral environmental agreements', and does so
without clearly granting to such multilateral agreements any concrete or
direct legal effect.[114] Such is one of the clear constraints of international
environmental law. There are numerous conventional instruments in
this area, and a number of customary rules and principles. However,
aside from the customary obligation to conduct an environmental impact
assessment in regard of any large-scale project,[115] they cannot easily be
directly transposed to investor action. Moreover, there is no easily

---

[108] See, e.g., US Model BIT (1994); Spain-Trinidad and Tobago BIT (1999); Bosnia and Herzegovina-Finland BIT (2000).

[109] See, e.g., Protocol and Art. 3 of the Mexico-Switzerland BIT (1995).

[110] North American Agreement on Environmental Cooperation between the Government of Canada, the Government of the United Mexican States and the Government of the United States of America, signed on 14 September 1993 (entered into force on 1 January 1994), 32 ILM 1482 (1993).

[111] Protocol of the Federal Republic of Germany-Pakistan BIT (1959), para. 2.

[112] See, e.g., Norway Model BIT (2015); India Model BIT (2016); SADC Model BIT (2012); US Model BIT (2012); Colombia Model BIT (2008); Ghana Model BIT (2008); Turkey Model BIT (2009); Canada Model BIT (2004).

[113] These include recent Brazilian treaties. See Annex II of the Angola-Brazil BIT (2015); Art. 15 of the Brazil-Chile BIT (2015); Art. 9 of the Brazil-Malawi BIT (2015); Art. 13 of the Brazil-Mexico BIT (2015); Annex II of the Brazil-Mozambique BIT (2015); and Art. 15.3 of the SADC Model BIT (2012) ('[i]nvestors and their investments shall not [establish,] manage or operate Investments in a manner inconsistent with international environmental, labour, and human rights obligations binding on the Host State or the Home State, whichever obligations are higher').

[114] Art. 12.1 of the US Model BIT (2012) ('[t]he Parties recognize that their respective environmental laws and policies, and multilateral environmental agreements to which they are both party, play an important role in protecting the environment').

[115] See note 56 *supra*.

identifiable 'core' of substantive international environmental obligations to which investors might be held.[116]

As a result, calls have been made upon States and the UNHRC to recognise a freestanding right to a healthy environment, as well as to clarify and solidify existing associated norms.[117] With specific relevance to climate change-related impacts, the International Bar Association also proposes to produce a Model Statute on Legal Remedies for Climate Change, which would 'provide for the identification of actionable rights available to individuals' and 'provide a clear definition of legal standing', while also addressing causation issues.[118] Such standards, once further developed, might be made subject to the models herein proposed.

Until such time, the obligation to conduct an environmental impact assessment and the existing framework of business and human rights may provide the most promising avenue for rendering international environmental obligations immediately actionable. Environmental impact assessments may be expected to identify potential harm that an investor must avoid or mitigate to the extent that he has 'caused', 'contributed', or been 'directly linked' to such adverse impacts. The same framework can then be used in relation to an investor's alleged involvement in non-compliance by the host State with binding international commitments,[119] or any

---

[116] J. H. Knox, *Report of the Independent Expert on the Issue of Human Rights Obligations Relating to the Enjoyment of a Safe, Clean, Healthy and Sustainable Environment, Mapping Report*, UN Doc. A/HRC/25/53 (2013), para. 26 ('while there is no shortage of statements on human rights obligations relating to the environment, the statements do not come together on their own to constitute a coherent set of norms').

[117] International Bar Association Climate Change Justice and Human Rights Task Force, *Achieving Justice and Human Rights in an Era of Climate Disruption* (2014) 9–10, 121–124 ('the Task Force recommends that, with the requisite state backing, the Human Rights Council adopt a resolution requesting that the UN Office of the High Commissioner for Human Rights (OHCHR) draft a report outlining a "minimum core" of rights and duties implicated by the right to a healthy environment, particularly as it pertains to climate change ... as a supplementary long-term goal, the Task Force recommends that states consider recognising freestanding human rights to a safe, clean, healthy and sustainable environment').

[118] Ibid. 11, 127–136.

[119] There have been a number of inter-State proceedings in recent years with significant environmental components. See *Case Concerning Pulp Mills on the River Uruguay* (Argentina v. Uruguay), Judgment, 2010 ICJ Reports 14; *Indus Waters Kishenganga Arbitration* (Pakistan v. India), PCA Case No. 2011-01, Partial Award, 18 February 2013 (concerning conventional and customary restrictions upon the right to divert waters of an international watercourse); *Rhine Chlorides Arbitration Concerning the Auditing of Accounts* (Netherlands v. France), PCA Case No. 2000-02, Award, 12 March 2004 (concerning a treaty obligation to reduce the level of chloride ions in the River Rhine and the applicability of the 'polluter pays' principle in relation to this particular treaty

environmentally-derived adverse impacts upon other established human rights.[120]

As with due diligence standards in other contexts, and given the challenges of identifying applicable universal standards, it may be advisable to define the scope of an impact assessment expressly, by reference to instruments adopted by either or both of the home State and the host State. Where an express approach is employed, the following international instruments may be of particular relevance:

- Convention on International Trade in Endangered Species of Wild Fauna and Flora (1973);
- United Nations Convention on the Law of the Sea (1982);[121]
- United Nations Framework Convention on Climate Change (1992), and associated instruments such as the Kyoto Protocol (1997) and Paris Agreement (2015);
- Convention on the Control of Transboundary Movements of Hazardous Wastes and their Disposal (Basel Convention) (1989);
- Convention on Biological Diversity (1992);
- Convention on the Conservation of Migratory Species of Wild Animals (Bonn Convention) (1979);
- Cartagena Protocol on Biosafety (2000);
- Vienna Convention for the Protection of the Ozone Layer (1988) and Montreal Protocol on Substances that deplete the Ozone Layer (1989);
- Stockholm Convention on Persistent Organic Pollutants (2001);
- Convention to Combat Desertification (1994);
- Convention on Long-Range Transboundary Air Pollution (1979); and
- Convention on Access to Information, Public Participation in Decision-Making and Access to Justice in Environmental Matters (Aarhus Convention) (1998).

---

obligation); and *Iron Rhine Arbitration* (Belgium v. Netherlands), PCA Case No. 2003-02, Award, 24 May 2005.

[120] In respect of the latter, often referred to as the 'greening' of human rights norms, see J. H. Knox, *Report of the Independent Expert on the Issue of Human Rights Obligations Relating to the Enjoyment of a Safe, Clean, Healthy and Sustainable Environment, Mapping Report*, UN Doc. A/HRC/25/53 (2013).

[121] There have been a number of inter-State proceedings under the United Nations Convention on the Law of the Sea bearing significant environmental components. See *The South China Sea Arbitration* (The Republic of Philippines v. The People's Republic of China), PCA Case No. 2013-19, Award, 12 July 2016; *Chagos Marine Protected Area Arbitration* (Mauritius v. UK), PCA Case No. 2011-03, Award, 18 March 2015; and *MOX Plant Case* (Ireland v. UK), PCA Case No. 2002-01, Procedural Orders of 22 January 2007 and 6 June 2008.

In addition, various regional instruments may be worthy of inclusion, especially in the realm of fisheries[122] or the conservation of specific protected areas.

By comparison, national laws on environmental protection are much more developed. The only challenge in this respect is how to define the scope, since the ambit of environmental regulation is not understood universally in the same manner. The US Model BIT defines 'environmental law' as follows:

> For purposes of this Article, 'environmental law' means each Party's statutes or regulations, or provisions thereof, the primary purpose of which is the protection of the environment, or the prevention of a danger to human, animal, or plant life or health, through the:
>
> (a) prevention, abatement, or control of the release, discharge, or emission of pollutants or environmental contaminants;
>
> (b) control of environmentally hazardous or toxic chemicals, substances, materials, and wastes, and the dissemination of information related thereto; or
>
> (c) protection or conservation of wild flora or fauna, including endangered species, their habitat, and specially protected natural areas,
>
> in the Party's territory, but does not include any statute or regulation, or provision thereof, directly related to worker safety or health.[123]

Such a definition may be easily adapted to non-treaty instruments as well.

Finally, two private sector initiatives bear mentioning. First, a 2010 compact provides for enterprises active in the area of genetically modified organisms to voluntarily accept binding arbitration of liability arising out of the 1992 Convention on Biological Diversity.[124] Secondly, the Gold Standard Foundation, a body that supervises a certification scheme for premium quality carbon credits generated by qualifying projects

---

[122] See, e.g., Convention on the Conservation and Management of High Seas Fisheries Resources in the North Pacific Ocean, signed on 24 February 2012 (entered into force on 19 July 2015), available at: http://npfc.r-cms.jp/files/user/docs/Convention%20Text.pdf. See also Convention on the Conservation and Management of High Seas Fishery Resources in the South Pacific Ocean, signed on 14 November 2009 (entered into force on 24 August 2012), available at: www.sprfmo.int/assets/Basic-Documents/Convention-web.pdf.

[123] Art. 12(4) of the US Model BIT (2012).

[124] *The Compact: A Contractual Mechanism for Response in the Event of Damage to Biological Diversity Caused by the Release of a Living Modified Organism*, 17 May 2010, available at: www.biodiversitycompact.org.

under the Kyoto Protocol's Clean Development Mechanism and other carbon-trading schemes, has successfully required that an open offer of arbitration be made for appeals against certification decisions on account of broader environmental and stakeholder interests.[125] Along with recent cases of investors consenting to jurisdiction over host State counter-claims,[126] these examples prove the common interest in and viability of the models in the environmental domain.

Indigenous Peoples' Rights

Indigenous peoples' rights emerge from the principle that these peoples hold a right to respect of their social, cultural, and economic conditions and political institutions that distinguish them from other sections of their national community.[127] Various international human rights

---

[125] *Rules for Appeals on Registration, Issuance and Labelling*, available at: www.goldstandard.org.

[126] See note 38 *supra*.

[127] For a general discussion of the interaction between indigenous rights and international investment law, see J. Levine, 'The Interaction of International Investment Arbitration and the Rights of Indigenous Peoples', in F. Baetens, *Investment Law within International Law: Integrationist Perspectives* (2013); V. S. Vadi, 'When Cultures Collide: Foreign Direct Investment, Natural Resources, and Indigenous Heritage in International Investment Law', 42 *Columbia Human Rights Law Review* 3 (2011); M. Krepchev, 'The Problem of Accommodating Indigenous Land Rights in International Investment Law', 6 *Journal of International Dispute Settlement* 1 (2015); F. Lenzerini, 'Investment Projects Affecting Indigenous Heritage', in V. S. Vadi and B. De Witte (eds.), *Culture and International Economic Law* (2015); T. Gazzini and Y. Radi, 'Foreign Investment with a Human Face – with Special Reference to Rights of Indigenous Peoples', in R. Hofmann, *International Investment Law and its Others* (2012); G. K. Foster, 'Foreign Investment and Indigenous Peoples: Options for Promoting Equilibrium between Economic Development and Indigenous Rights', 33 *Michigan Journal of International Law* 4 (2012). There are a number of arbitral and other decisions addressing indigenous rights in the context of international investment. See, e.g., *Grand River Enterprises Six Nations, Ltd., et al.* v. *United States of America*, NAFTA/UNICTRAL, Award, 12 January 2011, paras. 186–187, 210–219, 247; *Glamis Gold Ltd.* v. *United States of America*, NAFTA/UNCITRAL, Award, 8 June 2009; *Burlington Resources Inc.* v. *Republic of Ecuador*, ICSID Case No. ARB/08/05, Decision on Jurisdiction, 2 June 2010, paras. 316–318; *South American Silver Limited* v. *Plurinational State of Bolivia*, PCA Case No. 2013-15, Respondent's Objections to Jurisdiction, Admissibility and Counter-Memorial on the Merits, 31 March 2015, paras. 189–221; and *Vito G. Gallo* v. *Government of Canada*, PCA Case No. 2008-02, Canada's Counter-Memorial, 29 June 2010, paras. 137–155. See also *Case of the Kichwa Indigenous People of Sarayaku* v. *Ecuador*, Inter-American Court of Human Rights, Judgment of 27 June 2012 and *Indigenous Peoples of Sawhoyamaxa* v. *Paraguay*, Inter-American Court of Human Rights, Judgment of 29 March 2006.

instruments already protect the rights of indigenous peoples without addressing them as such. Three such instruments are the UDHR, the ICCPR, and the International Convention on the Elimination of All Forms of Racial Discrimination. Insofar as the right not to be discriminated against is enshrined in these instruments, they protect indigenous populations from discriminatory treatment. The first two instruments principally protect the rights of individuals,[128] and indigenous individuals naturally enjoy all rights listed therein. As for the last, Article 1 defines the term 'racial discrimination' as 'any distinction, exclusion, restriction or preference based on race, colour, descent, or national or ethnic origin which has the purpose or effect of nullifying or impairing the recognition, enjoyment or exercise, on an equal footing, of human rights and fundamental freedoms in the political, economic, social, cultural or any other field of public life'.[129] Most indigenous peoples would thus be susceptible of suffering racial discrimination within the meaning of this convention.

A more recent and focused effort to protect indigenous peoples is found in the UNDRIP.[130] The UNDRIP expressly recognises these peoples' right to the full enjoyment, *as a collective and as individuals*, of all human rights and fundamental freedoms as recognised in the Charter of the United Nations, the UDHR, and international human rights law. The ability of classes or collectives to vindicate non-individualised rights is thus particularly crucial in the sphere of indigenous rights. In particular, certain provisions in the UNDRIP call upon States to provide effective mechanisms for prevention of, and redress for, actions which have the aim *or effect* of dispossessing indigenous peoples of their lands, territories, or resources, as well as for forced population transfer which has the aim *or effect* of violating or undermining any of their rights.[131] As can be seen, the result of the actions, and not only the intention, is relevant for purposes of UNDRIP. In the light of the importance of lands and natural resources to indigenous peoples and the special protections that

---

[128] For a collective right, see, e.g., Art. 27 of the ICCPR ('[i]n those States in which ethnic, religious or linguistic minorities exist, persons belonging to such minorities shall not be denied the right, in community with the other members of their group, to enjoy their own culture, to profess and practise their own religion, or to use their own language').

[129] Art. 1 of the International Convention on the Elimination of All Forms of Racial Discrimination (1965).

[130] For the authoritative commentary on the Declaration, see M. Weller and J. Hohmann (eds.), *The UN Declaration on the Rights of Indigenous Peoples: A Commentary* (2017).

[131] See, e.g., Art. 8 of the UNDRIP.

attach thereto, and in view of the fact that exploitation of natural resources is often the object of foreign investment, it may be recognised that the interaction of investors' rights and indigenous peoples' rights may be complex.

In addition, a particularly relevant instrument (in the light of its legally binding nature) may be the ILO Convention No. 169. Even though it has obtained only twenty-two ratifications thus far, many of those are from States that have already encountered disputes with investors involving indigenous rights issues, and who seek to employ the ILO Convention No. 169 as a defence.[132]

Several ideas from the ILO Convention No. 169 specifically concern the making of investments in indigenous contexts. First, indigenous peoples are to have a say in measures or projects that affect them. In certain jurisdictions, they may even block the adoption of measures or the establishment or continuation of projects. Second, an impact assessment is required for any measure or project, to be conducted in cooperation with the peoples concerned, to assess the social, spiritual, cultural, and environmental impact upon them of planned development activities.[133] In addition, special safeguard measures are required for the persons, institutions, property, labour, cultures, and environment of the peoples concerned, such measures not being contrary to the freely expressed wishes of the peoples themselves.[134] Furthermore, a general obligation exists to consult with indigenous communities and peoples, and to take into account their position in matters that affect them. Apart from any obligations upon States that may stem from the convention, the need for investors to carry out community relations programmes is a reality in contexts where these rights are at stake, regardless of any legally established requirement in this regard.

As with human rights and labour rights, regional instruments of protection of indigenous rights may come into play depending upon the context in which a potential dispute might arise. Regional human rights régimes include protection against discrimination (for example, the American Convention on Human Rights (1969)) or rights of 'peoples', even without the qualifier 'indigenous'[135] (for example, the African Charter on Human and People's Rights (1981)). Worthy of mention is also the

---

[132] Another twenty-seven States have ratified ILO Convention No. 107, which also relates to indigenous people's rights, but is more assimilationist in character, in line with its time – seeing as it dates from 1959.

[133] Art. 7 of the ILO Convention No. 169.   [134] Art. 4 of the ILO Convention No. 169.

[135] See African Commission on Human and Peoples' Rights, *Indigenous Peoples in Africa: The Forgotten Peoples? The African Commission's Work on Indigenous Peoples in Africa*

American Declaration on the Rights of Indigenous Peoples, recently adopted by the Organisation of American States.[136]

Although not common, there are at least two States that have included provisions related to indigenous peoples' rights in their free trade agreements or bilateral investment treaties. New Zealand has included an exception as to measures taken in order to 'accord more favourable treatment to Maori' pursuant to the Treaty of Waitangi of 1840, so long as 'such measures are not used as a means of arbitrary or unjustified discrimination against persons of the other party or as a disguised restriction on trade in goods and services'.[137] South Africa has included in some of its treaties language qualifying the obligation to accord foreign investors national or most-favoured-nation treatment, which excludes from its purview State measures 'the purpose of which is to promote the achievement of equality in its territory, or designed to protect or advance persons or categories of persons, disadvantaged by unfair discrimination in its territory'.[138]

As may be seen from the foregoing, indigenous rights are tightly bound up in other human rights. Yet they additionally comprise unique rights of a collective nature that are not elsewhere fully captured. Where parties wish to render indigenous rights applicable within the models, it is advisable to make express reference to the UNDRIP and the ILO Convention No. 169, as well as any desired regional or national norms.

Anti-corruption

Corruption is universally condemned, not only from a moral point of view, but also from an economic perspective. Beyond attracting deserved moral opprobrium, it is widely recognised that corruption discourages investment flows, undermines economic growth, and is a significant contributing factor to other adverse impacts upon host States and their nationals. Investments derived from corruption thus stand in direct

---

(2006), available at: www.achpr.org/files/special-mechanisms/indigenous-populations/achpr_wgip_report_summary_version_eng.pdf.

[136] American Declaration on the Rights of Indigenous Peoples, AG/RES.2888 (XLVI-O/16), 167, available at: http://cdn7.iitc.org/wp-content/uploads/AG07150E06_web.pdf.

[137] See, e.g., Art. 205.1 of the New Zealand-China FTA (2008); Chapter 19, Article 3 of the New Zealand-Hong Kong Closer Economic Partnership Agreement (2010); Article 15.8 of the New Zealand-Thailand Closer Economic Partnership Agreement (2005); Article 74 of the New Zealand-Singapore Closer Economic Partnership Agreement (2000); and Article 17.6 of the New Zealand-Malaysia FTA (2009).

[138] See, e.g., Art. 3 of the South Africa-Mauritius BIT (1998).

opposition to investment instruments' stated object and purpose. It is therefore unsurprising that criminal sanctions, nullification of agreements, and the total barring of investment claims are the preferred remedies in case of corrupt acts by an investor.[139] Indeed, amongst the few investment instruments that address anti-corruption efforts in more than hortatory fashion, this is the most common approach.[140]

Absolute though such an approach may be, it does not fully address the multifaceted adverse impacts that corruption may yield upon host States and their nationals. The UNCAC, the principal (and only legally binding) universal anti-corruption instrument, thus recognises the need for a broader scope. In addition to a general need to ensure broader participation of society, it recognises the need to afford protection to whistle-blowers, witnesses, and victims,[141] as well as 'to ensure that entities or persons who have suffered damage as a result of an act of corruption have the right to initiate legal proceedings against those responsible for that damage in order to obtain compensation'.[142]

The UNCAC follows on other major regional and international anti-corruption instruments, including the Inter-American Convention against Corruption, the OECD Convention on Combating Bribery of Foreign Public Officials, and the African Union Convention on Preventing and Combating Corruption. It mandates States to establish offences regarding, *inter alia*, (i) bribery of foreign public officials and

---

[139] See, e.g., *World Duty Free Company Limited* v. *Republic of Kenya*, ICSID Case No. ARB/00/7, Award, 4 October 2006 and *Metal-Tech Ltd* v. *the Republic of Uzbekistan*, ICSID Case No. ARB/10/3, Award, 4 October 2013. As Judge Gunnar Lagergren famously held in his 1963 Award in ICC Case No. 1110, '[p]arties who ally themselves in an enterprise of the present nature must realise that they have forfeited any right to ask for assistance of the machinery of justice (national courts or arbitral tribunals) in settling their disputes.'

[140] See, e.g., Art. 10.1(k)(iv) of the Canada-Honduras FTA (2013); Art. 14(5) of the Norway Model BIT (2015) (precluding arbitration of an investor's claim 'where the investment has been made through fraudulent misrepresentation, concealment, corruption, or conduct amounting to an abuse of process'); and Art. 10 of the SADC Model BIT (2012) ('10.3. [a] breach of this article by an Investor or an Investment is deemed to constitute a breach of the domestic law of the Host State Party concerning the establishment and operation of an investment. 10.4. The State Parties to this Agreement, consistent with their applicable law, shall prosecute and where convicted penalize persons that have breached the applicable law implementing this obligation'). The commentary to paragraph 10.3 makes clear that 'an investment achieved by corruption . . . is no longer a covered investment and no longer has dispute settlement rights'. *SADC Model Bilateral Investment Treaty with Commentary* (2012) 32.

[141] Arts. 32–33 of the UNCAC.   [142] Art. 35 of the UNCAC.

officials of public international organisations;[143] (ii) embezzlement, misappropriation, or other diversion of property by a public official;[144] (iii) money laundering;[145] and (iv) obstruction of justice.[146] In addition, it asks States to 'consider adopting such legislative and other measures as may be necessary to establish as criminal offences' (i) trading in influence;[147] (ii) abuse of functions;[148] (iii) illicit enrichment;[149] (iv) bribery and embezzlement of property in the private sector;[150] and (v) concealment of illicit property.[151] All or any of these standards may be applied to investment activities, should parties wish to make them so applicable.

Given the clear consensus embodied in the UNCAC and the relevance to the conduct of foreign investors in a given host State, it is curious that anti-corruption efforts seldom find concrete expression in investment treaties.

---

[143] Art. 16 of the UNCAC ('the promise, offering or giving to a foreign public official or an official of a public international organization, directly or indirectly, of an undue advantage, for the official himself or herself or another person or entity, in order that the official act or refrain from acting in the exercise of his or her official duties, in order to obtain or retain business or other undue advantage in relation to the conduct of international business').

[144] Art. 17 of the UNCAC ('the embezzlement, misappropriation or other diversion by a public official for his or her benefit or for the benefit of another person or entity, of any property, public or private funds or securities or any other thing of value entrusted to the public official by virtue of his or her position').

[145] Art. 23 of the UNCAC.

[146] Art. 25 of the UNCAC ('[t]he use of physical force, threats or intimidation or the promise, offering or giving of an undue advantage to induce false testimony or to interfere in the giving of testimony or the production of evidence in a proceeding in relation to the commission of offences established in accordance with this Convention' or '[t]he use of physical force, threats or intimidation to interfere with the exercise of official duties by a justice or law enforcement official in relation to the commission of offences established in accordance with this Convention').

[147] Art. 18 of the UNCAC ('[t]he promise, offering or giving to a public official or any other person, directly or indirectly, of an undue advantage in order that the public official or the person abuse his or her real or supposed influence with a view to obtaining from an administration or public authority of the State Party an undue advantage for the original instigator of the act or for any other person').

[148] Art. 19 of the UNCAC ('[t]he performance of or failure to perform an act, in violation of laws, by a public official in the discharge of his or her functions, for the purpose of obtaining an undue advantage for himself or herself or for another person or entity').

[149] Art. 20 of the UNCAC ('[a] significant increase in the assets of a public official that he or she cannot reasonably explain in relation to his or her lawful income').

[150] Arts. 21–22 of the UNCAC.

[151] Art. 24 of the UNCAC ('[t]he concealment or continued retention of property when the person involved [without having participated in such offences] knows that such property is the result of any of the offences established in accordance with this Convention').

Only Canada's[152] and Japan's[153] recent investment agreements consistently speak to the issue, although a handful of further treaties do specifically address corruption in public procurement.[154] This may simply owe to the relatively recent emergence of the UNCAC, as increasing references in treaty

---

[152] See Art. 810 of the Canada-Peru FTA (2008) ('[e]ach Party should encourage enterprises operating within its territory or subject to its jurisdiction to voluntarily incorporate internationally recognized standards of corporate social responsibility in their internal policies, such as statements of principle that have been endorsed or are supported by the Parties. These principles address issues such as labour, the environment, human rights, community relations and anti-corruption'). See also, to similar effect, Art. 816 of the Canada-Colombia FTA (2008); Art. 9.17 of the Canada-Panama FTA (2010); Art. 16 of the Benin-Canada BIT (2013); Art. 15(2) of the Cameroon-Canada BIT (2014); Art. 16 of the Canada-Nigeria BIT (2014); Art. 16 of the Canada-Serbia BIT (2014); Art. 8.16 of the Canada-Republic of Korea FTA (2014); Art. 15.3 of the Canada-Mali BIT (2014); Art. 16 of the Canada-Senegal BIT (2014); Art. 15.2 of the Canada-Côte d'Ivoire BIT (2014); and Art. 16 of the Burkina Faso-Canada BIT (2015).

[153] See Art. 10 of the Cambodia-Japan BIT (2007); Art. 10 of the Japan-Lao People's Democratic Republic BIT (2008); Art. 10 of the Japan-Peru BIT (2008); Art. 9 of the Japan-Papua New Guinea BIT (2011); Art. 8 of the Colombia-Japan BIT (2011); Art. 9 of the Japan-Kuwait BIT (2012); Art. 9 of the Iraq-Japan BIT (2012); Art. 10 of the Japan-Mozambique BIT (2013); Art. 11 of the Japan-Myanmar BIT (2013); Art. 10 of the Japan-Kazakhstan BIT (2014); Art. 14 of the Japan-Uruguay BIT (2015); Art. 11 of the Japan-Ukraine BIT (2015); Art. 1.7 of the Japan-Mongolia Economic Partnership Agreement (2015); and Art. 8 of the Japan-Oman BIT (2015), all of which provide nearly identically as follows: 'Each Contracting Party shall ensure that measures and efforts are undertaken to prevent and combat corruption regarding matters covered by this Agreement in accordance with its laws and regulations.'

[154] See Art. 9.10 of the Bahrain-United States FTA (2004) ('[e]ach Party shall adopt or maintain procedures to declare ineligible for participation in the Party's procurements, either indefinitely or for a specified time, suppliers that the Party has determined to have engaged in fraudulent or illegal actions in relation to procurement. On request of the other Party, a Party shall identify the suppliers determined to be ineligible under these procedures, and, where appropriate, exchange information regarding those suppliers or the fraudulent or illegal action'); Art. 18 of the Hong Kong-New Zealand Closer Economic Partnership Agreement (2010) ('[e]ach Party shall ensure that criminal or administrative penalties exist to address corruption in its government procurement, and that its entities have in place policies and procedures to address any potential conflict of interest on the part of those engaged in or having influence over a procurement'); Art. 7.6 of the European Free Trade Association-Peru FTA (2010) ('[a] procuring entity shall conduct covered procurement in a transparent and impartial manner that: . . . (b) avoids conflicts of interest; and (c) prevents corrupt practices'); Art. 150(3) of the Japan-Peru FTA (2011) ('[e]ach Party shall ensure that its procuring entities conduct procurement in a transparent and impartial manner that: . . . (b) avoids conflicts of interest; and (c) prevents corrupt practices'); Art. 11.19 of the Trans-Pacific Strategic Economic Partnership Agreement (2004) (also known as the P4 Agreement) ('[e]ach Party shall ensure that criminal or administrative penalties exist to address corruption in its government procurement, and that its entities have in place policies and procedures to eliminate any potential conflict of interest on the part of those engaged in or having influence over a procurement').

preambles may betray.[155] However, no existing investment treaty yet provides for protection to whistle-blowers, witnesses, or victims (as foreseen under its Articles 32 and 33), or gives effect to its obligation to provide for civil recourse to entities or persons having suffered damage as a result of an act of corruption.

Alongside other national and international efforts to combat corruption and the denial of investment protections on account of corrupt acts, parties may wish to consider providing for recourse as directly against investors by host States and their nationals where victims of corruption, which may be done by simple reference to, for example, 'the offences, as well as the prohibition of intimidation, retaliation, and unjustified treatment, set forth in the *UN Convention against Corruption*' in an instrument effecting use of the models herein.[156] Some have proposed broadening the reach of such provisions to family members and close associates of relevant persons, or complementing them with robust transparency obligations.[157] However, recognising the high sensitivity of matters of corruption and other serious illegality, it bears repeating that the models take party autonomy as their starting point, and thus remain subject to the policy choices of States, investors, and other stakeholders in using the models as they wish, and with the substantive scope they deem best suited under the circumstances.

---

[155] Compare, for example, the Burkina Faso-Canada BIT (2015), including specific reference to the UNCAC, to the Canada-Serbia BIT (2014), referencing anti-corruption without specific reference to the Convention.

[156] Although little is publicly known of the claims other than that they were ultimately unsuccessful, the recent case of *Republic of Croatia* v. *MOL Hungarian Oil and Gas PLC*, PCA Case No. 2014-15, Award, 24 December 2016, would seem to prove the viability of this avenue for host States as well. See E. V. Gojkovic, 'An Unlikely Tandem of Criminal Investigations and Arbitral Proceedings: A Case Study of the INA – MOL Oil & Gas Proceedings', *Kluwer Arbitration Blog*, 26 January 2017, available at: http://kluwerarbitrationblog.com/2017/01/26/unlikely-tandem-criminal-investigations-arbitral-proceedings-case-study-ina-mol-oil-gas-proceedings. In the light of the international enforceability of arbitral awards, such claims may usefully complement the asset recovery mechanisms of the UNCAC itself. See Arts. 51–59 (Chapter V) of the UNCAC.

[157] J. A. VanDuzer, P. Simons, and G. Mayeda, 'Integrating Sustainable Development into International Investment Agreements: A Guide for Developing Countries', *Commonwealth Secretariat* (2012) 289, 335; *SADC Model Bilateral Investment Treaty with Commentary* (2012) 32–38.

6

Enforcement

In the same manner as foreign investors, host States and their nationals might reasonably desire an arbitral proceeding that produces an award enjoying the broadest international enforceability. The régime for enforcement of arbitral awards rendered in favour of the host State and its nationals falls largely across the two categories that exist with regard to investment arbitration generally. First, there is the ICSID Convention which, in addition to its framework for the conduct of proceedings, includes a self-contained enforcement mechanism. Secondly, awards falling outside the ambit of the ICSID Convention may rely upon those freestanding treaty instruments that govern the enforcement of international arbitral awards, the principal one amongst them being the New York Convention.

The ICSID Convention

The ICSID Convention features a robust enforcement mechanism. The Convention provides at Article 54 that '[e]ach Contracting State shall recognize an award rendered pursuant to this Convention as binding and enforce the pecuniary obligations imposed by that award within its territories as if it were a final judgment of a court in that State.'[1]

Thus, the treaty obligation of Article 54 requires that the courts of States party, where seized of an enforcement action, regard a duly rendered ICSID

---

[1] Art. 54(1) of the ICSID Convention. This assimilation of the status of an international arbitral award to that of a final court judgment has been emulated in other treaty instruments. See, e.g., Procedural Rules on Conciliation and Arbitration of Contracts Financed by the European Development Fund, Art. 33.3 of Annex IV of the Partnership Agreement between the Members of the African, Caribbean and Pacific Group of States of the one part, and the European Community and its Member States, of the other part, 317 *Official Journal of the European Union* (2000) (States party 'shall recognize as binding every award made pursuant to these rules and shall ensure that it is enforced in its territory, as if it were a final judgment of one of its own courts or tribunals').

decision as they would one of their own.[2] Such courts are prohibited from inquiring into the adequacy of the award, whether for any procedural defect or for any error on the merits. Rather, the sole recourse of an aggrieved award debtor lies in the internal ICSID mechanism of annulment.[3]

As for those models which do not allow for ICSID jurisdiction,[4] one possible resolution is that relevant treaties may include their own enforcement provision, whereby the States party commit to the recognition and enforcement in their own national courts of arbitral awards rendered thereunder. Indeed, enforcement provisions are a common feature of many contemporary investment treaties.[5] Where, however, an award debtor does not hold assets within the jurisdiction of any State party sufficient for the satisfaction of the adverse arbitral award, the prevailing party may be compelled to turn to other instruments for enforcement in third States.

Furthermore, where there is found to be no investment, where either the home State of the investor or the host State of the investment is not

---

[2] For those circumstances in which a contracting State would fail to do so, the Convention allows that the antiquity of diplomatic protection may be resurrected. See Art. 27(1) of the ICSID Convention ('[n]o Contracting State shall give diplomatic protection, or bring an international claim, in respect of a dispute which one of its nationals and another Contracting State shall have consented to submit or shall have submitted to arbitration under this Convention, unless such other Contracting State shall have failed to abide by and comply with the award rendered in such dispute').

[3] Under this mechanism, the powers of a committee to annul a duly rendered award are restricted to cases of procedural defects only. See Art. 52(1) of the ICSID Convention ('[e]ither party may request annulment of the award by an application in writing addressed to the Secretary-General on one or more of the following grounds: (a) that the Tribunal was not properly constituted; (b) that the Tribunal has manifestly exceeded its powers; (c) that there was corruption on the part of a member of the Tribunal; (d) that there has been a serious departure from a fundamental rule of procedure; or (e) that the award has failed to state the reasons on which it is based').

[4] See Direct Claims (I) Model, Chapter 2; see also Jurisdiction without Privity, Chapter 3.

[5] See, e.g., Art. 9(4) of the China Model BIT (1997) ('[t]he arbitration award shall be final and binding upon both parties to the dispute. Both Contracting Parties shall commit themselves to the enforcement of the award'); Art. VII(3) of the Turkey Model BIT (2000) ('[t]he arbitration awards shall be final and binding for all parties in dispute. Each Party commits itself to execute the award according to its national law'); Art. 10(3) of the Germany Model BIT (2005) ('[t]he award shall be enforced by the Contracting States as a final and absolute ruling under domestic law'); Art. 34(7) of the US Model BIT (2012) and Art. 1136(4) of the NAFTA ('[e]ach Party shall provide for the enforcement of an award in its territory'); and Art. 26(8) of the Energy Charter Treaty ('[e]ach Contracting Party shall carry out without delay any such award and shall make provision for the effective enforcement in its Area of such awards'). However, several of these model provisions appear on their faces not to be self-executing. Furthermore, even if properly implemented, these provisions are not helpful in securing enforcement in third States.

party to the ICSID Convention, or where ICSID jurisdiction is not engaged for any reason whatsoever, parties may have recourse to the New York Convention.

The New York Convention

As foreshadowed, prospects for enforcement under the New York Convention and other cornerstones of international commercial arbitration are broader. Unlike the ICSID Convention or investment treaties, these instruments do not place any restrictions upon the identities of the parties to arbitration, nor do they necessarily place any limitation upon the nature of the dispute. In a further departure, these instruments do not impose objective requirements for the *ex ante* existence of any arbitral jurisdiction, but rather only objective requirements which must be met in order for a State party's enforcement obligation to arise.

Universally known as the New York Convention, the treaty's official name is the Convention on the Recognition and Enforcement of Foreign Arbitral Awards of 1958.[6] Unlike the ICSID Convention, the New York Convention does not seek to establish the procedural framework of an arbitral mechanism. Rather, the New York Convention brings to bear its most significant legal effect after such time as an arbitral award is rendered. After such a time, States party to the New York Convention are obliged, where their courts are seized by an award creditor, to enforce the award, subject only to a closed list of permissive exceptions.[7]

---

[6] Convention on the Recognition and Enforcement of Foreign Arbitral Awards, 330 UNTS 38, 7 ILM 1046 (1968).

[7] Article V of the New York Convention provides as follows:

'1. Recognition and enforcement of the award may be refused, at the request of the party against whom it is invoked, only if that party furnishes to the competent authority where the recognition and enforcement is sought, proof that:

   (a) The parties to the agreement referred to in article II were, under the law applicable to them, under some incapacity, or the said agreement is not valid under the law to which the parties have subjected it or, failing any indication thereon, under the law of the country where the award was made; or

   (b) The party against whom the award is invoked was not given proper notice of the appointment of the arbitrator or of the arbitration proceedings or was otherwise unable to present his case; or

   (c) The award deals with a difference not contemplated by or not falling within the terms of the submission to arbitration, or it contains decisions on matters beyond the scope of the submission to arbitration, provided that, if the decisions on matters submitted to arbitration can be separated from those

The Role of the Lex Arbitri

One of these permissive grounds for declining to enforce an arbitral award envisages a parallel court procedure, for the New York Convention allows that

> [r]ecognition and enforcement of the award may be refused, at the request of the party against whom it is invoked ... if that party furnishes to the competent authority where the recognition and enforcement is sought, proof that: ... The award has not yet become binding on the parties, or *has been set aside or suspended by a competent authority of the country in which, or under the law of which, that award was made.*[8]

This provision is now widely accepted as allowing courts in States party to the Convention to accord weight only to an annulment of the arbitral award at the legal place of arbitration, commonly known as the arbitral seat.[9] While the Convention does not permit courts in the State wherein enforcement is sought to consider any ground for declining enforcement other than those expressly enumerated at Article V (of which annulment is one), the Convention equally does not prescribe any substantive grounds upon which an award may or may not be annulled by the courts at the place of arbitration. Thus, unlike in ICSID arbitration, where the grounds of annulment are expressly stated in a closed list within the ICSID Convention itself,[10] the grounds upon which an award may be set aside emerge from the *lex arbitri* at the chosen arbitral seat, which internal law is free from any constraint imposed by the New York Convention. In practice, however, parties tend to select arbitral seats

not so submitted, that part of the award which contains decisions on matters submitted to arbitration may be recognized and enforced; or

(d) The composition of the arbitral authority or the arbitral procedure was not in accordance with the agreement of the parties, or, failing such agreement, was not in accordance with the law of the country where the arbitration took place; or

(e) The award has not yet become binding on the parties, or has been set aside or suspended by a competent authority of the country in which, or under the law of which, that award was made.

2. Recognition and enforcement of an arbitral award may also be refused if the competent authority in the country where recognition and enforcement is sought finds that:

(a) The subject matter of the difference is not capable of settlement by arbitration under the law of that country; or

(b) The recognition or enforcement of the award would be contrary to the public policy of that country'.

[8] Art. V(1)(e) of the New York Convention (emphasis added).

[9] G. Born, *International Commercial Arbitration* (2014) 3621.   [10] See note 3 *supra*.

whose laws provide for grounds of annulment that are largely equivalent to those for refusal of enforcement at Article V of the New York Convention.[11] Lastly, upon the face of the New York Convention, the grounds for declining enforcement enumerated at Article V are, indeed, permissive.[12] There is presently a lively debate in the discipline regarding the weight that is properly accorded to an annulment at the arbitral seat under Article V(1)(e) of the Convention.[13]

---

[11] See G. Verhoosel, 'Annulment and Enforcement Review of Treaty Awards: To ICSID or Not to ICSID', in A. J. van den Berg (ed.), *50 Years of the New York Convention: ICCA International Arbitration Conference*, ICCA Congress Series, 14 *Kluwer Law International* (2009). It must also be noted that many States have enacted the UNCITRAL Model Law on International Commercial Arbitration (or a variation thereof) to fill the role of their *lex arbitri*, which essentially replicates the list of grounds for refusal of enforcement at Article V of the New York Convention. Art. 34(2) of the UNCITRAL Model Law on International Commercial Arbitration of 1985 (as amended in 2006) provides as follows:

An arbitral award may be set aside by the court . . . only if:

    (a) the party making the application furnishes proof that:

         (i) a party to the arbitration agreement referred to in article 7 was under some incapacity; or the said agreement is not valid under the law to which the parties have subjected it or, failing any indication thereon, under the law of this State; or

        (ii) the party making the application was not given proper notice of the appointment of an arbitrator or of the arbitral proceedings or was otherwise unable to present his case; or

      (iii) the award deals with a dispute not contemplated by or not falling within the terms of the submission to arbitration, or contains decisions on matters beyond the scope of the submission to arbitration, provided that, if the decisions on matters submitted to arbitration can be separated from those not so submitted, only that part of the award which contains decisions on matters not submitted to arbitration may be set aside; or

      (iv) the composition of the arbitral tribunal or the arbitral procedure was not in accordance with the agreement of the parties, unless such agreement was in conflict with a provision of this Law from which the parties cannot derogate, or, failing such agreement, was not in accordance with this Law; or

    (b) the court finds that:

        (i) the subject-matter of the dispute is not capable of settlement by arbitration under the law of this State; or

       (ii) the award is in conflict with the public policy of this State.

[12] Art. V(1) ('[r]ecognition and enforcement of the award may be refused . . . ') and Art. V(2) ('[r]ecognition and enforcement of an arbitral award may also be refused . . . ') of the New York Convention.

[13] See, e.g., *Global Arbitration Review*, 'Clash of the Singapore Titans: Menon and Born Disagree over Awards Annulled at the Seat', 12 October 2015, available at: http://globalarbitrationreview.com/article/1034834/clash-of-the-singapore-titans. Within the United States, for example, the federal District Court for the District of Columbia has found that US courts may

The Requirement of an 'Agreement in Writing'

It has been noted that where the home State of the foreign investor exercises its sovereign privilege to submit its nationals to the jurisdiction of an international tribunal,[14] the foreign investor has given no 'consent in writing' to the arbitral tribunal's jurisdiction, a defect that is likely fatal to ICSID jurisdiction, and thus also ICSID enforcement.[15] In such a case, there may equally be a failure of the agreement in writing as required between the disputant parties for an enforcement obligation to arise under the New York Convention.

Allied to the matter of consent is the concern for due process. In jurisdictions wherein the national court jurisprudence circumscribing international arbitration has matured, while the right of access to the courts for the adjudication of disputes remains a fundamental right, it is not an *inalienable* right.[16] It is now largely accepted that where there is *valid consent* to arbitration of disputes, there can be no due process objection. Important unanswered questions remain in regard to the *validity of consent* under this construct. Even where one looks to paternalistic models wherein sovereign States exercise judgment on behalf of their nationals, we arrive at only a form of constructive or contrived consent. In cases of derogation from the fundamental procedural right of access to a court of law, the strict consent of an arbitration agreement existing directly between two or more contracting parties or the arguably strict consent of the standing offer theory may be required as a matter of law, even in the world's most arbitration-friendly jurisdictions.

proceed to enforce an award annulled at the seat where it finds the annulment to be improperly obtained. *Chromalloy Aeroservices* v. *Arab Republic of Egypt*, 939 F. Supp. 907, D.D.C. (1996). In particular, the court found that 'Egypt's complaint that, "[t]he Arbitral Award is null under Arbitration Law, ... because it is not properly 'grounded' under Egyptian law," reflects this suspicious view of arbitration, and is precisely the type of technical argument that U.S. courts are not to entertain when reviewing an arbitral award.' Ibid. 911. See also *Corporación Mexicana de Mantenimiento Integral, S. de R.L. de C.V.* v. *Pemex-Exploración y Producción*, No. 13–4022, 2d Cir. (2016).

[14] See Jurisdiction without Privity, Chapter 3.

[15] See Art. 25(1) of the ICSID Convention. Professor Schreuer has observed that, for purposes of ICSID jurisdiction, '[c]onsent in writing must be explicit and not merely construed'. C. Schreuer, L. Malintoppi, A. Reinisch, and A. Sinclair, *The ICSID Convention: A Commentary*, 2nd edn. (2009) 191.

[16] See, e.g., *Judgment of 16 October 2001*, 2002 Rev. arb. 753, 756 (Swiss Fed. Trib.) ('Constitutional law (in Switzerland, Article 30(1) of the Federal Constitution applies) as well as treaty law (see Article 6(1) of the European Convention on Human Rights) afford each natural person and legal entity the right to be heard before a court established on the basis of statutory law. By submitting to arbitration a party waives such right').

This chasm between strict and constructive consent is of more than merely theoretical significance. In addition to the requirement of an 'agreement in writing', under the New York Convention, recognition and enforcement of an award 'may' be refused where '[t]he composition of the arbitral authority or the arbitral procedure was not in accordance with the agreement of the parties'.[17] Where the constitution of a tribunal or the applicable arbitral procedure are imposed not under an agreement existing between the disputant parties but rather by direct or indirect effect of an instrument of international law, questions might be raised as to whether such is 'in accordance with the agreement of the parties'.

The full text of the relevant section provides that enforcement may be refused where '[t]he composition of the arbitral authority or the arbitral procedure was not in accordance with the agreement of the parties or, failing such agreement, was not in accordance with the law of the country where the arbitration took place'.[18] On the face of this provision an argument emerges that it suffices for purposes of award enforceability that a tribunal is constituted and its proceedings conducted in conformity with the *lex arbitri* at the arbitral seat. While that argument appears textually correct, doubts remain as to whether this result may obtain in the absence of an 'agreement in writing' within the meaning of the New York Convention.

Similarly, with regard to an earlier stage in the life cycle of an arbitral proceeding, the New York Convention provides that '[t]he court of a Contracting State, when seized of an action in a matter in respect of which *the parties have made an agreement* within the meaning of this article, shall, at the request of one of the parties, refer the parties to arbitration.'[19] Where no arbitration agreement exists as effected directly between the disputant parties, national courts may not find themselves compelled (or even permitted) to foreclose actions before them. These treaty mechanisms may thus mark uncharted territory under the New York Convention.

In this regard, however, the analogous experience of the Iran-United States Claims Tribunal (and the enforcement of its awards under the New York Convention) offers reason for optimism.[20] Despite the lack of

---

[17] Art. V(1)(d) of the New York Convention.   [18] Ibid.

[19] Art. II(3) of the New York Convention.

[20] The Iran-United States Claims Tribunal, which was established and derives its jurisdiction from the Claims Settlement Declaration concerning the settlement of claims by the Government of the United States of America and the Government of the Islamic Republic of Iran, also renders awards on the basis of an agreement to which the private disputants

privity – both States having mandatorily submitted their nationals to the jurisdiction of the Tribunal for claims falling within the ambit of the Claims Settlement Declaration – various national courts have enforced the Tribunal's awards under the New York Convention, finding that the threshold requirement of an 'agreement in writing' was fulfilled. For instance, in *Ministry of Defense of the Islamic Republic of Iran v. Gould Inc., Gould Marketing, Inc., Hoffman Export Corporation, and Gould International*, the defendant contended that the US courts should refuse to enforce the arbitral award, arguing that, for the New York Convention to apply, it is necessary that arbitral awards 'derive from an arbitral agreement in writing to which the parties voluntarily submitted' and that the Claims Settlement Declaration 'do[es] not satisfy this require-ment'.[21] The court ruled:

> The real question is not whether Gould entered into a written agreement to submit its claims against Iran to arbitration, but whether the President – acting on behalf of Gould – entered into such an agreement. *The answer is clearly yes* ... [T]he requirements of Article II are satisfied. In addition, the Final Tribunal Rules of Procedure state that '[t]he Claims Settlement Declaration constitutes an agreement in writing by Iran and the United States, on their own behalfs and on behalf of their nationals submitting to arbitration within the framework of the Algiers Declarations and in accor-dance with the Tribunal Rules'.[22]

Such enforcement is also consistent with the general liberalisation over time of the requirement of an 'agreement in writing', in keeping with the Convention's strong pro-enforcement objective.[23]

---

lack privity. Declaration of the Government of the Democratic and Popular Republic of Algeria concerning the settlement of claims by the Government of the United States of America and the Government of the Islamic Republic of Iran (Claims Settlement Declaration), 19 January 1981, available at: www.iusct.net/General%20Documents/2-Claims%20Settlement%20Declaration.pdf. For relevant provisions of the Claims Settlement Declaration, see Chapter 4, note 28.

[21] *Ministry of Defense of the Islamic Republic of Iran v. Gould Inc.*, 887 F.2d 1357, 1363, 9th Cir. (1989).

[22] Ibid. 1364 (emphasis added). The court expressly rejected the opposing conclusion purported to have been reached in *Dallal v. Bank Mellat*, Queen's Bench Division (Commercial Court), [1986] 1 All ER 239. The award in *Dallal* was in any event recognised on the basis of international comity. See D. Caron and L. Caplan, *The UNCITRAL Arbitration Rules: A Commentary*, 2nd edn. (2013) 44 n 162.

[23] Recommendation Regarding the Interpretation of Article II, Paragraph 2, and Article VII, Paragraph 1, of the New York Convention, adopted by UNCITRAL on 7 July 2006 at its thirty-ninth session, Doc. No. A/CN.9/607, available at: https://documents-dds-ny.un .org/doc/UNDOC/GEN/V06/530/31/PDF/V0653031.pdf?OpenElement.

In this vein, seeing as the New York Convention may be disregarded where a more favourable framework for enforcement exists,[24] another solution might be found in the possibility that treaties in the mould of the International Institute for Sustainable Development model treaty or the early Netherlands-Indonesia treaty might include their own freestanding enforcement mechanism.[25] Further, in cases of mere bilateral treaties, or those with only a small number of States party, broader enforceability might be sought with a provision modelled upon the following, drawn from an innovative proposal within the world of international commercial arbitration:

> Both Parties declare their mutual desire and expectation that Arbitral Awards made by an arbitral tribunal pursuant to ... this Treaty be subject to recognition and enforcement by the Courts of other States in accordance with the provisions of the New York Convention. For the purposes of such recognition and enforcement proceedings, both Parties desire and expect that the provisions of ... this Treaty shall ... be deemed to constitute a valid agreement to arbitrate ... within the meaning of Articles II, IV and V(1)(a) of the New York Convention.[26]

---

[24] See Art. VII(1) of the New York Convention, providing as follows:

> The provisions of the present Convention shall not affect the validity of multilateral or bilateral agreements concerning the recognition and enforcement of arbitral awards entered into by the Contracting States nor deprive any interested party of any right he may have to avail himself of an arbitral award in the manner and to the extent allowed by the law or the treaties of the country where such award is sought to be relied upon.

[25] See Jurisdiction without Privity, Chapter 3.

[26] G. Born, *Draft Model Bilateral Arbitration Treaty*, Art. 6(4), available at: www.wilmer hale.com/uploadedFiles/Shared_Content/Editorial/News/Documents/Draft-Model-BAT.pdf. For a view into the theoretical and practical underpinnings of Mr. Born's proposal, see G. Born, *BITs, BATs, and Buts: Reflections on International Dispute Resolution* (2014), available at: www.wilmerhale.com/uploadedFiles/Shared_Content/Editorial/News/Documents/BITs-BATs-and-Buts.pdf.

Mr. Born further explains as follows:

> 88. The States that are party to the Treaty cannot bind other States to their expectations and intentions with respect to application of the New York Convention to awards under the Treaty; other States might take the view that the Convention's requirements for a valid arbitration agreement are not satisfied by the provisions of the Treaty. Nonetheless, it can be anticipated that other States will accord substantial weight to the expectations and intentions of the States party to the Treaty. Moreover, States that are not parties to the Treaty may elect to enforce awards made under the Treaty, even without formal application of the New York Convention, if they conclude that an award rendered under the Treaty nonetheless satisfies the requirements for recognition of national court judgments or administrative decrees.

The 'Commercial' Reservation

The New York Convention is inclusive of all awards, and does not impose any restriction by subject matter. However, aside from the possibility of annulment at the arbitral seat and the other permissive grounds for refusal of enforcement,[27] there is one further qualification in this regard. At the time of accession, a State may 'declare that it will apply the Convention only to differences arising out of legal relationships, whether contractual or not, which are considered as commercial under the national law of the State making such declaration'.[28] This provision is

> 89. As bilateral arbitration treaties become more common there will be an incentive for States to recognise and enforce awards rendered under substantially similar treaties even where the recognizing State is not a party to the treaty under which the award was rendered. This incentive can be formalized by an agreement among States party to different bilateral arbitration treaties to recognize and enforce awards made under such treaties in accordance with the terms of the New York Convention.

. . .

> 97. As with . . . the New York Convention . . . the Treaty should be interpreted in a robustly pro-enforcement manner. This is essential in order to ensure that the Treaty's benefits of efficiency, neutrality and finality are fully realized. Authorities decided under the New York Convention should, in general, be considered relevant to interpretation and application of the Treaty.

G. Born, *Explanatory Note to Draft Model Bilateral Arbitration Treaty*, paras. 88–89 and 97, available at: www.victoria.ac.nz/law/about/staff/petra-butler/Explanatory-Note-Draft-Model-Bilateral-Arbitration-Treaty.pdf. International comity provided sufficient grounds for the recognition and enforcement of the award in the aforementioned case of *Dallal* v. *Bank Mellat* where, despite finding the New York Convention inapplicable, the English courts nevertheless held that

> where two sovereign states have chosen to set up a tribunal to determine disputes between the nationals of their respective states in respect of choses in action for which the situs lies within the jurisdiction of those two states, there can be no warrant for the courts of this country to fail to recognise and treat as fully competent the decisions of that tribunal.

Dallal v. *Bank Mellat*, Queen's Bench Division (Commercial Court), [1986] 1 All ER 239.

[27] See note 7 *supra*.

[28] Art. I(3) of the New York Convention. In 2016, the Republic of Angola acceded to the New York Convention, thus becoming its 157th contracting State. Of these, forty-six have given declarations to enact a commercial reservation, or less than one third. Those recording the reservation include such established and emerging economies as the United States, Canada, Argentina, Poland, Turkey, Nigeria, Iran, India, Indonesia, Malaysia, South Korea, and the People's Republic of China. Those foregoing the reservation include six of the Group of Eight major economies, these being the United Kingdom,

commonly known as the commercial reservation.[29] Professor Albert Jan van den Berg has observed that the reservation 'was inserted because at the New York Conference of 1958 it was believed that, without this clause, it would be impossible for certain Civil Law countries, which distinguish between commercial and non-commercial transactions, to adhere to the Convention'.[30]

Herbert Kronke has written that '[w]ithout a doubt, a narrow interpretation is inconsistent with the underlying purpose of the Convention, which aims to facilitate enforcement within the framework of international commercial arbitration', and that '[i]n general, with respect to the implementation of the Convention, national courts are encouraged and often seize the opportunity to interpret the commercial reservation in the broadest sense'.[31] Other commentators have equally observed that '[i]n practice, the commercial reservation generally has not caused problems as the courts tend to interpret the coverage of "commercial" broadly', and that '[t]here is also a tendency to rely on the broad description of what constitutes "commercial" as is given in conjunction with the UNCITRAL Model Law on International Commercial Arbitration of 1985'.[32]

France, Germany, Italy, Japan, and Russia (presently suspended from the Group, following its annexation of Crimea in 2014). The ranks of the non-enacting States also include Austria, Belgium, Ireland, the Netherlands, Spain, Switzerland, Ukraine, Mexico, Brazil, Chile, Colombia, Peru, Saudi Arabia, the United Arab Emirates, Singapore, and Australia, as well as Kenya, Tanzania, Uganda, Angola, and South Africa.

[29] Under, for example, the Panama Convention, there is a default restriction to matters commercial in nature. See Art. 1 of the Inter-American Convention on International Commercial Arbitration, 1438 UNTS 245, 14 ILM 336 (1975) ('[a]n agreement in which the parties undertake to submit to arbitral decision any differences that may arise or have arisen between them with respect to a commercial transaction is valid').

[30] A. J. van den Berg, 'The New York Convention of 1958: An Overview', *International Council for Commercial Arbitration* (2003) 5. Further, '[t]he words "whether contractual or not" are intended to cover not only disputes arising out of contract but also tort.' Ibid.

[31] H. Kronke, P. Nacimiento, D. Otto, and N. C. Port (eds.), *Recognition and Enforcement of Foreign Arbitral Awards: A Global Commentary on the New York Convention* (2011) 35.

[32] Ibid. See also Note 2 of the UNCITRAL Model Law on International Commercial Arbitration of 1985 (as amended in 2006) ('[t]he term "commercial" should be given a wide interpretation so as to cover matters arising from all relationships of a commercial nature, whether contractual or not. Relationships of a commercial nature include, but are not limited to, the following transactions: any trade transaction for the supply or exchange of goods or services; distribution agreement; commercial representation or agency; factoring; leasing; construction of works; consulting; engineering; licensing; investment; financing; banking; insurance; exploitation agreement or concession; joint venture and other forms of industrial or business cooperation; carriage of goods or

Under the New York Convention, in an exception to the principle of autonomous interpretation, the ambit of 'commercial' is to be determined by reference to municipal law, which is to say the law of the State wherein enforcement is sought (if indeed such State has enacted the reservation).[33] Thus, for example, in the United States, awards are excluded from the scope of the New York Convention only where matters arise out of legal relationships, whether contractual or not, which are not considered as 'commercial' under the laws of the United States.[34]

Unsurprisingly, different States have interpreted and applied their reservations in divergent manners. A comparatively narrow scope of enforcement obligation has been assigned to the commercial reservation by a federal first instance court in the District of Columbia. In one case, the court refused to recognise and enforce an arbitral award that adjudicated claims of defamation and unfair competition.[35] The court looked to the text of the US Federal Arbitration Act, which serves as the implementing legislation of the New York Convention, and concluded that it is the nature of the relationship between the parties, not the nature of their

passengers by air, sea, rail or road') and Explanatory Note by the UNCITRAL Secretariat, para. 12 ('[i]n respect of the term "commercial", the Model Law provides no strict definition. The footnote to article 1 (1) calls for "a wide interpretation" and offers an illustrative and open-ended list of relationships that might be described as commercial in nature, "whether contractual or not". The purpose of the footnote is to circumvent any technical difficulty that may arise, for example, in determining which transactions should be governed by a specific body of "commercial law" that may exist in some legal systems').

[33] Art. I(3) of the New York Convention. It has, however, been observed that '[a]lthough the language of the Convention refers to the national law of the forum State (as an exception to the principle of autonomous interpretation), in practice courts also give consideration to the special circumstances of the case and to international practice'. International Council for Commercial Arbitration, *Guide to the Interpretation of the 1958 New York Convention: A Handbook for Judges* (2011).

[34] See J. Lew, L. Mistelis, and S. Kröll, *Comparative International Commercial Arbitration* (2003), para. 4.19.

[35] See *Diag Human S.E.* v. *Czech Republic-Ministry of Health*, 64 F. Supp. 3d 22, D.D.C. (2014). The facts of the case are as follows. The claimant, Diag Human S.E., was a large-scale blood plasma supplier. One of its principal commercial relationships was with the Danish company Novo Nordisk. Diag claimed that the Minister of Health of the Czech Republic sent a letter to Novo Nordisk regarding a public tender for blood plasma products that dissuaded Novo Nordisk from continuing to do business with Diag. Diag responded by suing the Ministry of Health in the Prague Commercial Court for defamation and unfair competition. The parties then agreed to arbitrate their dispute in the Czech Republic. The tribunal rendered a final award ordering damages and interest in favour of Diag. Diag then petitioned the District Court to enforce the award under the New York Convention.

dispute, which determines whether the reservation applies.[36] The court then found that, before the award-creditor instituted its action, there was no legal relationship between the parties of any kind whatsoever. The court thus held that the award did not fall within the enforcement obligation of the United States, as under the New York Convention.[37]

The law of this case is mentioned to demonstrate that the threshold of a legal relationship is attainable by use of the four models, even under a restrictive standard. Even where, for example, there is no contractual agreement as between the foreign investor and the host State of the investment, a legal relationship exists under an instrument which affords certain privileges to the foreign investor in exchange for the imposition of certain obligations (namely, the obligation to abide by certain rights which flow in favour of the host State or its nationals, and to submit to the arbitration of disputes arising therefrom).[38] As for host State nationals, their status as beneficiaries of obligations that fall upon the investor equally establishes their own legal relationship vis-à-vis such an investor.

Questions may arise, where applying the definition attributable to the word in the law of certain States party, as to whether this latter relationship is 'commercial', regardless of the nature of the underlying investment activity itself. While there may be a legal relationship, there is arguably no rapport that is commercial in character as directly between the foreign investor and the host State national where, for example, the latter merely suffers collateral consequences of the investor's otherwise commercial activity.[39]

Where an instrument grants rights to a non-party that are opposable to any or all of the parties to the instrument itself, a legal relationship exists not only bilaterally as between the non-party and each or all of the opposable parties, but multilaterally as amongst them all. Thus, in the

---

[36] Ibid. See also Federal Arbitration Act, 9 U.S.C. s. 202 ('[a]n arbitration agreement or arbitral award arising out of a legal relationship, whether contractual or not, which is considered as commercial, including a transaction, contract, or agreement described in section 2 of this title, falls under the Convention').

[37] Ibid. The decision has since been reversed and remanded on appeal. See *Diag Human S.E. v. Czech Republic-Ministry of Health*, 824 F.3d 131, D.C. Cir. (2016).

[38] See Chapter 3; see also Chapter 5.

[39] This absence of *quid pro quo* was precisely the stalling factor in the advancement of the doctrine of third party beneficiaries of contract at common law. Under the now-abandoned traditional view, any non-party to the relevant instrument could not gain enforceable rights vis-à-vis the foreign investor without giving consideration. See Chapter 2, note 6.

simplest example, and whether by treaty, contract, or host State law, a trilateral legal relationship is formed as between the host State, the foreign investor, and the host State national.[40] In this triangulation, the predominant purpose and even the *raison d'être* of the legal relationship lies in furtherance of commercial ends. Certain rights are granted to the host State and its national precisely in order to procure, in exchange, certain rights to the investor, in the pursuit of his investment.[41]

A proposed model treaty tailored to a different purpose has included a model definition of 'International Commercial Dispute'.[42] In that model,

---

[40] See Chapter 3.

[41] It must be noted that the strength of this proposition may be tested only in diverse national courts and under divergent national laws, once an enforcement action is brought under the New York Convention, and once the award debtor resists enforcement by invoking an applicable commercial reservation.

[42] The model definition provides as follows:

'International Commercial Dispute' means a dispute, disagreement, or controversy:

(a) arising between (1) one or more Enterprises of one Party; and (2) one or more Enterprises of the other Party; and

(b) arising out of commercial contracts, transactions, or activities, including, without limitation, any: trade transaction for the supply or exchange of goods or services; distribution agreement; commercial representation or agency; factoring; leasing; construction of works; consulting; engineering; licensing; investment; financing; banking; insurance; exploitation agreement or concession; joint venture or other form of industrial or business cooperation; mergers or acquisitions; carriage of goods or passengers by air, sea, rail or road; or any other activities the nature or purpose of which is the realization of a profit. Notwithstanding the foregoing, an 'International Commercial Dispute' does not include consumer disputes, employment or labor disputes, domestic relations disputes, marital or child custody disputes, inheritance disputes, or [____].

G. Born, *Draft Model Bilateral Arbitration Treaty*, Art. 1, available at: www.wilmerhale .com/uploadedFiles/Shared_Content/Editorial/News/Documents/Draft-Model-BAT.pdf.

Mr. Born further explains as follows:

13. The Treaty broadly defines 'International Commercial Dispute' as any dispute arising out of a commercial transaction, contract, or activity between 'Enterprises' in the States that are party to the Treaty. Sub-part (b) of the definition is drafted expansively, modelled on Article 1(1), note 2, of the UNCITRAL Model Law to cover any one of a list of transactions and any other activities or transactions whose nature or purpose is realization of a profit. In order to ensure a comprehensive and consistent regime, this definition is intended to cover any cause of action, however arising, provided it has some connection with a transaction or activity involving these States.

14. Claims in tort that are related to a commercial contract would therefore fall within the Treaty regime. A dispute that does not arise from or relate to an international commercial transaction would not fall

the definition serves at the jurisdictional threshold rather than the enforcement stage: this definition serves to delineate categories of disputes that would fall within the default jurisdiction of an arbitral tribunal where relevant commercial parties do not specify an alternative *modus* of dispute settlement. While the treaty calls upon third States to acknowledge the parties' 'mutual desire and expectation' that its mechanism be found to satisfy the requirement of an agreement to arbitrate for purposes of the New York Convention,[43] there is no call in a similar manner for third States to abide by its definition of commerciality.

Thus, a tribunal formed pursuant to a treaty emulating that model might apply its definition of 'International Commercial Dispute' to accept jurisdiction over the subject matter of given claims. Thereafter, a national court in a third State wherein enforcement is sought (and which has enacted the commercial reservation to the New York Convention) may abide by the wish of the States party to the treaty that its provisions 'shall ... be deemed to constitute a valid agreement to arbitrate',[44] but may nonetheless decline to enforce the award as falling on the wrong side of its own commercial reservation, under its own laws.

One model for overcoming any obstacle raised by a commercial reservation features within the US Model BIT and the NAFTA. Therein, it is stipulated that '[a] claim that is submitted to arbitration under this Section shall be considered to arise out of a commercial relationship or transaction for the purposes of Article I of the New York Convention and Article I of the [Panama] Convention.'[45] This provision might seem superfluous

within the Treaty. G. Born, *Explanatory Note to Draft Model Bilateral Arbitration Treaty*, paras. 13–14, available at: www.victoria.ac.nz/law/about/staff/petra-butler/Explanatory-Note-Draft-Model-Bilateral-Arbitration-Treaty.pdf.

[43] G. Born, *Draft Model Bilateral Arbitration Treaty*, Art. 6(4), available at: www.wilmerhale.com/uploadedFiles/Shared_Content/Editorial/News/Documents/Draft-Model-BAT.pdf.

[44] Ibid.

[45] Art. 34(10) of the US Model BIT (2012); Art. 1136(7) of the NAFTA. At first glance, this text would appear offensive to Professor Schreuer's admonition that it is 'futile to characterize disputes that may arise in the future' and that 'the tribunal would not be bound by such a clause'. C. Schreuer, L. Malintoppi, A. Reinisch, and A. Sinclair, *The ICSID Convention: A Commentary*, 2nd edn. (2009) 107. However one must recall yet again the fundamental difference between the posture of the ICSID Convention, to which Schreuer referred, on the one hand, and the New York and Panama Conventions, on the other. Under the latter, there is no concern with a tribunal applying objective requirements of jurisdiction, but rather the national courts of a given State applying a qualified obligation of enforcement. Under the New York Convention, the relevant definition of 'commercial' is determined not by the Convention itself, but rather in accordance with

where the same chapter also requires that '[e]ach Party shall provide for the enforcement of an award in its territory,'[46] appearing to impose a direct obligation of enforcement. However, upon closer inspection, this obligation is not self-executing. Thus, the stipulation that claims 'shall be considered to arise out of a commercial relationship or transaction' would appear to be designed to offer a further resort where States party might fail (whether by intention or mere neglect) to promulgate implementing legislation, or otherwise fail to respect the 'direct' obligation of enforcement.[47] This provision might also serve to facilitate or encourage enforcement in third States under the New York Convention, although such States' courts would not be bound.

Better than a stipulation of commerciality, and better than a duty to 'provide for the enforcement of an award in its territory', is for new treaties to simply dictate a self-executing obligation to enforce those awards rendered pursuant to their own arbitration mechanisms.[48] Such a duty may mirror or incorporate the standard of either the New York Convention or the ICSID Convention. In either case, this duty would serve to greatly expand the enforcement space, particularly where drafted into the forging of a new generation of multilateral instruments for maximum geographical reach. Such an expansion is of particular utility where relevant rights of host States and their nationals may arise from legal

municipal law, which municipal law now becomes constrained to consider any award resulting from the treaty's mechanism to be, indeed, commercial. Thus, the United States model treaty would impose a direct obligation upon all States party to consider awards resulting from its dispute settlement mechanism as commercial under their own laws, and thus to enforce such awards to the fullest extent of the New York and Panama Conventions. Enforcement of arbitral awards rendered in favour of the host State or its national might be resisted on other grounds given in the New York Convention. See, in particular, Art. V(2) of the New York Convention ('[r]ecognition and enforcement of an arbitral award may also be refused if the competent authority in the country where recognition and enforcement is sought finds that: (a) The subject matter of the difference is not capable of settlement by arbitration under the law of that country; or (b) The recognition or enforcement of the award would be contrary to the public policy of that country'). In one example, labour rights are sometimes considered non-arbitrable. In similar fashion to a treaty stipulation of commerciality, the relevant instrument might include a stipulation of arbitrability, thus imposing upon States party an obligation to regard those rights that fall within a tribunal's jurisdiction *ratione materiae* as arbitrable under their respective national laws.

[46] Art. 34(7) of the US Model BIT (2012); Art. 1136(4) of the NAFTA.

[47] It is, however, unclear whether States disregarding this obligation would be more inclined to abide by their obligations under the New York or Panama Conventions.

[48] See, e.g., Art. 10(3) of the Germany Model BIT (2005) ('[t]he award shall be enforced by the Contracting States as a final and absolute ruling under domestic law').

relationships falling on the periphery of what is considered commercial under the laws of certain States party to the New York Convention.

Conclusion

Where ICSID jurisdiction is chosen, its self-contained enforcement mechanism is available. Otherwise, the New York Convention supplies the requisite tools. In either case, an evaluation as to enforcement options must largely be made upon the basis of enforcement law within those jurisdictions where it is anticipated that an enforcement action might be brought, which is typically to say those jurisdictions wherein the assets of the parties may lie. Particularly in common law jurisdictions, the evaluation must be made in the light of the law's interpretation and application in the State's higher courts, including the manner in which those courts have interpreted and applied international obligations.

With regard to the New York Convention, this evaluation must take into account whether the relevant State has enacted a commercial reservation, as well as any national law regarding the definition of a commercial relationship. The commercial reservation (which, it is recalled, has been enacted by less than one third of States party)[49] presents a small pocket of uncertainty in a vast sea of enforcement, particularly where the Convention's evident object and purpose favour the broad enforceability of arbitral awards.

A final avenue is for a robust enforcement mechanism to be written directly into an opt-in convention that is crafted to confer treaty-born arbitral jurisdiction over certain categories of claims by the host State or its nationals.[50] In particular, such a convention may dictate an obligation upon all acceding States to recognise and enforce awards rendered pursuant to the underlying arbitral mechanisms. Furthermore, the enforcement obligation may be crafted in the mould of the ICSID Convention, thus removing any power of national courts before whom enforcement is sought to engage in any inquiry as to commerciality, arbitrability, or *ordre public*.

There is no great obstacle to the enforcement of awards rendered in favour of host States or their nationals. Rather, broad international enforceability is perhaps the greatest advantage in arbitrating the conduct of international investors.

---

[49] See note 28 *supra*.
[50] On the opt-in convention, see A Harmonisation Mechanism, Chapter 3.

~

Conclusion

Despite admirable advances, international law opens wide gaps in access to justice, for both States and non-State actors alike. One domain which prominently displays this deficit is international investment law.

One may fairly observe that the contemporary investment arbitration régime largely operates as a one-way street. The international investor is entitled to claim against the host State for alleged breach of investment protection guarantees, but the host State has been left with only an uncertain avenue to counterclaims while non-State actors within the host State are excluded entirely.[1]

In the absence of access to an international forum, the host State and its nationals are left to seek remedy in their own national courts or, where jurisdiction may be established, in the courts of the investor's home State (or, more remote still, in the courts of a third State). This default localisation has yielded an unsatisfactory result, namely the risk of multiplicitous proceedings across numerous national jurisdictions, with the accompanying potential to produce irreconcilable judgments, only some or none of which can be effectively enforced. On one end, there is the danger of excess liability to the investor; on the other, a denial of justice to the host State or its nationals.

The imbalances and inequities of the status quo need not prevail. An architecture to admit the interests of other stakeholders is eminently

---

[1] In the recent words of a prominent practitioner,

> [t]he potential for international arbitration to fill the dispute resolution lacuna for non-state actors . . . remains enormous. International arbitration remains a viable option – often still the only option – for a myriad of anticipated and as yet unanticipated public and private international law disputes in an increasingly uncertain and complicated world order where state sovereign rights must continue to be reconciled with individual, group, environmental and even commercial rights and protections.

W. Miles, 'The Abyei Arbitration: A Model for Peaceful Resolution of Disputes Involving Non-State Actors', in U. Franke, A. Magnusson, and J. Dahlquist (eds.), *Arbitrating for Peace: How Arbitration Made a Difference* (2016) 248.

attainable within the existing legal landscape. Where parties so desire, gains may be achieved in legal certainty and finality by the submission of all claims arising from a given investment to binding resolution in international arbitration. Aside from the inherent laudability of ensuring an effective adjudication forum to aggrieved investors, host States, and their nationals alike, as a fundamental matter of justice, there are other reasons to pursue this approach, all falling well within the realm of bounded rationality.

In but one scenario, where concerns of the host State or its nationals threaten to halt a promising investment initiative entirely, the investor may willingly assent to binding arbitration of certain present or future claims as a step in gaining entry. Thereafter, once the investment commences (or recommences), the investor will face every incentive to conduct himself with heightened responsibility, in order to reduce exposure to claims for loss or injury in arbitration. Where loss or injury incur, a wise investor might openly prefer a global settlement that establishes an exclusive arbitral tribunal or claims commission in order to foreclose years of multi-front litigation.[2]

Where merit is found in this volume's proposals, their utility may be harnessed to reach far beyond the particulars of any given investment dispute. A multilateral convention might serve as a tool to institutionalise inclusiveness while seeking to overcome the present fragmentation of international investment law, and thus to reach towards greater harmonisation and uniformity of a currently fractured landscape.[3] In this

---

[2] Furthermore,

> [i]f a dispute arises where the victims have no access to a court, a[] [multinational enterprise] might feel that even in spite of its legal immunity it should voluntarily submit to binding arbitration, motivated, positively, by its sense of corporate social responsibility or, more defensively, by a fear that its refusal to cooperate in a solution could boost negative reactions from the society at large. Moreover, companies that do not agree to refer human rights disputes to [a proposed International Arbitration Tribunal on Business and Human Rights] may find it difficult to compete in public procurement or to be included in World Bank finance programs. Sooner or later, such outsiders will not be welcome as business partners.

See C. Cronstedt and R. C. Thompson, 'A Proposal for an International Arbitration Tribunal on Business and Human Rights', 57 *Harvard International Law Journal* (2016) 68.

[3] See, e.g., J. Weber and C. Titi, 'UNCTAD's Roadmap for IIA Reform of Investment Dispute Settlement', 21 *New Zealand Business Law Quarterly* 4 (2015), available at: http://investmentpolicyhub.unctad.org/News/Report/Archive/523. See also, e.g., *The Addis Ababa Action Agenda of the Third International Conference on Financing for*

manner, existing treaties may be altered by opting into an emergent generation.

Where desired, the proposals of this book may be explored in order to reform investment arbitration from within, to preserve the viability of investments, and to better achieve access to justice, by arbitrating the conduct of international investors.

Development, endorsed by UNGA Res. 69/313, 27 July 2015, para. 87 ('[w]e will strengthen coherence and consistency among bilateral and regional trade and investment agreements') and para. 91 (requesting UNCTAD 'to continue its existing programme of meetings and consultations with Member States on investment agreements' for this and other purposes). On the presently prevailing inclination towards reform of international investment law, see also UNCTAD, *World Investment Report 2015: Reforming International Investment Governance* (2015) 140 (stating that '[the issue is] not about whether to reform or not, but about the what, how and extent of such reform').

ANNEX

The Model Texts

Model 1   Definitions

1. The 'Host State' for purposes of this [Agreement] [Law] shall be [INSERT HOST STATE].
   . . .
   The 'Host State' shall be that State in whose territory an investment is made which gives rise to a claim under this [Treaty].
2. A 'Host State National' for purposes of this [Agreement][Law] [Treaty] shall be: (i) any natural person holding the nationality of [or permanent residency in] the Host State; and (ii) any legal [person] [entity] constituted, organized, or recognized under the laws of the Host State, in either case as at the date of suffering a loss or injury giving rise to a claim under this [Agreement][Law][Treaty].
3. The 'Investor' for purposes of this [Agreement] shall be [INSERT NAME OF INVESTOR].
   . . .
   An 'Investor' for purposes of this [Law][Treaty] shall be any investor who holds the nationality of any [Contracting] State other than the Host State or is owned or controlled by an investor of any [Contracting] State other than the Host State, and makes an investment in the territory of the Host State which gives rise to a claim under this [Law][Treaty].
4. The 'Home State' for purposes of this [Agreement][Law][Treaty] shall be the State of nationality of the Investor or, where the Investor is a national of the Host State but is owned or controlled by an investor of any other State, that other State.

Commentary

1. The model definition of 'Host State National' is written in general terms to include any person holding the nationality of the host State at the relevant time. Parties may expand or contract this definition. In

172

particular, in addition to including permanent residents, parties may wish to extend access to, for example, stateless peoples such as nomadic or pastoralist tribes present within the territory of the host State.

2. In addition to natural persons, the model definition of 'Host State National' includes 'any legal [person] [entity] constituted, organized, or recognized under the laws of the Host State'. From this general formulation, language may be precisely targeted in order to include, for example, a collective of indigenous peoples (which may hold claims in its own right, separate and apart from any summation of individual claims held by its members).

3. It is noted that an abuse of rights or process may occur where a person or entity, though not yet actually injured, may 'foresee a specific future dispute as a very high probability and not merely as a possible controversy', and thus seek to acquire the host State's nationality.[1] Parties may wish to consider including express language to counter this eventuality.

4. The definition of 'Investor' as including those 'owned or controlled by an investor of any State other than the Host State' serves the important purpose of ensuring that a foreign investor cannot immunise himself from claims by conducting affairs via the vehicle of a local entity within the Host State.

5. As indicated, the definitions of 'Host State', 'Investor', and 'Home State' may vary depending on whether the instrument in question is a contract, investment law, or treaty. The definition of 'Host State National' may be used indistinctly in all three kinds of instruments.

Model 2   Contractual Arbitration Agreement

1. Any dispute, controversy or claim arising out of or in relation to this agreement, or the breach, termination or invalidity thereof, shall be finally resolved by international arbitration in accordance with the [INSERT ARBITRATION RULES]. The parties to this international arbitration agreement shall be (i) the Host State; (ii) the Investor; and (iii) such Host State National(s) as may seek to assert a claim or claims against the Investor as set forth in subparagraph 5 hereof, subject to the procedural rules as set forth below.

---

[1] *Pac Rim Cayman LLC* v. *Republic of El Salvador*, ICSID Case No. ARB/09/12, Decision on the Respondent's Jurisdictional Objections, 1 June 2012, para. 2.99.

2. The agreement is governed by [INSERT HOST STATE LAW OR OTHER APPLICABLE LAW] [except as relates to those subject-matters as set forth in subparagraph 5 hereof].

3. The arbitration shall be administered by [INSERT ADMINISTERING INSTITUTION, IF APPLICABLE].

   The appointing authority shall be [INSERT NAME OF INSTITUTION OR PERSON, IF APPLICABLE].

   The number of arbitrators shall be [INSERT NUMBER OF ARBITRATORS].

   The (legal) place of arbitration shall be [INSERT SEAT OF ARBITRATION].

   The language of the proceedings shall be [INSERT LANGUAGE OF ARBITRATION].

4. It is hereby restated, ratified, and agreed that the Investor irrevocably consents that the Host State and its Host State Nationals shall be entitled to submit the following claims to international arbitration:

   (i) those held by the Host State under subparagraph 5 of this agreement; and

   (ii) those held by any Host State Nationals under subparagraph 5 of this agreement.

   [For the avoidance of doubt, the Investor has further agreed and accepted that those claims held by any Host State National may be transferred or assigned to the Host State, provided that the Host State assumes any and all obligations of the transferor or assignor Host State National, including with respect to any and all jurisdictional defenses or counterclaims. Such transfer or assignment may include title or interest to any such claims, causes of action, or recoveries attaching to rights of the transferor or assignor Host State National with respect to any loss(es) or injury(ies) arising out of the investment, and which the Host State may acquire by any means including, without limitation, by way of subrogation or substitution under its laws.]

5. Without prejudice to any other rights as set forth elsewhere in this contract, the arbitral tribunal shall finally resolve any claims against the Investor submitted by the Host State or its Host State Nationals on the basis of the following laws [or rules] [as existing at the date of this Agreement]:

   5.1 [INSERT SUBJECT-MATTER AREA OF LAW]
   [Selected Host State Laws]

[Selected International Conventions]
[Other Instruments]

Commentary

1. Under this model text, an arbitration agreement within a contractual instrument serves to confer the investor's consent to arbitration of claims by the host State. Further, the agreement confers upon host State nationals the ability to bring claims opposable to the investor as third party beneficiaries.
2. The model text follows the model arbitration clause for contracts found in the UNCITRAL Arbitration Rules (as revised in 2010), which is nearly identical to the equivalent model clauses for the PCA Arbitration Rules 2012 and PCA Environmental Rules.
3. In addition to institutional arbitration, there is the option of ad hoc arbitration, or of an arbitration to be administered under the UNCITRAL Arbitration Rules at the Permanent Court of Arbitration.
4. As in many arbitration agreements generally, this one too is notable for the large number of applicable laws.
5. As in other model texts, the final clause of paragraph 4 serves to defuse possible concerns of abuse of rights or process arising from the transfer of claims as between the host State and its nationals. Such language is not necessary where the Direct Claims or *Qui Tam* Models are used.
6. In paragraph 5, the parties may wish to consider whether they desire to fix the obligations created as at the moment of conclusion of the agreement, or to allow for the specified categories, instruments, or rules to develop over time.

JURISDICTION ARISING FROM HOST STATE LAW

Model 3   Host State Investment Law

As a condition precedent to the enjoyment by an Investor of any and all rights or benefits granted under this Law, including but not limited to the right to submit a claim to international arbitration against the Host State as set forth in Article [X] of this Law, the Investor shall agree and accept in writing that the Host State and its Host State Nationals shall be entitled to submit the following claims to international arbitration under said Article [X]:

(i) those held by the Host State under Article [Y] of this Law;
(ii) those held by any Host State Nationals under Article [Y] of this Law.

[For the avoidance of doubt, the Investor shall agree and accept that those claims held by any Host State National may be transferred or assigned to the Host State, provided that the Host State assumes any and all obligations of the transferor or assignor Host State National, including with respect to any and all jurisdictional defenses or counterclaims. Such transfer or assignment may include title or interest to any such claims, causes of action, or recoveries attaching to rights of the transferor or assignor Host State National with respect to any loss(es) or injury(ies) arising out of the investment, and which the Host State may acquire by any means including, without limitation, by way of subrogation or substitution under its laws.]

Commentary

1. This model text is suited for inclusion within a host State's foreign investment law granting certain protections to the foreign investor. Under this model, the investor does not enjoy the protections as of right. Rather, they are conditioned upon the investor's consent to arbitration of certain categories of claims by the host State or its nationals.

2. One advantage of this model is that the conditionality of investment protections applies to all investors generally. Thus, the investor's consent to arbitration need not be individually contracted for.

3. The final paragraph of this model text serves to confer the investor's consent to a transfer or assignment of claims from a host State national to the host State itself, as may occur under the Espousal or Hybrid Model, with a view to avoiding objections for abuse of rights or process. Further, such may include a scenario in which the host State disburses compensation to its nationals and then proceeds to prosecute their claims as opposable to the investor. This language is not necessary where the Direct Claims or *Qui Tam* Models are used.

4. Article X would contain the investor-State arbitration provision, appropriately adapted so as to encompass claims by the host State and its nationals under the four models.

5. Article Y would set forth the *ratione materiae* scope of jurisdiction in respect of claims brought through these models.

Model 4   Investment License

This Investment License has been issued in favour of the Investor for purposes of granting authorization to make one or more investment(s) in the territory of the Host State pursuant to the Foreign Investment Law (the 'Law').

As a condition precedent to the granting of this Investment License and to the enjoyment by the Investor of any and all rights and benefits established in the Law, including but not limited to the right to submit a claim to international arbitration against the Host State as set forth in Article [X] of the Law, the Investor has agreed and accepted that the Host State and its Host State Nationals shall be entitled to submit the following claims to international arbitration under said Article [X]:

(i) those held by the Host State under Article [Y] of the Law; and
(ii) those held by any Host State Nationals under Article [Y] of the Law.

[For the avoidance of doubt, the Investor has further agreed and accepted that those claims held by any Host State National may be transferred or assigned to the Host State, provided that the Host State assumes any and all obligations of the transferor or assignor Host State National, including with respect to any and all jurisdictional defenses or counterclaims. Such transfer or assignment may include title or interest to any such claims, causes of action, or recoveries attaching to rights of the transferor or assignor Host State National with respect to any loss(es) or injury(ies) arising out of the investment, and which the Host State may acquire by any means including, without limitation, by way of subrogation or substitution under its laws.]

Commentary

1. In contrast to the Host State Investment Law, which requires the investor's consent to arbitration of certain categories of claims by the host State or its nationals as a condition of investment protection, the Investment License operates to obtain the investor's consent as a condition of entry, and thus prior to any particular dispute having arisen.

2. In similar manner to the Host State Investment Law, one advantage of this model is that the conditionality applies to all investors generally. This model may thus operate to obtain the consent to arbitration of those investors legally present within the territory of the host State.

3. However, such need not require a blanket investment licensing scheme of general applicability. Rather, many industries – including precisely those featuring large-scale investments most liable to cause injury to the host State and its nationals – operate within regulatory environments to which licensure requirements already attach. The investor's consent to arbitration may be obtained via these processes.

4. As in other model texts, the final paragraph serves to defuse possible concerns of abuse of rights or process arising from the transfer of claims as between the host State and its nationals. Such language is not necessary where the Direct Claims or *Qui Tam* Models are used.

5. Article X would contain the investor-State arbitration provision, appropriately adapted so as to encompass claims by the host State and its nationals under the four models.

6. Article Y would set forth the *ratione materiae* scope of jurisdiction in respect of claims brought through these models.

Model 5   Tender Rules

As a condition precedent to participation in this International Call for Tenders for [INSERT PROJECT] (the 'Project'), [INSERT TENDERER] (the 'Tenderer') shall execute and submit to the Host State a letter in accordance with Annex [A] hereof, agreeing and accepting that the Host State and its Host State Nationals shall be entitled to submit the following claims relating to or arising out of the Project to international arbitration in accordance with Article [X] of these Tender Rules:

(i) those held by the Host State under Article [Y] of these Tender Rules; and

(ii) those held by any Host State Nationals under Article [Y] of these Tender Rules.

[For the avoidance of doubt, the Tenderer shall agree and accept that those claims held by any Host State National may be transferred or assigned to the Host State, provided that the Host State assumes any and all obligations of the transferor or assignor Host State National, including with respect to any and all jurisdictional defenses or counterclaims. Such transfer or assignment may include title or interest to any such claims, causes of action, or recoveries attaching to rights of the transferor or assignor Host State National with respect to any loss(es) or injury(ies) arising out of the investment, and which the Host State may acquire by any means including, without limitation, by way of subrogation or substitution under its laws.]

Commentary

1. In contrast to the Investment License (which requires the investor's consent to arbitration of certain categories of claims by the host State or its nationals as a condition of entry) and the Contractual Arbitration Agreement (which gains the investor's consent to arbitration once a contract is signed), the Tender Rules operate to obtain a tenderer's consent at the pre-investment phase.[2]

2. In this manner, jurisdiction may vest over claims opposable to a putative investor for misconduct in the tender phase, even where no investment ultimately results (including where the tenderer is unsuccessful in his tender). As an example, it has now become a common feature of many tender rules to include an actionable anti-corruption provision.

3. It is noted that those categories of claims arising in the pre-investment phase might primarily vest in the host State itself rather than its nationals, as there might be limited potential for harm to the latter during this time. However, in pursuit of efficiencies, a structure may be designed such that if the tenderer is successful and an agreement is ultimately entered into, the agreement simply incorporates the earlier arbitration provision by reference. Alternatively, such agreement may contain a superseding provision, as per the Contractual Arbitration Agreement.

4. Further, where the parties wish, the Tender Rules might include, for example, an actionable duty to consult that operates in favour of host State nationals.

5. As in other model texts, the final paragraph serves to defuse possible concerns of abuse of rights or process arising from the transfer of claims as between the host State and its nationals. Such language is not necessary where the Direct Claims or *Qui Tam* Models are used.

---

[2] It is noted that claims brought regarding pre-investment conduct might not fall within the ambit of ICSID jurisdiction, as it might be argued that there is not yet an 'investment'.

6. Article X would contain the arbitration provision, appropriately adapted so as to encompass claims by the host State and its nationals under the four models.
7. Article Y would set forth the *ratione materiae* scope of jurisdiction in respect of claims brought through these models.

JURISDICTION ARISING FROM TREATY

Model 6   Contingent Consent Clause

The Contracting Parties hereby agree that, as a condition precedent to the enjoyment by the Investor of any and all rights or benefits under this Treaty, including but not limited to the right to submit a claim to international arbitration against the Host State as set forth in Article [X] of this Treaty, the Investor shall agree and accept in writing that the Host State and its Host State Nationals shall be entitled to submit the following claims to international arbitration under said Article [X]:

 (i)   those held by the Host State under Article [Y] of this Treaty; and
 (ii) those held by any Host State Nationals under Article [Y] of this Treaty.

[For the avoidance of doubt, the Investor shall further agree and accept that those claims held by any Host State National may be transferred or assigned to the Host State, provided that the Host State assumes any and all obligations of the transferor or assignor Host State National, including with respect to any and all jurisdictional defenses or counterclaims. Such transfer or assignment may include title or interest to any such claims, causes of action, or recoveries attaching to rights of the transferor or assignor Host State National with respect to any loss(es) or injury(ies) arising out of the investment, and which the Host State may acquire by any means including, without limitation, by way of subrogation or substitution under its laws.]

Commentary

1. This model operates in similar manner to Model 3 (Host State Investment Law). Under this model, the investor does not enjoy the protections of an investment treaty as of right. Rather, they are

conditioned upon the investor's consent to arbitration of certain categories of claims by the host State or its nationals.

2. Article X would contain the investor-State arbitration provision, appropriately adapted so as to encompass claims by the host State and its nationals under the four models.

3. The model text has been drafted in the form of a condition precedent to the host State's consent to arbitration in order to leave clear that non-compliance with this requirement would defeat the jurisdiction of an arbitral tribunal constituted under Article [X] over any claim advanced by an investor. Alternatively, such a provision may be drafted in the form of a denial-of-benefits clause, although this may have the effect of shifting the burden of proof to the host State as to compliance with this requirement.

4. In order to facilitate (where desired) the selection of provisions within the host State's laws as a basis of claims by the host State or its nationals, it is suggested that Article [Y] of the Treaty – which regulates *ratione materiae* jurisdiction – include a list of those selected provisions as to each State party.

5. As in other model texts, the final paragraph serves to defuse possible concerns of abuse of rights or process arising from the transfer of claims as between the host State and its nationals. Such language is not necessary where the Direct Claims or *Qui Tam* Models are used.

Model 7   Jurisdiction without Privity

The Contracting Parties hereby agree that the Host State and its Host State Nationals shall be entitled to submit the following claims against an Investor having the nationality of [the other] [another] Contracting Party to international arbitration under Article [X] of this Treaty:

(i) those held by the Host State under Article [Y] of this Treaty; and

(ii) those held by any Host State Nationals under Article [Y] of this Treaty.

[For the avoidance of doubt, such claims may include those transferred or assigned by any Host State National to the Host State, provided that the Host State assumes any and all obligations of the transferor or assignor Host State National, including with respect to any and all jurisdictional defenses or counterclaims. Such transfer or assignment may include title or interest to any such claims, causes of action, or recoveries attaching to rights of the transferor or assignor Host State National with respect to any loss(es) or injury(ies) arising out of the investment, and which the Host State may acquire by any means including, without limitation, by way of subrogation or substitution under its laws.]

Commentary

1. The first paragraph of this model text is inspired by an early Netherlands-Indonesia economic treaty.[3] Parties may also wish to consider a similar model proposed by the International Institute for Sustainable Development.[4]
2. Under international law, the State holds the power to submit its investor-nationals to the jurisdiction of an international tribunal. It is noted that such a step might be subject to constitutional challenge under the internal laws of the relevant home State.
3. Article X would contain the investor-State arbitration provision, appropriately adapted so as to encompass claims by the host State and its nationals under the four models.
4. In order to facilitate (where desired) the selection of provisions within the host State's laws as a basis of claims by the host State or its nationals, it is suggested that Article [Y] of the Treaty – which regulates *ratione materiae* jurisdiction – include a list of those selected provisions as to each State party.
5. As in other model texts, the final paragraph serves to defuse possible concerns of abuse of rights or process arising from the transfer of claims as between the host State and its nationals. Such language is not necessary where the Direct Claims or *Qui Tam* Models are used.

Model 8   Opt-In Convention

1. The Contracting Parties agree, with respect to all investment treaties as concluded amongst them, that any offer of arbitration to the Investor shall be conditioned upon the Investor's consent in

---

[3] See Art. 11 of the Netherlands-Indonesia Agreement on Economic Cooperation (with Protocol and Exchanges of Letters dated 17 June 1968), signed on 7 July 1968 (entered into force on 17 July 1971), 799 UNTS 13.

[4] See Art. 4 at Annex A of the International Institute for Sustainable Development Model International Agreement on Investment for Sustainable Development (2005), available at: www.iisd.org/pdf/2005/investment_model_int_agreement.pdf.

writing that the Host State and its Host State Nationals be entitled to submit the following claims to international arbitration under Article [X] of this Treaty:

(i) those held by the Host State as set forth in Annex [A]; and
(ii) those held by any Host State Nationals as set forth in Annex [A].

[For the avoidance of doubt, such claims may include those transferred or assigned by any Host State National to the Host State, provided that the Host State assumes any and all obligations of the transferor or assignor Host State National, including with respect to any and all jurisdictional defenses or counterclaims. Such transfer or assignment may include title or interest to any such claims, causes of action, or recoveries attaching to rights of the transferor or assignor Host State National with respect to any loss(es) or injury(ies) arising out of the investment, and which the Host State may acquire by any means including, without limitation, by way of subrogation or substitution under its laws.]

2. The Contracting Parties further agree that, where an Investor accepts an offer of arbitration extended in a Contracting Party's investment treaty but the Investor's Home State is not party to this Convention, such Contracting Party shall request that the Investor consent in writing that the Host State Nationals be entitled to submit claims as set forth in Annex [A].

3. For purposes of this Convention, the term 'investment treaty' means any bilateral or multilateral treaty, including any treaty commonly referred to as a free trade agreement, economic integration agreement, trade and investment framework or cooperation agreement, or bilateral investment treaty, which contains provisions on the protection of investments or investors and a right for investors to resort to arbitration against contracting parties to that investment treaty.

Commentary

1. This model text is inspired by an innovative proposal for an opt-in convention that is in turn modeled upon the United Nations Convention on Transparency in Treaty-Based Investor-State Arbitration, commonly known as the Mauritius Convention.[5] Under

---

[5] See G. Kaufmann-Kohler and M. Potestà, 'Can the Mauritius Convention Serve as a Model for the Reform of Investor-State Arbitration in Connection with the Introduction of a Permanent Investment Tribunal or an Appeal Mechanism? Analysis and Roadmap', *CIDS-Geneva Center for International Dispute Settlement* (2016).

this model, acceding States alter the effect of prior investment treaties existing as between them, such that the foreign investor does not enjoy their protections as of right, but rather must give his consent to the arbitration of certain categories of claims by the host State or its nationals, as under Model 6 (Contingent Consent Clause).

2. In order to enable the broadest possible accession, as well as to facilitate (where desired) the selection of provisions within a given host State's laws as a basis of claims by the host State or its nationals, it is suggested that Annex [A] of the Treaty include a list of those selected provisions as to each acceding State.

3. Article X would contain an arbitration provision for claims by host States and its nationals, which may be adapted from Model 2 (Contractual Arbitration Agreement) or inspired by existing treaty texts and models.

4. As in other model texts, the final paragraph serves to defuse possible concerns of abuse of rights or process arising from the transfer of claims as between the host State and its nationals. Such language is not necessary where the Direct Claims or *Qui Tam* Models are used.

Model 9   Mass Claims Settlement Agreement

1. This Settlement Agreement by and between [INSERT HOME STATE] and [INSERT HOST STATE] addresses the compensation of any and all Host State Nationals who have suffered a loss or injury as a consequence of those events defined in Annex [X], caused by [INSERT INVESTOR] as an investor in the territory of [INSERT HOST STATE].

2. [INSERT INVESTOR] and [INSERT HOST STATE] have agreed to establish a compensation fund in accordance with Annex [Y].

3. Applications for compensation under this Agreement shall be made within one year of the effective date of this Settlement Agreement and shall be administered by the [International Bureau of the Permanent Court of Arbitration], in accordance with the rules as set forth in Annex [Z], as well as such other supplementary rules as may be established by the [International Bureau of the Permanent Court of Arbitration].

4. [Where the amount of the damage assessed exceeds the balance of the compensation fund, the compensation to be granted shall be reduced in proportion to the funds available.]

5. The right to compensation cannot be assigned or pledged. If the person entitled to compensation has died as of the date of this Settlement Agreement, the surviving spouse and the surviving children shall be entitled to equal compensation. Benefits under this Settlement Agreement may be applied equally by the grandchildren, or if they are no longer living, by the siblings, if the entitled person has left neither spouses nor children. If no application is made by these persons, the heirs who are appointed in a will are entitled to apply.

6. Host State Nationals who are juridical persons shall not be entitled to compensation. [This paragraph shall not apply to indigenous or religious communities or organizations, or their legal successors.]

7. In the application, any and all persons entitled to compensation shall submit a declaration that, upon receipt of compensation under this Settlement Agreement, they shall not be entitled to any further assertion of claims in connection with those events defined in Annex [X]. Such declaration shall have the force of a waiver of claims for compensation from [INSERT INVESTOR] or any affiliate thereof, before any forum other than the [arbitral tribunal] [claims commission] established in this Settlement Agreement, including without limitation the courts of [INSERT HOME STATE] and [INSERT HOST STATE]. [INSERT HOME STATE] and [INSERT HOST STATE] declare their mutual desire and expectation that the exclusivity of the [arbitral tribunal] [claims commission] established under this Settlement Agreement be respected by the Courts of other States.

Commentary

1. This model text is designed to establish the exclusivity of an arbitral tribunal or a claims commission to adjudicate all claims arising out of a particular event or sequence of events.

2. Further, where desired, the States party to the treaty may stipulate a fixed negotiated sum that is not required to be replenished and is, therefore, the limit of the investor's liability, in order to achieve greater certainty and finality, and thereby obtain the investor's willing participation.

3. Certain parties might also wish to consider the usage of private instruments. As an example, the host State might conclude a settlement agreement with the foreign investor intended to achieve a similar effect, although such agreement may not serve to foreclose the possibility of claims in the courts of the home State.

4. The Permanent Court of Arbitration or another international institution may be entrusted with the administration of this sort of process. The Permanent Court of Arbitration has accumulated significant experience in the administration of mass claims, and 'continues to gather information concerning various mass claims tribunals and processes to create a conveniently accessible source of useful information for those involved in existing mass claims tribunals as well as those responsible for the design of future ones'.[6]

5. It is noted that this mechanism may be subject to constitutional challenge under the internal laws of the relevant States.

OTHER MODEL TEXTS

Model 10   Jurisdiction *Ratione Materiae*

Without prejudice to any other rights as set forth elsewhere in this [Agreement][Law][Treaty], the arbitral tribunal constituted in accordance with Article [X] of this [Agreement][Law][Treaty] shall finally resolve any claims submitted by the Host State and its Host State Nationals insofar as they are based on any of the following laws [or rules] [as existing at the date of this [Agreement][Law][Treaty]]:

[INSERT SUBJECT-MATTER AREA OF LAW]
[Selected Internal Laws]
[Selected International Conventions]
[Other Instruments]

Commentary

1. Under the paramount principle of autonomy, parties may submit any body (or bodies) of substantive rights and obligations they might wish to the jurisdiction of an arbitral tribunal.

2. Depending on the subject matter in question, parties might find that the best-suited bodies of law are to be found in municipal sources (including, for example, the host State's laws of extra-contractual liability), in international sources (such as widely subscribed international conventions, the UN Guiding Principles on Business and Human Rights, or the OECD Guidelines for Multinational Enterprises), or in a

---

[6] Permanent Court of Arbitration, *116th Annual Report* (2016) 16.

combination of both. Parties may also wish to consider whether or not to include general references to broad categories of rights – such as internationally recognized human rights, internationally accepted labour standards, or internationally recognised standards of corporate social responsibility – alongside an enumerated list of specific instruments or rules.

3. Parties may also wish to consider whether they desire to fix the obligations created as at the moment of conclusion of the agreement, or to allow for the specified categories, instruments, or rules to develop over time.

Model 11 Waiver of Claims

Where the Host State or any Host State Nationals commence an arbitration against the Investor or seek to be joined in an already commenced arbitration proceeding against the Investor, the Host State or such Host State Nationals shall be deemed to have waived any and all rights to initiate or continue any proceeding in any other forum with respect to the same claim or claims, except where the arbitral tribunal declines to hear any claim, in which case the waiver shall have no effect as to such claim.

[Notwithstanding the foregoing, the Host State or such Host State Nationals may initiate or continue an action that seeks interim injunctive relief, provided that the action is brought for the sole purpose of preserving the Host State's or Host State Nationals' rights and interests during the pendency of the arbitration.]

Commentary

1. A waiver provision such as this one is advised for inclusion in order to ensure the principle of *ne bis in idem*. This model text is inspired by the 'no U-turn' rule contained in Article 1121 of the North American Free Trade Agreement, as well as various other bilateral investment treaties and free trade agreements. The provision operates to ensure that where elected by a claimant host State or host State national, international arbitration serves as the exclusive forum.

2. It is noted that the language of this model provision does not yield a broad effect of claim preclusion (as that doctrine is sometimes known in the common law tradition). In other words, the waiver becomes operative only as to those claims actually brought.

3. If a tribunal declines to hear any claim, then the waiver does not take effect, lest a denial of justice occur.

Model 12   Exclusivity of Remedy

The Contracting Parties hereby agree that the Host State and Host State Nationals, being entitled to bring claims in international arbitration against the Investor as under Article [X] this Treaty, shall not be entitled to assert any of those claims indicated at Article [Y] of this Treaty against the Investor in any other forum whatsoever, including without limitation the courts of the Contracting Parties. The Contracting Parties declare their mutual desire and expectation that the exclusivity of arbitration as under Article [X] of this Treaty be respected by the Courts of other States.

[Each Contracting Party shall, in any case in which it is notified that a claim indicated at Article [Y] of this Treaty has been asserted in its courts against the Investor, inform such courts that it is a matter of public order that arbitration as under Article [X] of this Treaty be the exclusive remedy and forum for resolving such claims.]

Commentary

1. This model text is inspired in part by the Agreement between the Government of the United States of America and the Government of the Federal Republic of Germany concerning the Foundation 'Remembrance, Responsibility and the Future', by which it was sought to establish an exclusive forum for the resolution of claims arising from the use of forced labour by Germany at the time of the Second World War.[7]
2. It is noted that this mechanism may be subject to constitutional challenge under the internal laws of the relevant States.
3. Article X would contain an arbitration provision for claims by host States and their nationals, which may be adapted from Model 2 (Contractual Arbitration Agreement) or inspired by existing treaty texts and models.

---

[7] See the Agreement between the Government of the United States of America and the Government of the Federal Republic of Germany concerning the Foundation 'Remembrance, Responsibility and the Future', signed 17 July 2000 (entered into force 19 October 2000), 2130 UNTS 249.

Model 13   Host State Appointment of Representative

1. Subject to the provisions of this Law, Host State Nationals shall be entitled to seek appointment as legal representative of the Host State for purposes of prosecuting claims against Investors in international arbitration for losses or injuries arising from or related to an investment in its territory, including such claims as may be transferred or assigned by any Host State Nationals to the Host State.
2. A Host State National seeking such appointment shall file an application with the Host State in accordance with the requirements set forth in Annex [A]. The Host State shall then conduct an evaluation and render a decision in accordance with the procedure set forth in Annex [B].
3. Where the application is approved, the Host State shall issue all required governmental authorizations, including but not limited to such letters and documents as may be requested by the arbitral tribunal or institution. [The Host State National shall be entitled to reimbursement of reasonable costs in accordance with the schedule in Annex [C], and to a share of any compensation awarded to the Host State in accordance with the schedule in Annex [D].]
4. Where the application is denied, the Host State National shall be entitled to participate in any Host State prosecution of the claim by making written submissions, which the Host State shall present to the arbitral tribunal.

Commentary

1. This text serves as a model provision for adoption within the host State's internal laws, designed to regulate the appointment of host State nationals as representatives of their State for the purpose of prosecuting its claims against the investor in arbitration, as under the *Qui Tam* and Hybrid Models.
2. Under such a law, interested or affected host State nationals may receive appointment in order to seek a remedy for and on behalf of their State. Such includes, where applicable, the power to prosecute claims originally held by the representative himself (or other host State nationals) but later transferred or assigned to the host State.
3. Annexes [A] and [B] would regulate the application requirements and procedure for host State nationals to be appointed as representatives

under the *Qui Tam* and Hybrid Models. Annexes [C] and [D] would in turn regulate the reimbursement and compensation provided to such representatives, if and when appointed. Under the *Qui Tam* Model, depending upon preferences in the internal legislative process, such representatives might be entitled to receive, for example, only costs and expenses of litigation, a modest quantum of compensation, or a percentage of damages recovered.

Model 14   Home State Insurer or Guarantor

Where the Home State acts as an insurer or guarantor of obligations of the Investor with respect to an investment made in the territory of the Host State or accepts transfer or assignment of the Investor's liabilities arising from a claim or claims as may be brought by any Host State Nationals under Article [X] hereof, such Host State Nationals shall be entitled to bring those claims in international arbitration against the Home State.

Commentary

1. Where desired, a home State scheme of investment insurance or guarantee may extend to include liabilities that the investor may accrue towards the host State or its nationals, as under the Direct Claims (II) Model.
2. Where properly structured, such scheme may allow for the home State to be a proper respondent, thus opening the door to ICSID jurisdiction over claims by host State nationals.

INDEX